INTRODUCTION TO PATTERN RECOGNITION

STATISTICAL, STRUCTURAL, NEURAL AND FUZZY LOGIC APPROACHES

SERIES IN MACHINE PERCEPTION AND ARTIFICIAL INTELLIGENCE*

Editors: **H. Bunke** (Univ. Bern, Switzerland)
P. S. P. Wang (Northeastern Univ., USA)

---

*For the complete list of titles in this series, please write to the Publisher.

Series in Machine Perception and Artificial Intelligence – Vol. 32

INTRODUCTION TO PATTERN RECOGNITION

STATISTICAL, STRUCTURAL, NEURAL AND FUZZY LOGIC APPROACHES

Menahem Friedman
Nuclear Research Center-Negev, Israel

Abraham Kandel
University of South Florida, USA
&
Tel-Aviv University, Israel

World Scientific

NEW JERSEY • LONDON • SINGAPORE • BEIJING • SHANGHAI • HONG KONG • TAIPEI • CHENNAI

Published by

Imperial College Press
57 Shelton Street
Covent Garden
London WC2H 9HE

Distributed by

World Scientific Publishing Co. Pte. Ltd.
5 Toh Tuck Link, Singapore 596224
USA office: 27 Warren Street, Suite 401-402, Hackensack, NJ 07601
UK office: 57 Shelton Street, Covent Garden, London WC2H 9HE

Library of Congress Cataloging-in-Publication Data
Friedman, Menahem.
   Introduction to pattern recognition : statistical, structural,
neural, and fuzzy logic approaches / Menahem Friedman, Abraham
Kandel.
      p. cm. -- (Series in machine perception and artificial
intelligence ; vol. 32)
   Includes bibliographical references.
   ISBN 9810233124
   1. Pattern recognition systems. I. Kandel, Abraham. II. Title.
III. Series.
TK7882.P3F75   1999
0006.4--dc21
                                               98-32406
                                               CIP

British Library Cataloguing-in-Publication Data
A catalogue record for this book is available from the British Library.

First published 1999
Reprinted 2000, 2005

Printed in Singapore.

In memory of

Rabbi Simcha and Hana Friedman

Joseph and Goldie Winters

Dina Kandel and Bernard Balanov

Contents

PREFACE

This text is an introduction to pattern recognition, meant to be used by undergraduate and graduate students in Computer Science as well as in related fields in science and technology. The only prerequisite for using this book is a one semester course in discrete mathematics and knowledge of the basic preliminaries of calculus, linear algebra and probability theory. Since most of the topics covered in this text are accompanied by algorithms and applications which involve a considerable amount of computations, we expect the students to be familiar with at least one programming language. This is eventually a necessity, because to solve any nontrivial problem in pattern recognition, one should be able to program a specific algorithm and run it on a digital computer.

A student who takes a course in pattern recognition is usually motivated by one of the following reasons:

1. The need to fulfill the requirements of a degree program in computer science or engineering.

2. A desire to expand one's horizons of knowledge in a subject which has become tremendously important and useful in recent years.

3. The possibility of successfully adapting the studied algorithms for solving real-world problems in various fields.

Although the book is primarily intended for use by students who qualify for classes (2) and (3), it is also written to be at least partially favored by students who belong to class (1).

The purpose of this manuscript is to present the student with the classical topics in pattern recognition, and illustrate the theory by solving practical problems with emphasis on obtaining intuitive understanding of both the application and the appropriate algorithm. Above all this text is meant to provide the student with sufficient knowledge for relatively independent work in the field. An accumulated teaching experience in Computer Science and Applied Mathematics shows that intuitive understanding of algorithms by the student is almost always a guarantee for the student to successfully repeat, apply and modify these algorithms later.

The first chapter is introductory in nature. It concentrates on the importance and usefulness of pattern recognition in a modern world by discussing real applications from the disciplines of computer science, engineering, biology, medicine, psychology and other related sciences. In the second chapter we discuss the concept of *decision functions* emphasizing the principal function of a pattern recognition system: providing *decisions* related to the class membership of incoming patterns. Prior to the remaining chapters which may be read in a non-sequential order, it is recommended that the student masters the first two chapters as well as Chapter 3 in which we introduce the concept of clustering.

A review of the probabilistic approach to pattern recognition is given in Chapter 4. In Chapter 5 we discuss the problem of feature selection and feature extraction. The interaction between fuzzy logic and pattern classification is presented in Chapter 6. Syntactic pattern recognition is introduced in Chapter 7 and the use of neural networks for pattern classification is presented in Chapter 8.

Even though the material in this volume may be considered to be classical in nature, novel topics such as *fuzzy pattern recognition* and *pattern recognition via neural networks*, which are essentials in any modern text on pattern recognition, present a major portion of this text. However, courses in fuzzy logic and neural networks are not prerequisites, since proper introductions to these subjects are given in this book as well.

The content of this text was successfully tested and modified through the many classes taught by both of us in both Computer Science and Electrical Engineering since the late 1970's.

Completing this text would not have been possible without the encouragement and support of Professor Horst Bunke, Dean of the Institut fur Informatick und Angewandte Mathematik, Universitat Bern, Switzerland, Professor Michael Kovac, Dean of the College of Engineering at the University of South Florida and Professor Uri Shaked, Dean of the Faculty of Engineering at Tel-Aviv University. Finally, we would like to give special thanks to Mrs. Judy Hyde from the College of Engineering at the University of South Florida for her enormous help during the final stages of preparing the manuscript.

Menahem Friedman
Abraham Kandel

Tampa, December 1997

1 INTRODUCTION

1.1 BASIC CONCEPTS IN PATTERN RECOGNITION

Pattern recognition is characteristic to all living organisms. However, different creatures recognize differently. If a human would recognize another human by sight, by voice or by handwriting, a dog may recognize a human or other animal by smell thirty yards away which most humans are incapable of doing. Yet most dogs are unimpressed by looking at the mirror since they do not actually *recognize* another dog over there. A blind person would recognize various items just by touching them. But recognition is not restricted to objects that can be identified using biological senses. In a conversation we can suddenly identify an old argument that we heard years ago. All of these examples are classified as *recognition*.

The object which is inspected for the "recognition" process is called a *pattern*. Usually we refer to a pattern as a *description* of an object which we want to recognize. In this text we are interested in spatial patterns like humans, apples, fingerprints, electrocardiograms or chromosomes. In most cases a pattern recognition problem is a problem of discriminating between different populations. For example we may be interested among a thousand humans to discriminate between four different types: (a) tall and thin (b) tall and fat (c) short and thin (d) short and fat. We thus want to *classify* each person in one of four populations. The recognition process thus turns into *classification*. To determine which *class* the person belongs to, we must first find which *features* are going to determine this classification. The age of the person is clearly not a feature in this case. A reasonable choice of course is the pair of numbers (height, weight) and we thus perform a *feature selection* for this particular problem. Getting these measurements is called *feature extraction*.

At times feature selection may be an easy task while feature extraction is too costly. In this case we may look for an alternative way of selecting features or go ahead and extract the features of the original selection. It is not recommended to start compromising and choose less adequate features which are easier to extract. Suppose for example that a certain medical test, very expensive, is necessary to determine (together with other tests) whether a patient has some severe disease. No competent doctor would even consider dropping that test in order to 'simplify' the feature extraction.

Forecasting the weather is based upon inspecting a weather map. The map itself is raw input data on which we perform *preprocessing*. The features to look for are usually known to the professional due to vast experience. The preprocessing here includes extracting these features and identify *noise*. For an expert, one glance at a weather map is enough to produce a reasonable weather forecast. The expert knows what features to look for and if extracting them is not complicated, forecasting is straightforward. In general we may insert the knowledge acquired by experts in this field into an expert system that will replace the expert and will (almost) always provide a good weather forecast.

Medical diagnosis is another example of a pattern recognition problem where feature selection is a very delicate process since quite often human life is in stake. The features are usually some test results like blood pressure or blood sugar rate, or symptoms like 'coughing at night' or not having feeling in the forefinger'. Features of a completely different nature are 'no heart problem in the family' or 'the patient had already this disease'. An appropriate feature extraction in medical diagnosis rely first on the objective test results and then on the patient's ability to provide an accurate description of the symptoms and 'related facts' in his family history. It is more than relevant for example for a person who is treated for hearing loss, to mention whether there are deaf people in his family.

In designing a *pattern recognition system*, i.e. a system that will be able to obtain an unknown incoming pattern and classify it in one (or more) of several given classes, we clearly want to employ all the available related information that was previously accumulated. We assume that some *sample patterns* with known classification are available. These patterns with their typical attributes form a *training set* which provides relevant information how to associate between input data and *decision making*. By using the training set the pattern recognition system may learn various types of information like statistical parameters, relevant features, etc.

The dominant concept in pattern recognition is that of *clustering*. A *cluster* consists of a number of *similar* objects (patterns) which are grouped together. We may consider a cluster of points in the *n*-dimensional space, a cluster of stars which seem to be grouped together or a cluster of people in the community whose annual income is under $20,000 per year. If we consider a cluster of people with 'low' income we take a further step and define a *fuzzy cluster*. Clustering given input data is a major subject in pattern recognition. It consists of dividing the data into clusters and establishing the *cluster centers* and *cluster boundaries*. An *a priori* knowledge of the number of clusters and their approximate locations definitely simplifies our task. We then carry a *supervised learning* process. If the data is of no known characteristic we obtain an *unsupervised learning* process.

Given input data it can be clustered in several ways. For example let the input consist of all the schools in town. If we cluster them geographically we get one set of clusters. If on the other hand we find *similarity* between schools only if the number of their students is similar, we obtain a different set of clusters. If we consider the attribute 'quality' we obtain a third set of clusters and this last partition is even ambiguous since people measure 'quality' differently.

1.2 CLASSIFIERS

The final goal in pattern recognition is classification of a pattern. From the original information that we obtain about the pattern we first identify the relevant features and then use a *feature extractor* to measure them. These measurements are then passed to a *classifier* which performs the actual classification, i.e., determines at which of the existing classes to classify the pattern. If the pattern is for example 'noise' it is rejected by the classifier.

In this section we assume the existence of *natural grouping*, i.e. we have some *a priori* knowledge about the classes and the data. For example we may know the exact or approximate number of the classes and the correct classification of some given patterns which are called the *training patterns*. Usually, it is this type of information and the type of the features that may suggest which classifier to apply for a given application.

Decision Functions

When the number of classes is known and when the training patterns are such that there is geometrical separation between the classes we can often use a set of decision functions to classify an unknown pattern. Consider for example a case where two classes C_1 and C_2 exist in R^n and a hyperplane $d(x) = 0$ which separates between their patterns can be found. Then we can use the *decision function* $d(x)$ as a *linear classifier* and classify each new pattern by

$$d(x) > 0 => x \in C_1$$

$$(1.2.1)$$

$$d(x) < 0 => x \in C_2$$

The hyperplane $d(x) = 0$ is called a *decision boundary*. If a set of hyperplanes can separate between m given classes in R^n, these classes are *linearly separable*. Quite often a set of classes cannot be discriminated by linear decision functions. In this case we can either use *generalized decision functions* (nonlinear) in the original *pattern space*, i.e. use a *nonlinear classifier* or transform the problem to a space of a much higher dimension where classification is carried using linear boundaries.

Minimum-Distance Classifiers

If the training patterns seem to form clusters we often use classifiers which use distance functions for classification. If each class is represented by a single prototype called the *cluster center*, we can use a *minimum-distance classifier* to classify a new pattern. A similar modified classifier is used if every class consists of several clusters. The *nearest-neighbor* classifier classifies a new pattern by measuring its distances from the training patterns and choosing the class to which the nearest neighbor belongs.

Sometimes the *a priori* information is the exact or approximate number of classes *c*. Each training pattern is in one of these classes but its specific classification is not known. In this case we use algorithms to determine the cluster (class) centers by minimizing some performance index. These centers are found iteratively and then a new pattern is classified using a minimum-distance classifier. One such algorithm is *c*-Means where the exact number of classes is known. A more ambiguous situation is assumed by the ISODATA algorithm. We only have a *desired* number *k* of clusters and the final number of classes which is determined by the algorithm cannot be much higher or much lower than *k*.

Statistical Approach

Many times the training patterns of various classes overlap for example when they are originated by some statistical distributions. In this case a statistical approach is appropriate, particularly when the various distribution functions of the classes are known. A statistical classifier must also evaluate the *risk* associated with every classification which measures the probability of *misclassification*. The *Bayes classifier* based on Bayes formula from probability theory minimizes the total expected *risk*. To use Bayes classifier one must know a priori the pattern distribution function for each class. If these distributions are not known they must be approximated using the training patterns. Sometimes the functional form of these distributions is known and one must only estimate its parameters. However, in some applications even the distribution's form is unknown and must (approximately) be found. To do so we may for example perform functional approximation using expansions by orthogonal functions.

Fuzzy Classifiers

Quite often classification is performed with some degree of uncertainty. Either the classification outcome itself may be in doubt, or the classified pattern x may belong in some degree to more than one class. Fore example a person 5'8" tall does not fully belong to the class 'tall', yet at the same time he cannot be fully accepted in the class 'short' (provided that only these two classes exist). We thus naturally introduce *fuzzy classification* where a pattern is a member of every class with some grade of membership between 0 and 1. In this text we are mainly interested in fuzzy classification using equivalence relations and in fuzzy clustering. The *crisp c-Means* algorithm is generalized and replaced by the *fuzzy c-Means* and after the cluster centers are determined, each incoming pattern is given a final set of *grades of membership* which determine the degrees of its classification in the various clusters.

Syntactic Approach

Unlike the previous approaches, the *syntactic pattern recognition* utilizes the *structure* of the patterns. Instead of carrying an analysis based strictly on quantitative characteristics of the pattern, we emphasize the interrelationships between the *primitives*, the components which compare the pattern. Typical patterns which are subject to syntactic pattern recognition research are therefore characters, fingerprints, chromosomes, etc. The analogy between the structure of some patterns and the syntax of a language which has a solid theoretical basis is very attractive. By introducing the concept of a formal grammar and language we are able to design syntax classifiers that can classify a given pattern which is now presented as a string of symbols. In general, given a specific class, a grammar whose language consists of patterns in this class is designed. For an unknown new pattern a syntax classifier analyzes the pattern (a string) in a process called *parsing* and determines whether or not that string belongs to the language (class).

Neural Nets

The neural net approach assumes as other apporaches before that a set of training patterns and their correct classifications is given. The *architecture* of the net which includes *input layer*, *output layer* and *hidden layers* may be very complex. It is characterized by a set of weights and activation function which determine how any information (input signal) is being transmitted to the output layer. The neural net is trained by training patterns and adjusts the weights until the correct classifications are obtained. It is then used to classify arbitrary unknown patterns. There are several popular neural net classifiers, from the simple *perceptron* to the more advanced *backpropagation classifier.*

Pattern recognition and classification have been used for numerous applications. A detailed list is given below:

1. *Scientific Applications*:
   (a) Astronomy: telescope resolution improvements and atmospheric degradation removal.
   (b) Geology—planetary exploration: crater counts, color analysis, robotics, topography, atmospheric measurements and analysis, landing site and related evaluations, and terrestrial geologic feature analysis and charting.
   (c) Geology—cartography and geodesy: mosaicing, surface model fitting, and maps (making and alteration).
   (d) Bubble chamber tracking and electron microscope crystallography.
   (e) Satellite data analysis.
   (f) Sensing for life and date analysis on remote planets.
2. *Life and Behavioral Sciences*:
   (a) Anthropology.
   (b) Archeology.
   (c) Entomology.
   (d) Biology and botany: microbiology, ecology, and zoology.
   (e) Psychology: sociological aspects and criminological aspects.
   (f) Cybernetics.
   (g) Information management systems.
   (h) Education.
   (i) Communication.
3. *Industrial Applications*:
   (a) Character recognition.
   (b) Image controlled machines (process control).
   (c) Signature analysis.
   (d) Speech analysis.

(e) Photographic recognition.

(f) Mineral exploration (subsurface analysis).

(g) Internal flow detection (X-ray and sonic).

(h) Commercial photograph enhancement.

(i) Multimedia and animation.

(j) Electronic toys design.

(k) Automated cytology.

4. *Medical Applications*:

(a) Microscopic examination and biomedical data: blood cell counting and blood tests, cancer cell identification and tests, neuron measurements, chromosome karyotyping, bone composition analysis, automated focusing and positioning, and brain-tissue studies.

(b) Radioisotope examination.

(c) X-ray examination and tomography: blood vessel thickness measurements, heart size measurements, breast cancer detection, intracranial blood vessel constriction detection, dental charting and analysis, bone structure analysis, pulmonary disease diagnosis, and skeletal structure analysis.

(d) Electrocardiogram and vectorcardiogram analysis.

(e) Electroencephalogram tracing and neurobiological signal processing.

(f) Drug interaction.

(g) Chromosome properties for genetic studies.

5. *Agricultural Applications*:

(a) Crop analysis.

(b) Soil evaluation.

(c) Process control.

(d) Earth-resource photography.

6. *Governmental Applications*:

(a) Weather prediction: cloud tracking and water temperature measurements.

(b) Public systems: traffic analysis and control, urban growth determination, smog detection and measurement, and air traffic radar data reduction.

(c) Earth-resource data and remote sensing.

7. *Some Specific Military Applications*:
    (a) Aerial photography and remote sensing.
    (b) Sonor detection and classification.
    (c) ATR: Automatic Target Recognition.

1.3 DATA MINING AND KNOWLEDGE DISCOVERY

Even though this text represents only the fundamental entities in the field of pattern recognition, we feel that it will not be complete without devoting a small section to the subject of data mining and knowledge discovery, in which classification plays a major role.

Throughout the text when we talk about classification, what we have in mind is the process assigning an item to its "natural group". In a more concrete sense, the objective of clustering is to sort a data set into categories such that the degree of "natural association" is high among members of the same category and low between members of different categories. In many cases, however, classification means *finding* the categories themselves from a given set of unclassified data. In essence this is what knowledge discovery and data mining is all about. When acquiring knowledge from data, the problem at times may be in the data itself, which may have limited breadth or coverage. While the development of databases has provided us with an effective tool for storage and lookup of large data sets, the issues related to knowledge discovery in these data glut, depends heavily on the field of pattern classification, since the notion of finding useful patterns (which in essence are just nuggets of knowledge) from raw data is the essence of information harvesting, which this text is all about.

Knowledge discovery (KD) and data mining (DM) systems draw upon methods and techniques from the field of pattern recognition, as well as related topics in database systems, artificial intelligence, machine learning, statistics, and expert systems, where the unifying goal is extracting knowledge from large volumes of data.

In their edited volume "Advances in Knowledge Discovery and Data Mining", Fayyad et.al. provide us with the following statement:

> *Knowledge discovery in databases (KDD) is the non-binial process of identifying valid, novel, potentially useful, and ultimately understandable patterns in data.*

They use the notion of *interestingness* to denote the *overall* measure of pattern value, combining validity, novelty, usefulness, and simplicity. The data mining step in the knowledge discovery process is therefore concerned with *means* by which patterns are extracted (as well as enumerated) from the raw data. In essence, the knowledge discovery process itself involves the evaluation and interpretation of the different patterns in order to provide decision-making with additional information on what constitutes knowledge and what does not. We should keep in mind, however, that in the context of knowledge discovery, *description* (finding human-interpretable patterns describing the data) tends to be more important than *prediction* (using some variables in the database in order to predict unknown other variables of interest), which is in contrast to pattern recognition, where prediction is usually the major goal of the analysis process.

One particular approach which we would like to mention is that of extracting fuzzy rules from raw data, which allows relationships in the raw data to be modelled by Fuzzy IF-THEN rules that are easy to validate and understand. Because fuzzy logic allows us to express nonlinear relationships by simple sets of qualitative IF-THEN rules, we can easily capture the essence of data behavior. Capturing that behavior, which is in essence knowledge discovery, in the form of Fuzzy IF-THEN rules, rather than by neural networks or surface approximation, provide us with a set of fuzzy rules which are easy to verify, validate, understand, explain and extend. This is a powerful framework not only for capturing the behavior of high dimensional data sets but also for explaining the behavior of the data sets, especially in non-stationary cases as well as in those cases where missing and noisy data is an acute pattern or when complex relationships exist between fields representing the data in a database. With the increase awareness of the advantages of representing classifiers in the form of sets of fuzzy IF-THEN rules, extracting fuzzy rules from raw data, with or without neural networks (for adaptive learning) will result in efficient and robust algorithms, especially for high dimensional and noisy data.

1.4   REFERENCES

For additional information on pattern recognition we refer the reader to the following sources. These include many classical monographs which explore in depth a variety of topics covered in our text.

[Agarwala 1977] AGARWALA, A.K., (ed.), *Machine Recogniton of Patterns*, IEEE Press, 1977.

[Anderberg 1973] ANDERBERG, M.R., *Cluster Analysis for Applications*, Academic Press, New York, 1973.

[Anderson/Rosefeld 1988] ANDERSON, J.A., AND E. ROSENFELD (eds.), *Neuro-computing: Foundations of Research*, MIT Press, Cambridge, Mass., 1988.

[Backer 1995] BACKER, E., *Computer-assisted Reasoning in Cluster Analysis*, Prentice Hall, Great Britain, 1995.

[Bezdek 1981] BEZDEK, J., *Pattern Recognition with Fuzzy Objective Function Algorithms*, Plenum Press, New York, 1981.

[Bezdek/Pal 1992] BEZDEK, J.C. AND S.K. PAL (eds.), *Fuzzy Models for Pattern Recognition: Methods that Search for Pattern in Data*, IEEE Press, New York, 1992.

[Bow 1984] BOW, S.T., *Pattern Recognition*, Marcel Dekker, New York, 1984.

[Bunke 1982] BUNKE, H., 'Attributed Programmed Graph Grammars and Their Application to Schematic Diagram Interpretation,' *IEEE Transactions on Pattern Analysis and Machine Intelligence*, Vol. PAMI-4, No. 6, Nov. 1982, pp. 574-582.

[Carpenter 1989] CARPENTER, G., 'Neural Network Models for Pattern Recognition and Associative Memory,' *Neural Networks*, Vol. 2, 1989, pp. 243-257.

[Chen 1973] CHEN, C.H., *Statistical Pattern* Recognition, Hayden, Washington, D.D., 1973.

[Chien 1978] CHIEN, Y.T., *Interactive Pattern* Recognition, Marcel Dekker, New York, 1978.

[Coleman/Andrews 1979] COLEMAN, G.B., AND H.C. ANDREWS, 'Image Segmentation by Clustering,' *Proceedings of the IEEE*, Vol. 67, May 1979, pp. 773-785.

[Devijver/Kittler 1982] DEVIJVER, P., AND J. KITTLER, *Pattern Recognition: A Statistical Approach*, Prentice-Hall, Englewood Cliffs, N.J., 1982.

[Dubois/Pvade 1979] DUBOIS, D. AND H. PVADE, *Fuzzy Sets and Systems: Theory and Applications*, Academic Press, New York, 1979.

[Duda/Hart 1973] DUDA, R.O., AND P.E. Hart, *Pattern Classification and Scene Analysis*, John Wiley & Sons, New York, 1973.

[Everitt 1977] EVERITT, B., *Cluster Analysis*, Heinemann Educational Books, 1977.

[Fausett 1994] FAUSETT, L., *Fundamentals of Neural Networks*, Prentice Hall, Englewood Cliffs, N.J., 1994.

[Fayyad/et.al. 1996] FAYYAD, U.M. et. al. (eds.) Advances in Knowledge Discovery and Data Mining, AAAI Press/the MIT Press, Merile lPark, California, 1996.

[Fu 1968] FU, K.S., *Sequential Methods in Pattern Recognition and Machine Learing*, Academic Press, New York, 1968.

[Fu 1974] FU, K.S., *Syntactic Methods in Pattern Recognition*, Academic Press, New York, 1974.

[Fu 1980] FU, K.S., '*Recent Developments in Pattern Recognition*,' IEEE Transactions on Computers, Vol. C-29, No. 10, Oct. 1980, pp. 845-857.

[FU 1 1982] FU, K.S., *Syntactic Pattern Recognition and Applications*, Prentice-Hall, Englewood Cliffs, N.J., 1982.

[Fu 2 1982] FU, K.S. (ed), *Application of Pattern Recognition*, CRC Press, Cleveland, OH, 1982.

[Fu/Young 1985] FU, K.S., AND T.Y. YOUNG (eds.), *Handbook of Pattern Recognition and Image Processing*, Academic Press, New York, 1985.

[Fukunaga 1972] FUKUNAGA, K., *Introduction to Statistical Pattern Recognition*, Academic Press, New York, 1972.

[Gonzales/Thomason 1978] GONZALEZ, R.C., AND M.G. Thomason, *Syntactic Pattern Recognition*, Addison-Wesley, Reading, Mass., 1978.

[Haralick 1978] HARALICK, R.M., 'Structural Pattern Recognition, Homomorphisms, and Arrangements,' *Pattern Recognition*, Vol. 10, 1978, pp. 223-236.

[Hartigan 1975] HARTIGAN, J.A., *Clustering Algorithms*, John Wiley & Sons, New York, 1975.

[Hopfield/Tank 1986] HOPFIELD, J.J., AND D.W. TANK, 'computing with Neural Circuits: A Model,' *Science*, Vol. 233, Aug. 1986, pp. 625-633.

[Hwang et al. 1986] HWANG, V.S., L.S. DAVIS, AND T. MATUSUYAMA, 'Hypothesis Integration in Image Understanding Systems,' *Computer Vision, Graphics and Image Processing*, Vol. 36, 1986, pp. 321-371.

[Jain/Dubes 1988] JAIN, A.K., AND R. Dubes, Algorithms for Clustering Data, Prentice-Hall, Englewood Cliffs, N.J., 1988.

[Jang/et.al. 1997] JANG, J.-S.R., C.-T. SUN, AND E. MIZUTANI *Neuro-Fuzzy and Soft Computing*, Prentice Hall, Upper Saddle River, N.J., 1997.

[Kanal 1979] KANAL, L.N., 'Problem-solving Models and Search Strategies for Pattern Recognition,' *IEEE Transactions on Pattern Analysis and Machine Intelligence*, Vol. PAMI-1, April 1979, pp. 194-201.

[Kandel/Yelowitz 1974] KANDEL, A. AND Yelovitz, Fuzzy Chairs, IEEE Transactions on System, Man and Cybernetics, SMC-4, pp. 472-475, 1974.

[Kandel 1975] KANDEL, A., Fuzzy Hierarchical Classifications Of Dynamic Patterns, *Invited presentation at NATO A.S.I. on Pattern Recognition and Classification*, France, September 3-17, 1975.

[Kandel 1979] KANDEL, A., 'Fuzzy Techniques In the Clustering of Static And Dynamic Patterns', *Proceedings of the 1979 International Conference on Cybernetics and Society*, Denver, October 1979.

[Kandel 1982] KANDEL, A., *Fuzzy Techniques in Pattern Recognition*, Wiley Intersciences, New York, 1982.

[Kandel 1986] KANDEL, A., *Mathematical Techniques with Applications*, Addison-Wesley Publishing Co., Reading, Mass., 1986.

[Kandel et.al 1997] KANDEL, A., Y.Q. ZHANG, H. BUNKE, 'A Genetic Fuzzy Neural Network for Pattern Recognition,' *Proceedings of FUZZ-IEEE 1997*, pp. 11-21, July 1997, Barcelona, Spain.

[Khanna 1990] KHANNA, T., *Foundations of Neural Networks*, Addison-Wesley, Reading, Mass., 1990.

[Klir/Yuan 1995] KLIR, G.J. AND B. YUAN, *Fuzzy Sets and Fuzzy Logic: Theory and Applications*, Prentice Hall, Upper Saddle River, N.J., 1995.

[Kohonen 1984] KOHONEN, T., *Self-Organization and Associative Memory*, Springer-Verlag, Berlin, 1984.

[Kosko 1990] KOSKO, B., 'Unsupervised Learning in Noise,' *IEEE Transactions on Neural Networks*, Vol. 1, No. 1, March 1990, pp. 44-57.

[Kosko 1991] KOSKO, B., *Neural Networks and Fuzzy Systems*, Prentice Hall, Englewood Cliffs, NY, 1991.

[Miclet 1986] MICLET, L., *Structural Methods in Pattern Recognition*, Springer-Verlag, New York, 1986.

[Pal/Majumder 1986] PAL, S.K., AND D.K.D. MAJUMDER, *Fuzzy Mathematical Approach to Pattern Recognition*, John Wiley & Sons, New York, 1986.

[Pal/Pal 1986] PAL, N.R., K. PAL AND J.C. BEZDEK, 'A Mixed *c*-Means Clustering Model,' *Proceedings of FUZZ-IEEE 1997*, pp. 11-21, July 1997, Barcelona, Spain.

[Pao 1989] PAO, Y.H., Adaptive *Pattern Recognition and Neural Networks*, Addison-Wesley, Reading, Mass., 1989.

[Patrick 1972] PATRICK, E. A., *Fundamentals of Pattern Recognition*, Prentice-Hall, Englewood Cliffs, N.J., 1972.

[Pavlidis 1977] PAVLIDIS, T., *Structural Pattern Recognition*, Springer-Verlag, New York, 1977.

[Pedrycz 1990] PEDRYCZ, W., *Fuzzy Sets in Pattern Recognition Methodology and Methods, Pattern Recognition*, vol. 23, pp. 121-146, 1990.

[Pedrycz 1995] PEDRYCZ, W., *Fuzzy Sets Engineering*, CRC Press, Boca Raton, Florida, 1995.

[Rosenfeld 1979] ROSENFELD, A., *Picture Languages*, Academic Press, new York, 1979.

[Rosenfeld 1984] ROSENFELD, A., *The Fuzzy Geometry of Image Subjects, Pattern Recognition Letters*, vol. 2, pp. 311-317, 1984.

[Ross 1995] ROSS, T.J., *Fuzzy Logic With Engineering Applications*, McGraw-Hill, Inc., 1995.

[Rummelhart/McClelland 1 1986] RUMMELHART, D.E., AND J.L. McCLELLAND, *Parallel Distributed Processing—Explorations in the Microstructure of Cognition, Volume 1: Foundations*, MIT Press, Cambridge, Mass., 1986.

[Rummelhart/McClelland 2 1986] RUMMELHART, D.E., AND J.L. McCLELLAND, *Parallel Distributed Processing—Explorations in the Microstructure of Cognition, Volume 2: Psychological and Biological Models*, MIT Press, Cambridge, Mass., 1986.

[Ruspini 1969] RUSPINI, E., 'A New Approach to Clustering,' *Inf. Control*, Vol. 15, pp. 22-32.

[Schalkoff 1989] SCHALKOFF, R.J., *Digital Image Processing and Computer Vision*, John Wiley & Sons, New York, 1989.

[Schalkoff 1992] SCHALKOFF, R.J., *Pattern Recognition: Statistical, Structural and Neural Approaches*, John Wiley & Sons, 1992.

[Simpson 1990] SIMPSON, P.K., *Artificial Neural Systems*, Pergamon Press, Elmsford, New York, 1990.

[Sklansky 1973] SKLANSKY, J. (ed.), *Pattern Recognition: Introduction and Foundations*, Dowden, Hutchinson and Ross, Straudsburg, Pa., 1973.

[Tamura/et al 1971] TAMURA, S., S. HIGUCHI, and K. TANAKA, 'Pattern classification Based on Fuzzy Relations,' *IEEE Trans. Syst. Man Cybern.*, vol. 1, pp. 61-66.

[Therrien 1989] THERRIEN, C.W., *Decision Estimation and Classification: An Introduction to Pattern Recognition and Related Topics*, John Wiley & Sons, New York, 1989.

[Thomason 1975] THOMASON, M.G., *Finite Fuzzy Automata, Regular Languages and Pattern Recognition*, Pattern Recognition, vol. 5, pp. 383-390, 1975.

[Tou/Gonzalez 1974] TOU, J., AND R. GONZALEZ, *Pattern Recognition Principles*, Addison Wesley, Reading, Mass., 1974.

[Turksen 1993] Turksen, I.B. AND S. Jiang, *Rule Base Reorganization and Search with a Fuzzy Cluster Analysis*, International Journal of Approximate Reasoning, vol. 9., no. 3, pp. 1267-196, 1993.

[Watanable 1985] WATANABE, S., *Pattern Recognition: Human and Mechanical*, John Wiley & Sons, New York, 1985.

[Yager/Zadeh 1992] YAGER, R.R. AND L.A. Zadeh (eds.), An Introduction to Fuzzy Logic Applications in Intelligent Systems, Kluwer, Boston, 1992.

[Yager/Zadeh 1994] YAGER, R.R. AND L.A. ZADEH (eds.), *Fuzzy Sets, Neural Networks and Soft Computing*, Von Nostrand Reinhold, New York, 1994.

[Yager/Filev 1994] YAGER, R.R. AND D.P. FILEV, *Essentials of Fuzzy Modeling and Control*, John Wiley & Sons, New York, 1994.

[Young/Calvert 1974] YOUNG, T.Y., AND T.W. CALVERT, *Classification, Estimation and Pattern Recognition*, Elsevier, New York, 1974.

[Zadeh 1965] ZADEH, L., 'Fuzzy Sets,' *Inf. Control*, 8 pp. 338-353, 1965.

[Zadeh 1971] ZADEH, L., 'Similarity Relations and Fuzzy Orderings,' *Inf. Sci.*, vol. 3, pp. 177-200.

[Zadeh 1975] ZADEH, L., et.al., *Fuzzy Sets and Their Applications to Cognitive and Decision Processes*, Academic Press, New York, 1975.

[Zimmerman 1985] ZIMMERMAN, H.J., *Fuzzy Set Theory and its Applications*, Kluwer, Boston, 1985.

[Zimmerman 1987] ZIMMERMAN, H.J., *Fuzzy Sets, Decision Making and Expert Systems*, Kluwer, Boston, 1987.

The following journals contain major papers on the theory of pattern recognition and its applications:

Pattern Recognition

Pattern Recognition - letters

IEEE Transactions on Pattern Analysis and Machine Intelligence

IEEE Transactions on Neural Networks

IEEE Transactions on Fuzzy Systems

IEEE Transactions on Systems, Man and Cybernetics

Fuzzy Sets and Systems

Information Sciences

International Journal of Pattern Recognition and Artificial Intelligence

2 DECISION FUNCTIONS

The main task of a pattern recognition system is to provide decisions based on given samples, by which incoming patterns can be classified. In this chapter we introduce the first approach - using decision functions.

2.1 BASIC CONCEPTS

We start with a simple example. Let C_1 and C_2 be two pattern classes, samples of which are shown in Fig. 2.1.1. Each sample pattern is a vector $x = (x_1, x_2)^T$ in the $x_1 - x_2$ plane, denoted by either $\bullet \, (x \in C_1)$ or $\circ \, (x \in C_2)$.

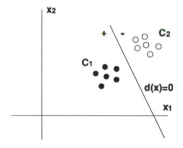

■ **Figure 2.1.1** Linear decision function; two pattern classes.

The two populations can be clearly separated by a straight line. Let $d(x) = 0$ be such a line. Then, its coefficients given by

$$d(x) = w_1 x_1 + w_2 x_2 + w_3 = 0 \qquad (2.1.1)$$

can be rearranged such that $d(x) > 0$ for all $x \in C_1$ and $d(x) < 0$ for all $x \in C_2$. For any incoming x known *a priori* to belong to either C_1 or C_2, we can calculate $d(x)$ and *decide* that $x \in C_1$ if $d(x) > 0$ and $x \in C_2$ if $d(x) < 0$. Thus, $d(x)$ is a linear *decision function* of C_1.

This particular example can be easily extended to the case of two pattern classes C_1, C_2 in the n-dimensional Euclidean vector space R^n. Assume the classes to be geometrically separated by the hyperplane

$$d(x) = w_1 x_1 + w_2 x_2 + \ldots + w_n x_n + w_{n+1} = w_0^T x + w_{n+1} = 0 \qquad (2.1.2)$$

where $w_0 = (w_1, w_2, \ldots, w_n)^T$ is the *weight* vector, such that

$$d(x) > 0, \quad \text{for} \ \ x \in C_1$$
$$\qquad (2.1.3)$$
$$d(x) < 0, \quad \text{for} \ \ x \in C_2$$

Then, for an arbitrary incoming x at $C_1 \cup C_2$, we can decide

$$d(x) > 0, \ \Rightarrow \ x \in C_1$$
$$\qquad (2.1.4)$$
$$d(x) > 0, \ \Rightarrow \ x \in C_2$$

Usually, x and w_0 of Eq. (2.1.2) are replaced by the *augmented* pattern and weight vectors $x = (x_1, x_2, \ldots, x_n, 1)^T$ and $w = (w_1, w_2, \ldots, w_{n+1})^T$ for which one gets

$$d(x) = w^T x \qquad (2.1.5)$$

A decision function may not be linear. In Fig. 2.1.2 the two pattern classes are separated by the circumference $d(x) = 1 - x_1^2 - x_2^2 = 0$. Since $d(x) > 0$ for all $x \in C_1$ and $d(x) < 0$ for all $x \in C_2$, $d(x)$ is a *nonlinear* decision function of C_1. The membership of an incoming x in either C_1 or C_2 will be decided by using Eq. (2.1.4).

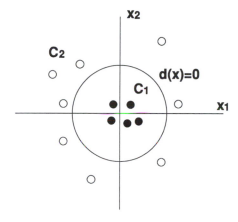

■ **Figure 2.1.2** Nonlinear decision function; two pattern classes.

In general there are m pattern classes $\{C_1, C_2, \ldots, C_m\}$ in R^n and a decision function is defined as follows.

■ **Definition 2.1.1** Let $C_1, C_2, \ldots, C_m$ be m pattern classes in R^n. If a surface $d(x) = 0$, $x \in R^n$ separates between some C_i and the remaining C_j, $j \neq i$, i.e.

$$d(x) > 0, \quad x \in C_i$$

$$d(x) < 0, \quad x \in C_j, \quad j \neq i$$

(2.1.6)

then $d(x)$ will be called a *decision function* of C_i.

Naturally, the domain of definition for $d(x)$ must include the union of $C_1, C_2, \ldots, C_m$.

For the sake of simplicity, pattern classes would be often denoted in figures by the boundaries of the regions where the given sample patterns fall.

■   **Example 2.1.1** Let C_1 and C_2 be the pattern classes of Fig. 2.1.3. The parabola $x_1^3 - x_2 = 0$ is a decision function of C_1.   Usually, the number of legitimate decision functions is infinite. In this particular case, $d^*(x) = x_1 - x_2$ is also a possible decision function.

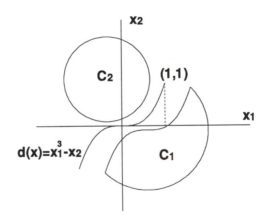

■   **Figure 2.1.3**   A decision function for Example 2.1.1.

■   **Example 2.1.2**   Let C_1, C_2, C_3 be the pattern classes of Fig. 2.1.4. The parabola $d_1(x) = 1 - x_1^2 - x_2 = 0$ is a decision function for C_1, while $d_2(x) = 6x_1 + 7x_2 - 21$ is a decision function of C_2.   Unlike in the previous example, a linear decision function for C_1 does not exist.

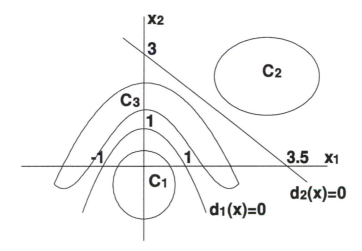

■ **Figure 2.1.4**   Decision functions for Example 2.1.2.

♠

Throughout the next section we shall discuss various cases where the given pattern classes are *linearly separable,* i.e. where linear decision functions that separate between the pattern classes may be found.

PROBLEMS

1. Two possible linear decision functions for C_1 and C_2 are $d_1(x) = 2 - x_1$ and $d_1^*(x) = 3 - x_1$.   Which one is a better choice? Explain.

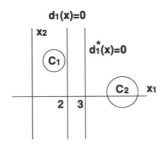

2. Let $x, y \in C_1$ and let $z = \dfrac{x + y}{2}$ (vector sum) belong to C_2. Are C_1 and C_2 linearly separable? Explain.

3. Repeat and solve problem 2 for

   (a) $z = 2x - y$

   (b) $z = x - y$

2.2   LINEAR DECISION FUNCTIONS

Given m pattern classes $C_1, C_2, \ldots, C_m$ in R^n we distinguish between two cases.

I. Absolute separation

If each pattern class C_i has a linear decision function $d_i(x)$, i.e.

$$d_i(x) = w_i^T x = \begin{cases} > 0, & x \in C_i \\ < 0, & \text{otherwise} \end{cases} \tag{2.2.1}$$

for $1 \leq i \leq m$, where w_i is the weight vector associated with $d_i(x)$, then *absolute separation* exist between $C_1, C_2, \ldots, C_m$ or $\{C_i\}_{i=1}^m$ are *absolutely separable*. In other words $\{C_i\}_{i=1}^m$ are absolutely separable if each C_i is linearly separated from the remaining pattern classes.

■ **Example 2.2.1**   Consider the pattern classes C_1, C_2, C_3 in Fig. 2.2.1. The straight lines $d_1(x) = 2 - x_2 = 0$, $d_2(x) = -x_1 + x_2 - 2 = 0$ and $d_3(x) = x_1 + x_2 - 4 = 0$ provide decision functions for C_1, C_2, C_3 respectively , i.e. C_1, C_2 and C_3 are absolutely separable.

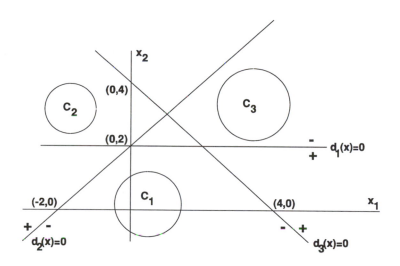

■ **Figure 2.2.1.** Absolute separation.

Given absolutely separable pattern classes $\{C_i\}_{i=1}^m$, how do we classify an incoming pattern x? Let us consider the previous example. For each $y \in C_1$ three fragments of knowledge are available, namely, $d_1(y) > 0$, $d_2(y) < 0$ and $d_3(y) < 0$. Without further information, it is reasonable to classify x as a member of C_1 if $d_1(x) > 0$, $d_2(x) < 0$ and $d_3(x) < 0$. This leads to the following definition.

■ **Definition 2.2.1** (decision region): Let the pattern classes $\{C_i\}_{i=1}^m$ be absolutely   separable   by   the   linear   decision   functions $d_1(x), d_2(x), \ldots, d_m(x)$ respectively. Then the vector sets

$$D_i = \left\{ x \mid d_i(x) > 0; \ d_j(x) < 0, \ j \neq i \right\}, \ 1 \leq i \leq m \qquad (2.2.2)$$

are called the *decision regions* of $C_1, C_2, \ldots, C_m$ respectively.

Note that each pattern class C_i, is a subset of its associated decision region D_i and that decision regions depend directly on the particular choice of decision functions.

■ **Example 2.2.2**   The decision regions associated with the previous example are the shaded are as in Fig. 2.2.2.

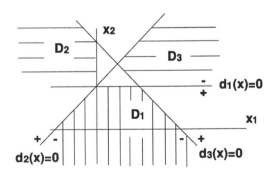

■ **Figure 2.2.2.** Decision regions for Example 2.2.1.

It should be noted that while pattern classes are usually bounded, their associated decision regions may not be.

■ **Example 2.2.3** The pattern classes C_1, C_2, C_3, C_4 in Fig. 2.2.3 are such that no linear decision function exists for C_4. However, any three of the four classes are absolutely separable.

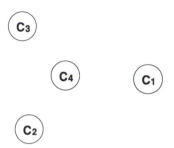

■ **Figure 2.2.3** A case with no absolute separation.

♠

II. Pairwise separation

In the absence of absolute separation, partial separation between pattern classes, can still occur if each pair of them can be separated by a linear decision function. In this case the pattern classes are said to be *pairwise separable*. Each pair of classes C_i and C_j are associated with a linear decision function d_{ij} such that

$$d_{ij}(x) > 0 \ \textit{for all } x \in C_i$$

$$d_{ij}(x) < 0 \ \textit{for all } x \in C_j \tag{2.2.3}$$

Consequently, for all $x \in C_i$ we have

$$d_{ij}(x) > 0 \ \textit{for all } j \neq i \tag{2.2.4}$$

Also, for all i and j: $d_{ji}(x) = -d_{ij}(x)$.

Since, Eq. (2.2.4) provides the maximum possible knowledge about C_i, associated with the particular decision function set $\{d_{ij}(x)\}_{i,j=1}^{m}$, it suggests a natural procedure for classifying incoming patterns. A pattern x will belong to C_i, if and only if Eq. (2.2.4) holds.

■ **Example 2.2.4**   Let C_1, C_2 and C_3 be the pattern classes shown in Fig. 2.2.4. The linear decision functions $d_{12}(x) = x_1 - 5$, $d_{23}(x) = -x_2 + 3$ and $d_{13}(x) = x_1 - 2x_2 + 2$ separate between the pairs (C_1, C_2), (C_2, C_3) and (C_1, C_3) respectively. Therefore C_1, C_2 and C_3 are pairwise separable.

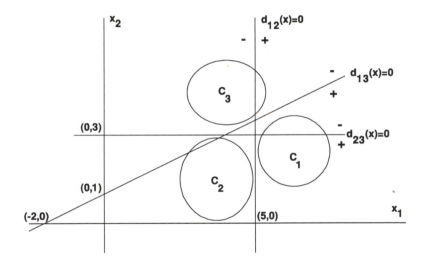

■ **Figure 2.2.4** Pairwise separation.

Decision regions in the case of pairwise separation are defined as follows.

■ **Definition 2.2.2** (decision region). Let the pattern classes $C_1, C_2, \ldots, C_m$ be pairwise separable by the linear decision functions $\{d_{ij}(x)\}_{i,j=1}^{m}$. Then the vector sets

$$D_i = \{x \mid d_{ij}(x) > 0, \ j \neq i\}, \ 1 \leq i \leq m \qquad (2.2.5)$$

are called the decision regions of $C_1, C_2, \ldots, C_m$ respectively.

■ **Example 2.2.5** The decision regions of C_1, C_2, C_3 in the previous example are shown in Fig. 2.2.5. In order to get D_2 we take $d_{21}(x) = -d_{12}(x)$, and to obtain D_3 we use $d_{31}(x) = -d_{13}(x)$ and $d_{32}(x) = -d_{23}(x)$.

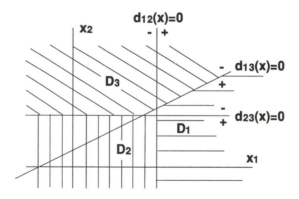

■ **Figure 2.2.5** Decision regions for Example 2.2.5.

In both cases, i.e. absolute separation and pairwise separation, the union of the decision regions is usually not the whole space. Thus, an incoming pattern x may not be classified as a member of any of the existing pattern classes. For obvious reasons the ambiguous region is larger in the case of absolute separation, than in the case of pairwise separation.

A common particular case of pairwise separation occurs when linear functions $d_1(x)$, $d_2(x),\ldots,d_m(x)$ such that for all $x \in C_i$, $1 \le i \le m$

$$d_i(x) > d_j(x) \ \text{ for all } \ j \ne i \tag{2.2.6}$$

exist. It is easily seen that by defining $d_{ij}(x) = d_i(x) - d_j(x)$ for $1 \le i, j \le m$, we obtain a case of pairwise separation. However, the union of the decision regions is now the whole space, i.e. no ambiguous region exists. Indeed, for any incoming pattern x we can find i for which

$$d_i(x) = \max[d_j(x)], \ 1 \le j \le m \tag{2.2.7}$$

and then classify x as a member of C_i. If the maximum is achieved for several $i's$ we choose (for example) the smallest.

If Eq. (2.2.6) holds, there is a simple geometric interpretation to the empty ambiguous region: The straight lines $d_{12}(x)$, $d_{23}(x)$, $d_{13}(x)$, intersect at one point. Indeed, if $d_1(x) - d_2(x) = 0$ and $d_2(x) - d_3(x) = 0$ then clearly $d_1(x) - d_3(x) = 0$ as well.

PROBLEMS

1. Sketch an example of three pattern classes where no pair is linearly separable.

2. The samples of the pattern classes C_1 and C_2 are located within unit circles centered at (1,0) and (4,0) respectively. Choose a linear decision function, if in addition, it is known that any incoming pattern $x = (x_1, x_2)^T$ which belongs to C_1, must satisfy $x_1 \le 2.5$. Explain.

3. Let $C_1, C_2,\ldots, C_m$ be a pattern classes 'represented' by the vertices of a convex polygon. Show that $\{C_i\}_{i=1}^m$ are absolutely separable.

4. Let C_1 be a pattern class whose patterns are inside a unit circle centered at $(1,0)$. The patterns of a second class C_2 are located inside a unit circle centered at $(4,0)$ except for a single pattern y which is located elsewhere. Sketch the forbidden region for y if C_1 and C_2 are linearly separable.

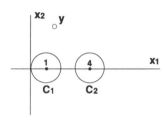

5. Let $d_1(x) = x_1 - 1$, $d_2(x) = x_2 - 2$ and $d_3(x) = x_1 - x_2 - 1$ denote decision functions associated with three given pattern classes C_1, C_2 and C_3 respectively. Sketch the decision regions in the following cases.

(a) Absolute separation
(b) Pairwise separation with $d_{ij}(x) = d_i(x) - d_j(x)$.

In case (a) compare the decision regions to those of Example 2.2.2.

6. Consider the problem where each pattern class consists of a single pattern.

(a) Are three pattern classes absolutely separable? What is the exception?
(b) Sketch a nontrivial example of four pattern classes which is not absolutely separable.
(c) Can you sketch a five-class problem where absolute separation occurs for every four classes but not for the complete problem?

2.3   GENERALIZED DECISION FUNCTIONS

Classes which do not share a single pattern may always be separated. However, decision boundaries which separate between classes, may not always be linear (see Fig. 2.1.2). The complexity of these boundaries may sometimes request the use of highly nonlinear surfaces. A popular approach to generalize the concept of linear decision functions is to consider a *generalized decision function* defined as

$$d(x) = w_1 f_1(x) + \ldots + w_N f_N(x) + w_{N+1} \tag{2.3.1}$$

where $f_i(x)$, $1 \leq i \leq N$ are scalar functions of the pattern x, $x \in R^n$. Introducing $f_{N+1}(x) = 1$ we get

$$d(x) = \sum_{i=1}^{N+1} w_i f_i(x) = w^T x^* \tag{2.3.2}$$

where

$$w = \begin{pmatrix} w_1 \\ w_2 \\ \vdots \\ w_N \\ w_{N+1} \end{pmatrix}, \quad x^* = \begin{pmatrix} f_1(x) \\ f_2(x) \\ \vdots \\ f_N(x) \\ f_{N+1}(x) \end{pmatrix} \tag{2.3.3}$$

The representation of $d(x)$ by Eqs. (2.3.2) and (2.3.3) implies that *any* decision function defined by Eq. (2.3.1) can be treated as linear, provided that we first transform *all* the original patterns x into x^* by calculating $f_i(x)$, $1 \leq i \leq N$ for every individual x. Although $d(x)$ is linear in the $(N+1)-$ dimensional space whose dimension $N+1$ is usually considerably greater than n, it certainly maintains its nonlinearity characteristics in R^n.

As expected, the most commonly used generalized decision function is $d(x)$ for which $f_i(x)$, $1 \le i \le N$ are polynomials. If these functions are all linear in R^n, then $d(x)$ can be rewritten as

$$d(x) = (w^*)^T x \qquad (2.3.4)$$

where w^* is a new weight vector, which can be calculated from the original w and the original linear $f_i(x)$, $1 \le i \le N$ in Eq. (2.3.1). The expression in Eq. (2.3.4) is identical to that in Eq. (2.1.2) from the previous section.

Let us now consider quadratic decision functions. For 2-dimensional patterns (i.e. $n = 2$), the most general decision function is

$$d(x) = w_1 x_1^2 + w_2 x_1 x_2 + w_3 x_2^2 + w_4 x_1 + w_5 x_2 + w_6 \qquad (2.3.5)$$

i.e. $w = (w_1, w_2, \ldots, w_6)^T$ and $x^* = (x_1^2, x_1 x_2, x_2^2, x_1, x_2, 1)^T$. For patterns $x \in R^n$ the most general quadratic decision function is given by

$$d(x) = \sum_{i=1}^{n} w_{ii} x_i^2 + \sum_{i=1}^{n-1} \sum_{j=i+1}^{n} w_{ij} x_i x_j + \sum_{i=1}^{n} w_i x_i + w_{n+1} \qquad (2.3.6)$$

The number of terms at the right-hand side of Eq. (2.3.6) is

$$l = N + 1 = n + \frac{n(n-1)}{2} + n + 1 = \frac{(n+1)(n+2)}{2} \qquad (2.3.7)$$

This is the total number of weights which are the free parameters of the problem. If for example $n = 3$, the vector x^* is 10-dimensional. For $n = 10$ we already have a considerably large $N = 65$.

In the case of polynomial decision functions of order m, a typical $f_i(x)$ in Eq. (2.3.1) is given by

$$f_i(x) = x_{i_1}^{e_1} x_{i_2}^{e_2} \ldots x_{i_m}^{e_m} \qquad (2.3.8)$$

where $1 \leq i_1, i_2, \ldots, i_m \leq n$ and e_i, $1 \leq i \leq m$ is 0 or 1. It is clearly a polynomial with a degree between 0 and m. To avoid repetitions we request $i_1 \leq i_2 \leq \ldots \leq i_m$.

■ **Theorem 2.3.1.** Let $d^m(x)$ denote the most general polynomial decision function of order m. Then

$$d^m(x) = \sum_{i_1=1}^{n} \sum_{i_2=i_1}^{n} \cdots \sum_{i_m=i_{m-1}}^{n} w_{i_1 i_2 \ldots i_m} x_{i_1} x_{i_2} \ldots x_{i_m} + d^{m-1}(x) \qquad (2.3.9)$$

where $d^0(x) = w_{n+1}$.

The proof using mathematical induction is straightforward.

■ **Example 2.3.1** Let $n = 3$ and $m = 2$. Then

$$d^2(x) = \sum_{i_1=1}^{3} \sum_{i_2=i_1}^{3} w_{i_1 i_2} x_{i_1} x_{i_2} + w_1 x_1 + w_2 x_2 + w_3 x_3 + w_4$$

$$= w_{11} x_1^2 + w_{12} x_1 x_2 + w_{13} x_1 x_3 + w_{22} x_2^2 + w_{23} x_2 x_3 + w_{33} x_3^2$$

$$+ w_1 x_1 + w_2 x_2 + w_3 x_3 + w_4$$

♠

■ **Example 2.3.2** Let $n = 2$ and $m = 3$. Then

$$d^3(x) = \sum_{i_1=1}^{2} \sum_{i_2=i_1}^{2} \sum_{i_3=i_2}^{2} w_{i_1 i_2 i_3} x_{i_1} x_{i_2} x_{i_3} + d^2(x)$$

$$= w_{111} x_1^3 + w_{112} x_1^2 x_2 + w_{122} x_1 x_2^2 + w_{222} x_2^3 + d^2(x)$$

where

$$d^2(x) = \sum_{i_1=1}^{2} \sum_{i_2=i_1}^{2} w_{i_1 i_2} x_{i_1} x_{i_2} + d^1(x)$$

$$= w_{11} x_1^2 + w_{12} x_1 x_2 + w_{22} x_2^2 + w_1 x_1 + w_2 x_2 + w_3$$

♠

The number of terms needed to represent a general quadratic decision function is $\dfrac{(n+1)\,(n+2)}{2}$ where n is the original patterns space's dimension. It can be shown, that in the case of order m, this number is

$$M(n,m) = \binom{n+m}{m} = \frac{(n+m)!}{n!\,m!} \tag{2.3.10}$$

and it clearly increases fast as a function of n and m. For practical purposes it is not always necessary to apply all the terms in Eq. (2.3.9). If in Example 2.3.2 one can construct an appropriate cubic decision function which does not include quadratic or linear elements, one then needs to consider only four coefficients, namely $w_{111}, w_{112}, w_{122}, w_{222}$.

The commonly used quadratic decision function can be easily represented as the general $n-$dimensional quadratic surface

$$d(x) = x^T A x + x^T b + c \tag{2.3.11}$$

where the matrix $A = (a_{ij})$, the vector $b = (b_1, \ldots, b_n)^T$ and c, depend on the weights w_{ii}, w_{ij}, w_i of Eq. (2.3.6). If A is positive definite, the decision function is a hyperellipsoid with axes in the directions of the eigenvectors of A. In the particular case where A is the identity matrix of order n, the decision function is simply the $n-$dimensional hypersphere. If A is negative definite the decision function describes a hyperhyperboloid. Thus, it is only A which determines the shape and characteristics of the decision function.

PROBLEMS

1. Consider a 3-D pattern space and cubic polynomial decision functions. How many terms are needed to represent a decision function if only cubic and linear functions are assumed.

2. Present the general 4-th order polynomial decision function for a 2-D pattern space.

3. Calculate $M(n,m)$ of Eq. (2.3.10) for $1 \le n, m \le 5$.

4. Let R^3 be the original pattern space and let the decision function associated with the pattern classes C_1 and C_2 be

$$d(x) = 2x_1^2 + x_3^2 + x_2 x_3 + 4x_1 - 2x_2 + 1$$

for which $d(x) > 0$ if $x \in C_1$ and $d(x) < 0$ if $x \in C_2$.

   (a) Rewrite $d(x)$ in the form of Eq. (2.3.11).
   (b) Determine the class of each of the following pattern vectors: (1,1,1), (1,10,0), (0,1/2,0).

2.4   GEOMETRICAL DISCUSSION

Since linear decision functions play a significant role in pattern recognition, it is essential to provide a complete geometrical interpretation of their properties. Such an interpretation which includes the concepts of hyperplanes and dichotomies is given below.

2.4.1   Hyperplanes

Let R^n be the original patterns' space and consider a two-class or a multiclass problem. A linear decision function which separates one class from another, is determined by an equation such as

$$d(x) = w_1 x_1 + w_2 x_2 + \ldots + w_n x_n + w_{n+1} = 0 \qquad (2.4.1)$$

which defines a *linear decision boundary*. The linear decision function itself, is the left-hand side of Eq. (2.4.1). For $n = 2$, the linear decision boundary is a straight line. It is a plane for $n = 3$ and a *hyperplane* for $n > 3$. The vector form of Eq. (2.4.1) is

$$d(x) = w_0^T x + w_{n+1} = 0 \tag{2.4.2}$$

where $x = (x_1, x_2, \ldots, x_n)^T$ and $w_0 = (w_1, w_2, \ldots, w_n)^T$.

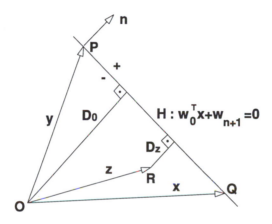

■ **Figure 2.4.1** Basic properties of hyperplane.

Consider now the hyperplane H of Eq. (2.4.2) as shown in Fig. 2.4.1. Let n be a unit normal vector at some point P of H, pointing to its positive side. Let $y = \overrightarrow{OP}$ and let $x = \overrightarrow{OQ}$ denote any arbitrary point on the hyperplane. Then, the equation of the hyperplane can be rewritten as

$$n^T \cdot \overrightarrow{QP} = n^T \cdot (x - y) = 0 \tag{2.4.3}$$

or as

$$n^T x = -n^T y \tag{2.4.4}$$

To compare with Eq. (2.4.2) we normalize the previous equation and divide it by

$$\|w_0\| = (w_1^2 + w_2^2 + \ldots + w_n^2)^{1/2}$$

to get

$$\frac{w_0^T x}{\|w_0\|} = -\frac{w_{n+1}}{\|w_0\|} \tag{2.4.5}$$

Since Eqs. (2.4.4) and (2.4.5) represent the same hyperplane and since n and $w_0/\|w_0\|$ are unit vectors, we must have either $n = w/\|w_0\|$ or $n = -w_0/\|w_0\|$. But n was chosen to point to the positive side of the hyperplane, implying

$$w_0^T(y + n) + w_{n+1} > 0 \tag{2.4.6}$$

and since $w_0^T y + w_{n+1} = 0$ we get $w_0^T n > 0$. Therefore

$$n = \frac{w_0}{\|w_0\|} \tag{2.4.7}$$

and consequently, by virtue of Eqs. (2.4.4) and (2.4.5)

$$n^T y = \frac{-w_{n+1}}{\|w_0\|} \tag{2.4.8}$$

The quantity $|n^T y|$ measures the normal distance D_0 between the origin and the hyperplane H. Thus

$$D_0 = \frac{|w_{n+1}|}{\|w_0\|} \tag{2.4.9}$$

The distance between an arbitrary point R, associated to a vector z, from the hyperplane, is

$$D_z = |n^T(y-z)| = |n^T(z-y)| \tag{2.4.10}$$

and by applying Eqs. (2.4.7) and (2.4.8) we get

$$D_z = \left| \frac{w_0^T}{\|w_0\|}(z-y) \right| = \left| \frac{w_0^T z + w_{n+1}}{\|w_0\|} \right| \tag{2.4.11}$$

In the particular case $w_{n+1} = 0$, the hyperplane H passes through the origin, since $D_0 = 0$.

■ **Example 2.4.1** Consider the decision boundary

$$3x_1 + 4x_2 - 5 = 0$$

in R^2. Here $\|w_0\| = (3^2 + 4^2)^{1/2} = 5$ and the normal unit vector pointing at the positive side of the straight line is $n = w_0 / \|w_0\| = \left(\frac{3}{5}, \frac{4}{5} \right)^T$. The distance of a pattern located at $(1,2)^T$ from the decision boundary is

$$D_{(1,2)} = \left| \frac{(3,4)\,(1,2)^T - 5}{5} \right| = \left| \frac{3+8-5}{5} \right| = 1.2$$

♠

■ **Example 2.4.2** Consider a two-class pattern classification of a given 3-D pattern set, using the plane

$$2x_1 - x_2 + 2x_3 - 7 = 0$$

as a linear decision boundary. If patterns whose normal distance from the plane is less than 0.01 are excluded, one should eliminate all the patterns (y_1, y_2, y_3) for which

$$\left| \frac{2y_1 - y_2 + 2y_3 - 7}{\|w_0\|} \right| = \left| \frac{2y_1 - y_2 + 2y_3 - 7}{3} \right| < 0.01$$

If a pattern is located at (0.51,0,3), it is excluded since

$$\left| \frac{2 \cdot 0.51 - 0 + 2 \cdot 3 - 7}{3} \right| = \frac{0.02}{3} < 0.01$$

♠

2.4.2   Dichotomies

A common numerical approach to estimate the discriminatory potential of decision functions is to consider the number of possible classifications of a given set of patterns using these decision functions. Each *two-class* classification of a given set of patterns is called a *dichotomy*. Clearly, several decision functions may provide the same dichotomy. Each dichotomy is represented by an ordered pair of its pattern classes (C_1, C_2) and is therefore counted twice. A dichotomy obtained by a linear decision boundary is a *linear dichotomy*.

■ **Example 2.4.3** Consider a three 2-D pattern set $\{x_1, x_2, x_3\}$ and assume that the patterns are not located on one straight line (Fig. 2.4.2). Using linear decision boundaries, *all* the possible eight two-class groupings are attainable. Each of the four decision boundaries yields two two-class classifications of the set. For example, line 3 produces

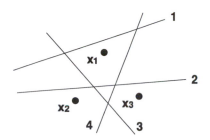

■ **Figure 2.4.2**   Linear dichotomies for three patterns.

$(\{x_1, x_3\}, \{x_2\})$ and $(\{x_2\}, \{x_1, x_3\})$. Thus, we have a total of eight linear dichotomies.

If all the possible two-class groupings, using linear decision boundaries, were available, the total number of the dichotomies for a given $m-$ pattern set would have been

$$\binom{m}{0} + \binom{m}{1} + \ldots + \binom{m}{m-1} + \binom{m}{m} = 2^m \qquad (2.4.12)$$

However, this is not the case. Even in the previous example, if the three patterns are located on a single straight line, the number of dichotomies drops to six as can be easily seen. In the next 2-D example, no straight line passes through three patterns, yet certain two-class classifications using linear decision boundaries are not feasible.

■ **Example 2.4.4** Consider four *regularly distributed* patterns $\{x_i\}_{i=1}^4$, i.e. each three patterns are not located on a single straight line (Fig. 2.4.3). Clearly, a linear decision boundary which separates between x_4 and $\{x_1, x_2, x_3\}$, does not exist. The total number of linear dichotomies is 14. Each straight line in Fig. 2.4.3 provides two dichotomies.

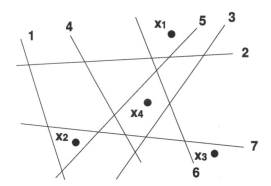

■ **Figure 2.4.3**   Linear dichotomies for four regularly distributed 2-D
                patterns.

■ **Definition 2.4.1**   An $m-$pattern set in R^n is said to be *regularly
distributed*, if none of its $(n+1)-$pattern subsets is located on a
hyperplane in R^n.
    The following result is given without a proof.

■ **Theorem 2.4.1**   Given a regularly distributed $m-$pattern set in R^n,
the number of its linear dichotomies is

$$D(m,n) = \begin{cases} 2\sum_{i=0}^{n}\binom{m-1}{i}, & m > n \\ \\ 2^m & , \quad m \leq n \end{cases}$$

$$(2.4.13)$$

In the particular case $m = n+1$, both expressions for $D(m,n)$ are identical.

If nonlinear decision functions and boundaries are considered, we can still maintain the use of linear dichotomies, except that their total may increase significantly. For example, consider five 2-D patterns regularly distributed, with a total of $2\sum_{i=0}^{2}\binom{5-1}{i} = 22$ linear dichotomies. If we decide to use general quadratic decision functions, the dimensionality of the patterns increases from 2 to 5 (the number of the non-constant terms in Eq. (2.3.5)) and the number of linear dichotomies - from 22 to $D(5,5) = 2^5 = 32$.

A large number of applicable dichotomies, increases our chances to obtain solutions to pattern classification problems, using decision functions.

Let us consider a regularly distributed m − pattern set and generalized decision functions which transform the original n − dimensional patterns into N − dimensional ones. The number of linear dichotomies that can be obtained is $D(m,N)$, compared with the total number of two-class groupings which is 2^m. Thus, the probability for a random dichotomy (i.e. a random two-class grouping of the pattern set) to be *linearly implementable* is

$$p(m,N) = \frac{D(m,N)}{2^m} = \begin{cases} 2^{-(m-1)}\sum_{i=0}^{N}\binom{m-1}{i}, & m > N \\ \\ 1 & , \quad m \le N \end{cases} \quad (2.4.14)$$

Consequently, if the number of patterns does not exceed the new dimensionality of the pattern space, each two disjoint pattern classes whose union is the whole pattern set, are linearly separable in the N - dimensional space.

■ **Example 2.4.5** Consider the four 2-D patterns in Fig. 2.4.4. There is no way that the classes $\{x_1, x_3\}$, $\{x_2, x_4\}$ will be linearly separated. However, by using quadratic decision functions and boundaries, we get

$N = 5$ and since $m = 4 < 5$ linear separation in R^5 is possible. In the original space, we simply use a quadratic parabola.

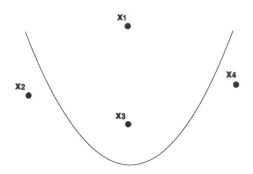

■ **Figure 2.4.4** A 2-D problem linearly separable only in R^5.

♠

If we substitute $m = 2(N + 1)$ in Eq. (2.4.14), we get

$$p(2(N+1), N) = 2^{-(2N+1)} \sum_{i=0}^{N} \binom{2N+1}{i} = 2^{-(2N+1)} \cdot \frac{2^{2N+1}}{2} = \frac{1}{2} \qquad (2.4.15)$$

Thus, if the number of the given patterns does not exceed $2(N+1)$, there is probability of at least 0.5 to find an $(N+1)-$parameter generalized decision function that will separate a given two-class groupings of the given pattern set. Denote $a = m/(N+1)$. The fact that

$$\lim_{N \to \infty} p(a(N+1), N) = 1, \quad 0 \le a < 2 \qquad (2.4.16)$$

motivates one to define the *dichotomization capacity* of generalized decision functions defined by $(N+1)$ parameters as $2(N+1)$. For example, the dichotomization capacity of a general quadratic surface in R^n is $(n+1)(n+2)$ as follows from Eq. (2.3.7).

PROBLEMS

1. Consider the linear decision boundary $x_1 + x_2 - x_3 + x_4 - 2 = 0$ in R^4.

    (a) Find the normal distance from the origin to the given hyperplane.
    (b) Obtain the normal unit vector to the hyperplane which points to its positive side.
    (c) Given a set of patterns, obtain a rule which eliminates all the patterns that are on the negative side of the hyperplane and are located at a distance of at least 10 from it.

2. Find all the linear dichotomies for a four-pattern set in R^2, where three patterns are known to be on a straight line.

3. Repeat and solve problem 2 for a five-pattern set where three patterns are located on a straight line and the remaining two - on a second straight line - parallel to the first.

4. Obtain a table for $D(m,n)$ of Eq. (2.4.13), for $1 \le m, n \le 5$.

5. Given a seven-pattern set in R^2, is it always possible to separate each couple of disjoint subsets of three and four patterns using a quadratic decision function?

2.5   ORTHOGONAL FUNCTIONS

This section is a brief introduction to systems of orthogonal functions in one and several variables.   Orthogonal systems are often used in constructing decision functions, approximating probability decision functions, and play an important role in designing pattern recognition systems.

2.5.1   Univariate Functions

We assume that $u(x), v(x)$ are real-valued integrable functions of one variable, defined over the interval $a \le x \le b$, denoted $I = [a, b]$.   The function $w(x)$ denotes a nonnegative integrable function over I for which

$$\int_a^b w(x)dx > 0 \tag{2.5.1}$$

■ **Definition 2.5.1** The integral

$$(u, v) = \int_a^b u(x)v(x)dx \tag{2.5.2}$$

is called the *inner product* of $u(x), v(x)$ over I.

■ **Definition 2.5.2** The nonnegative number

$$(u, u)^{1/2} = \left(\int_a^b u^2(x)dx \right)^{1/2} \tag{2.5.3}$$

is called the *norm* of $u(x)$ over I.

■ **Definition 2.5.3** The functions $u(x)$, $v(x)$ are said to be *orthogonal* over I with respect to the *weight* function $w(x)$, if

$$\int_a^b w(x)u(x)v(x)dx = 0 \tag{2.5.4}$$

■ **Definition 2.5.4** A set of integrable functions $u_1(x)$, $u_2(x),\ldots,u_m(x)$ defined over I is said to be an *orthogonal system* over I with respect to $w(x)$, if

$$\int_a^b w(x)u_i(x)u_j(x)dx = A_i \delta_{ij}, \quad 1 \le i, j \le m \tag{2.5.5}$$

where $A_i \neq 0$ are constants and δ_{ij} is Kronecker's delta function defined as

$$\delta_{ij} = \begin{cases} 0, & i \neq j \\ 1, & i = j \end{cases} \qquad (2.5.6)$$

If $A_i = 1$ for all i, the set is an *orthonormal system*.

Definition 2.5.4   Is not restricted to finite sets.   The extension to the infinite case is straightforward.

■ **Definition 2.5.5**   A set of integrable functions $u_1(x)$, $u_2(x),\ldots,u_m(x)$ over I, is said to be *linearly independent* if the relation

$$c_1 u_1(x) + c_2 u_2(x) +\ldots+ c_m u_m(x) = 0 , \quad a \leq x \leq b \qquad (2.5.7)$$

holds if and only if $c_1 = c_2 \ldots = c_m = 0$.

The following result is a direct consequence of Definitions 2.5.4 and 2.5.5

■ **Theorem 2.5.1.**   An orthogonal system is linearly independent.

Proof.

Let $u_1(x)$, $u_2(x),\ldots$, $u_m(x)$ be orthogonal over I with respect to $w(x)$ such that Eq. (2.5.7) is satisfied for some $c_1, c_2,\ldots,c_m$. Multiplying this equation by $w(x)u_i(x)$ and integrating over I provides

$$\sum_{j=1}^{m} \int_a^b c_i w(x) u_i(x) u_j(x) dx = 0 \qquad (2.5.8)$$

and by virtue of Eq. (2.5.5) we get

$$c_i A_i = 0 \qquad\qquad (2.5.9)$$

Since $A_i \neq 0$ we must have $c_i = 0$ which completes the proof.

□

■ **Example 2.5.1** The functions $\{1,\ \cos(mx),\ \sin(mx)\}$, $m \geq 1$ are orthogonal over the interval $[0,\ 2\pi]$ with respect to $w(x) = 1$. The proof is left as an exercise for the reader.

♠

An orthogonal system can be easily replaced by an orthonormal one. We simply define

$$u_i^*(x) \ = \ \frac{1}{\sqrt{A_i}}\, u_i(x) \qquad\qquad (2.5.10)$$

The new functions are clearly orthogonal to each other and also

$$\int_a^b w(x) u_i^*(x) u_i^*(x) dx = \frac{1}{\sqrt{A_i}} \frac{1}{\sqrt{A_i}} A_i = 1 \qquad\qquad (2.5.11)$$

■ **Definition 2.5.6** Let $f(x)$ be a piecewise continuous function and $\{u_1(x),\ u_2(x),...\}$ a system of functions, defined over the same domain. If

$$\lim_{i \to \infty} u_i(x) = f(x), \quad f \ \text{is continuous at} \ x$$

$$\qquad\qquad (2.5.12)$$

$$\lim_{i \to \infty} u_i(x) = \frac{1}{2}\left[f(x_+) + f(x_-) \right], \quad f \ \text{has a jump at} \ x$$

the sequence $\{u_i(x)\}$ is said to approximate $f(x)$ arbitrarily closely *in the mean*.

■ **Definition 2.5.7** A system of functions S defined over a domain D is called *complete*, if for any given piecewise continuous function over D, a sequence $\{u_i(x)\}$ whose elements are finite linear combinations of the elements of S can be found, such that $\{u_i(x)\}$ approximates $f(x)$ arbitrarily closely in the mean.

■ **Example 2.5.2** The system of Example 2.5.1 is known to be complete over the interval $[0,\ 2\pi]$.

♠

One should note that a complete system of functions may not be an orthogonal system.

2.5.2 Multivariate Functions

In this subsection we will present a simple mechanism for constructing a complete orthogonal systems of multivariate functions.

Let $\{u_1(x), u_2(x), ...\}$ be a complete orthogonal system over the interval $[a,b]$ with respect to a weight function $w(x)$. The next result relates to 2-D systems.

■ **Theorem 2.5.2**   The system of functions

$$\{u_i(x_1)u_j(x_2)\}, \quad 1 \le i, j \tag{2.5.13}$$

defined over the rectangle $a \le x_1, x_2 \le b$ is a complete orthogonal system over this rectangle with respect to the 2-D weight function

$$w^{(2)}(x) = w^{(2)}(x_1, x_2) = w(x_1)w(x_2) \tag{2.5.14}$$

The proof of orthogonality is simple. Indeed, let $v_k(x_1, x_2), v_l(x_1, x_2)$ denote arbitrary 2-D functions defined as

$$v_k(x) = v_k(x_1, x_2) = u_i(x_1)u_j(x_2)$$

$$\tag{2.5.15}$$

$$v_l(x) = v_l(x_1, x_2) = u_{i'}(x_1)u_{j'}(x_2)$$

Then

$$\int_a^b \int_a^b w^{(2)}(x_1, x_2)v_k(x_1, x_2)v_l(x_1, x_2)dx_1dx_2$$

$$= \int_a^b \int_a^b w(x_1)w(x_2)u_i(x_1)u_j(x_2)u_{i'}(x_1)u_{j'}(x_2)dx_1dx_2$$

$$= \left(\int_a^b w(x_1)u_i(x_1)u_{i'}(x_1)dx_1 \right) \left(\int_a^b w(x_2)u_j(x_2)u_{j'}(x_2)dx_2 \right)$$

$$= \delta_{ii'} \, \delta_{jj'}$$

The result vanishes unless $i = i', j = j'$ which consequently implies (Eq. (2.5.15)) $k = l$. This completes the proof of the orthogonality of the new system. Showing completeness is beyond the scope of this book and is omitted.

The extension of the scheme defined by Eqs. (2.5.13) and (2.5.14) to the $n-$ dimensional case is straightforward. We define a system of functions

$$\{u_{i_1}(x_1)u_{i_2}(x_2) \dots u_{i_n}(x_n)\}, \quad 1 \le i_1, i_2, \dots, i_n \tag{2.5.16}$$

with an attached weight function

$$w^{(n)}(x) = w(x_1)w(x_2)\ldots w(x_n)$$ (2.5.17)

and choose any one to one correspondence between the vectors $(i_1, i_2, \ldots i_n)^T$, $1 \le i_1; i_2, \ldots, i_n$ and the positive integers. Let k and l correspond to $(i_1, i_2, \ldots i_n)^T$ and $(i'_1, i'_2, \ldots i'_n)^T$ respectively. Then, it is easily seen that the functions

$$v_k(x) = u_{i_1}(x_1)u_{i_2}(x_2)\ldots u_{i_n}(x_n)$$

$$v_l(x) = u_{i'_1}(x_1)u_{i'_2}(x_2)\ldots u_{i'_n}(x_n)$$ (2.5.18)

satisfy

$$\int_a^b \int_a^b \ldots \int_a^b w^{(n)}(x)v_k(x)v_l(x)dx = \delta_{kl}$$ (2.5.19)

where $dx = dx_1 dx_2 \ldots dx_n$ and the integration is carried over the $n-$dimensional hypercube

$$a \le x_i \le b, \quad 1 \le i \le n$$ (2.5.20)

The system defined by Eq. (2.5.16) is also complete.

■ **Example 2.5.3** Starting with the system given in Example 2.5.1 we get the 2-D system which includes the functions 1, $\cos(mx_2)$, $\sin(mx_2)$, $\cos(mx_1)$, $\cos(mx_1)$, $\cos(nx_2)$ $\cos(mx_1)$, $\sin(nx_2)$ $\sin(mx_1)$, $\sin(mx_1)$, $\cos(nx_2)$ $\sin(mx_1)$ $\sin(nx_2)$ for arbitrary $m, n \ge 1$.

♠

Several systems of orthogonal *polynomial* functions are commonly used in pattern recognition. The most popular are the Legendre, Laguerre and Hermite polynomials.

Legendre Polynomials

The Legendre polynomials $p_n(x)$, $n \geq 0$ defined by

$$p_0(x) = 1, \ p_1(x) = x \tag{2.5.21}$$

and the recursive equation

$$np_n(x) - (2n - 1)xp_{n-1}(x) + (n - 1)p_{n-2}(x) = 0 \ , \ n \geq 2 \tag{2.5.22}$$

are orthogonal over the interval $[-1, 1]$ with the weight function $w(x) = 1$.

Laguerre Polynomials

The Laguerre polynomials $L_n(x)$, $n \geq 0$ defined by

$$L_0(x) = 1 \ , \ L_1(x) = -x + 1 \tag{2.5.23}$$

and the recursive equation

$$L_n(x) - (2n - 1 - x)L_{n-1}(x) + (n - 1)^2 L_{n-2}(x) = 0 \ , \ n \geq 2 \tag{2.5.24}$$

are orthogonal over the semi-infinite interval $[0, \infty)$ with respect to the weight function e^{-x}, i.e.

$$\int_0^\infty e^{-x} L_i(x) L_j(x) dx = \delta_{ij} \tag{2.5.25}$$

■ **Example 2.4.4** By substituting $n = 2$ in Eq. (2.5.24) we get

$$L_2(x) - (3 - x)L_1(x) + L_0(x) = 0$$

i.e.

$$L_2(x) = (3-x)(1-x) - 1 = x^2 - 4x + 2$$

For $n = 3$ we have

$$L_3(x) - (5-x)L_2(x) + 4L_1(x) = 0$$

i.e.

$$L_3(x) = (5-x)(x^2 - 4x + 2) - 4(-x+1) = -x^3 + 9x^2 - 18x + 6$$

♠

■ **Example 2.5.5** The 2-D orthogonal Laguerre polynomials of order ≤ 2 are :

$$1 , \quad -x_2 + 1 , \quad x_2^2 - 4x_2 + 2 , \quad -x_1 + 1 , \quad (-x_1 + 1)(-x_2 + 1) , \quad x_1^2 - 4x_1 + 2$$

and they are orthogonal over the semi-infinite rectangle $0 \leq x_1 < \infty, \; 0 \leq x_2 < \infty$ with respect to the weight function

$$w^{(2)}(x_1, x_2) = e^{-x_1} e^{-x_2} = e^{-(x_1 + x_2)}$$

♠

Hermite Polynomials

The third frequently used orthogonal system is the Hermite system defined by

$$H_0(x) = 1 , \quad H_1(x) = 2x \tag{2.5.26}$$

and the recursive equation

$$H_n(x) - 2xH_{n-1}(x) + 2(n-1)H_{n-2}(x) = 0 , \quad n \geq 2 \tag{2.5.27}$$

These functions form a complete orthogonal system over the infinite interval $(-\infty, \infty)$ with respect to the weight function e^{-x^2}.

The complete orthogonal systems introduced in this subsection are often used for representing or approximating generalized decision functions. The ability to approximate a given function by a finite linear combination of orthogonal functions, follows from the *completeness* of the orthogonal system to which these functions belong. While an infinite number of functions may be necessary to fully represent the given function, only a small number of these functions are usually needed to approximate it within a given tolerance.

PROBLEMS

1. The system $\{1, \cos(mx), \sin(mx)\}_{m=1}^{\infty}$ is orthogonal over the interval $[0, 2\pi]$ with respect to the weight function $w(x) = 1$. *Normalize* the system, i.e. multiply its functions by appropriate coefficients to get an orthonormal system.

2. Find all the 2-D Legendre orthogonal functions of order ≤ 3.

3. Find all the 4-D Hermite orthogonal functions of order ≤ 3.

4. Given a 1-D orthogonal system, write a procedure to obtain a 1-D orthonormal system with respect to $w(x) = 1$.

5. Repeat and solve problem 4 for an $n-$ dimensional orthogonal system which was initiated by a 1-D system using Eq. (2.5.18).

3 CLASSIFICATION BY DISTANCE FUNCTIONS AND CLUSTERING

3.1 INTRODUCTION

If a pattern is simulated by a vector in R^n, then the statement 'x and y are similar' simply means that the two vectors are 'close', i.e. that the distance between them is 'small.' Thus, if C_1 and C_2 are classes of patterns such that patterns at each class are 'all similar to each other,' we may expect the patterns to be distributed for example as in Fig. 3.1.1 but not as in Fig. 3.1.2.

■ **Figure 3.1.1**   Two classes – each consisting of 'similar' patterns.

Still, an appropriate classification problem may be geometrically represented as in Fig. 3.1.2. Suppose for example that every incoming pattern is represented by an ordered pair of numbers $x = (x_1, x_2)$ such that $0 \leq x_1 \leq 0.75$ and that there are only two types of patterns, classified as follows:

$$\alpha_1 = x_1 - x_2 \sim 1 \Rightarrow x \in C_1$$

(3.1.1)

$$\alpha_2 = x_1 + x_2 \sim 1 \Rightarrow x \in C_2$$

Such a case is illustrated in Fig. 3.1.2.

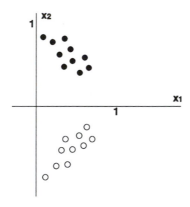

■ **Figure 3.1.2**   Classes with non-similar patterns.

While in Fig. 3.1.1 each class *clusters* around a single vector - the *cluster center*, each of the classes in Fig. 3.1.2 includes patterns which are not similar to each other in R^2. For example, the patterns $x^{(1)} = (0.2, -0.7)$ and $x^{(2)} = (0.71, -0.25)$ will certainly be classified in C_1 since they yield

$(\alpha_1, \alpha_2) = (0.9, -0.5)$ and $(0.96, 0.47)$ respectively.   Yet, the distance between the patterns in R^2

$$\left\| x^{(1)} - x^{(2)} \right\| = \left((0.2 - 0.71)^2 + (-0.7 + 0.25)^2 \right)^{1/2} = 0.68$$

is not small at all.

If a pattern classification problem is of the type portrayed in Fig. 3.1.1, i.e. if each class is a cluster and can be represented by a single *prototype* or *typical value*, the classification can be performed simply by measuring the distances of an incoming pattern from all the prototypes. If however, the existing classes do not cluster around single prototypes, the classification problem becomes significantly more difficult. For example, consider the single incoming pattern **x**   and the two existing pattern classes in Fig. 3.1.3.

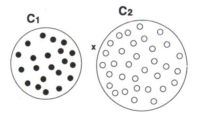

■ **Figure 3.1.3**   A complex decision making problem.

Although we may be tempted to classify **x** in C_2 since

$$\min_{y \in C_2} \| x - y \| < \min_{y \in C_1} \| x - y \|$$

we cannot rule out the opposite choice, since for example the *average* distance from **x** to C_1 is shorter than from **x** to C_2. However, unless we have *a priori* information for example such as in Eq. (3.1.1), classification in a case as illustrated in Fig. 3.1.3 can be complex and possesses a substantial degree of uncertainty.

   In this chapter the *proximity* of an incoming pattern to the patterns of all the existing classes, will serve as a sole measure in determining its pattern class. Since each pattern classification requires that a minimum distance is obtained, we will refer to this approach as *minimum-distance classification procedure.*   Such procedures are expected to perform efficiently as long as each pattern class can be represented by a single prototype or by several prototypes around which the patterns cluster.

3.2   MINIMUM-DISTANCE CLASSIFICATION

We will first discuss the simple case, where the patterns of each class are *very close* to each other. In this case, each class can be represented by a single prototype.

3.2.1   Single Prototypes

Let $C_1,\ldots,C_m$ denote m pattern classes in R^n, represented by the single prototype vectors $y_1,\ldots,y_m$ respectively.   The distances between an incoming pattern x and the prototype vectors are

$$D_i = \|x - y_i\| = \left((x - y_i)^T (x - y_i)\right)^{1/2}, \ 1 \leq i \leq m \qquad (3.2.1)$$

and a minimum-distance classifier will classify x at $C_j \left(\text{or to } y_j\right)$ for which D_j is minimum, i.e.

$$D_j = \min\|x - y_i\|, \ \ 1 \leq i \leq m \qquad (3.2.2)$$

If the minimum is achieved by several j's, x is classified at the first C_j (for example) for which a minimum is found, or not classified at all. Minimizing D_i^2 is equivalent to minimizing D_i but is more convenient. Indeed

$$D_i^2 = (x - y_i)^T(x - y_i) = x^T x - 2x^T y_i + y^T y_i$$

and since the constant $x^T x$ can be removed, we should only minimize $-2x^T y_i + y^T y_i$ or instead maximize

$$2x^T y_i - y^T y_i, \quad 1 \leq i \leq m \tag{3.2.3}$$

Thus, we can define

$$d_i(x) = x^T y_i - \frac{1}{2} y_i^T y_i, \quad 1 \leq i \leq m \tag{3.2.4}$$

as decision functions and apply the classifier

$$x \in C_i \text{ iff } d_i(x) > d_j(x), j \neq i \tag{3.2.5}$$

The decision functions are linear, i.e.

$$d_i(x) = w_i^T x, \quad 1 \leq i \leq m \tag{3.2.6}$$

where x is the augmented vector $(x_1, x_2, \ldots, x_n, 1)^T$ and $w_i = (w_{i1}, w_{i2}, \ldots, w_{in}, w_{i,n+1})^T$, $1 \leq i \leq m$ are determined by $y_i = (y_{i1}, y_{i2}, \ldots, y_{in})^T$, $1 \leq i \leq m$ as

$$w_{ij} = y_{ij}; 1 \leq i \leq m, 1 \leq j \leq n$$

$$w_{i,n+1} = -\frac{1}{2} y_i^T y_i, 1 \leq i \leq m \tag{3.2.7}$$

In the case of two pattern classes the decision boundary associated with the minimum-distance classification is

$$d_{12}(x) = d_1(x) - d_2(x) = x^T(y_1 - y_2) - \frac{1}{2}y_1^T y_1 + \frac{1}{2}y_2^T y_2 = 0 \qquad (3.2.8)$$

This is a hyperplane in normal direction to the vector $y_1 - y_2$. By substituting $x = (y_1 + y_2)/2$ in Eq. (3.2.8) we get

$$d_{12}(x) = \frac{1}{2}(y_1 + y_2)^T(y_1 - y_2) - \frac{1}{2}y_1^T y_1 + \frac{1}{2}y_2^T y_2 = 0$$

The decision boundary is therefore the hyperplane which is perpendicular to the vector connecting the two prototypes and bisects it (Fig. 3.2.1).

- **Figure 3.2.1** Minimum-distance classification - two single prototypes.

If more than two classes exist, the decision boundaries are no longer hyperplanes but piecewise linear.

- **Example 3.2.1** Consider a three-class single-prototype classification problem in R^2 with prototypes y_1, y_2 and y_3 representing the classes C_1, C_2 and C_3.

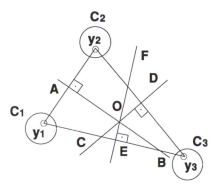

■ **Figure 3.2.2**   Piecewise linear boundaries - three prototypes.

The decision boundaries for y_1, y_2 and y_3 are the piecewise linear curves AOE, AOD and EOD respectively.   Unless a pattern is located on a decision boundary, it is uniquely classified in one of the existing classes.

♠

3.2.2   Multiprototypes

We will now discuss the case where each class consists of several clusters. Each cluster is represented by a single prototype-the cluster's center, and therefore each class is characterized by a finite number of prototypes.   For example, a two-class problem where C_1 has the prototypes y_1 and y_2 and the second class C_2 consists of three prototypes y_3, y_4 and y_5 is illustrated in Fig. 3.2.3.

In the case of multiprototypes, the minimum-distance classification represented in the previous subsection, can be implemented as follows. Let $C_1, \ldots, C_m$ denote the various classes of a multiclass-multiprototype problem, and let C_i include the prototypes $y_i^{(1)}, y_i^{(2)}, \ldots, y_i^{(n_i)}$ for $1 \le i \le m$. The distance of an incoming pattern z from C_i is defined as

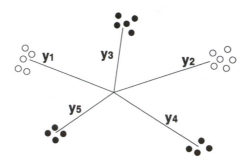

■ **Figure 3.2.3**   Two-class case; multiprototypes.

$$D_i = \min_{1 \leq j \leq n_i} \left\| z - y_i^{(j)} \right\| \tag{3.2.9}$$

As previously discussed, D_i can be found by maximizing $z^T y_i^{(j)} - \frac{1}{2}(y_i^{(j)})^T y_i^{(j)}$ for $1 \leq j \leq n_i$. Let the maximum occur for $j = j(i,z)$. Then the decision functions for *this particular z* are

$$d_i(z) = z^T (y_i^{(j(i,z))})^T y_i^{(j(i,z))} , \ 1 \leq i \leq m \tag{3.2.10}$$

and z is classified in C_i if and only if

$$d_i(z) > d_j(z) , \quad \text{for all } j \neq i \tag{3.2.11}$$

■ **Example 3.2.2** Consider a three-class problem in R^2 where each class is represented by its prototypes as follows:

$$C_1 \ : \ (1,0), \ (1,1)$$
$$C_2 \ : \ (0,1), (3,1)$$
$$C_3 \ : \ (1,2), \ (0,0), \ (-1,1)$$

Given the incoming pattern $z = (1,-1)$ we get

$$j(1,z) = 1 \;,\; y_1^{(j(1,z))} = (1,0)^T$$
$$j(2,z) = 1 \;,\; y_2^{(j(2,z))} = (0,1)^T$$
$$j(3,z) = 2 \;,\; y_3^{(j(3,z))} = (0,0)^T$$

and the decision functions are

$$d_1(\mathbf{x}) = (x_1, x_2)(1,0)^T - (1,0)(1,0)^T = x_1 - \tfrac{1}{2}$$
$$d_2(\mathbf{x}) = (x_1, x_2)(0,1)^T - (0,1)(0,1)^T = x_2 - \tfrac{1}{2}$$
$$d_3(\mathbf{x}) = (x_1, x_2)(0,0)^T - (0,0)(0,0)^T = 0$$

and the decision boundaries are

$$d_{12}(\mathbf{x}) = d_1(\mathbf{x}) - d_2(\mathbf{x}) = x_1 - x_2 = 0$$
$$d_{23}(\mathbf{x}) = d_2(\mathbf{x}) - d_3(\mathbf{x}) = x_2 - \frac{1}{2} = 0$$
$$d_{31}(\mathbf{x}) = d_3(\mathbf{x}) - d_1(\mathbf{x}) = \frac{1}{2} - x_1 = 0$$

Since $d_1(z) = \dfrac{1}{2}$, $d_2(z) = -\dfrac{3}{2}$, $d_3(z) = 0$ we classify $y \in C_1$ (Fig. 3.2.4).

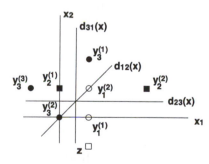

■ **Figure 3.2.4** Minimum-distance classification;
         three-class-multiprototypes.

As previously stated in Example 3.2.1, the minimum-distance classifier using single or several prototypes, classifies *every* incoming pattern in one of the existing classes, i.e. there are no indeterminate regions. This is an immediate consequence of the specific linear boundaries imposed by the minimum-distance approach.

A classifying algorithm based on the minimum-distance approach, for a multiclass (MC) multiprototype (MP) problem, is given next.

Algorithm 3.2.1.

(A minimum-distance classifier: MC-MP). Given a set of classes and prototypes in R^n this algorithm uniquely classifies an arbitrary incoming pattern using the minimum-distance approach with Euclidean norms.

Input: $n -$ the problem's dimension.

             $m -$ the number of classes.

             $n_i -$ number of prototypes for the $i-$ th class for $1 \leq i \leq m$.

             $\{y_i^{(j)}\}, 1 \leq j \leq n_i -$ the prototypes of the *i*-th class for $1 \leq i \leq n$

             $x -$ an incoming pattern

Output: $k -$ the number of class into which x is classified.

Step 1.   For $i = 1, 2, \ldots, m$ find $j(i, x)$ which yields

$$x^T y_i^{(j(i,x))} - \frac{1}{2}(y_i^{(j(i,x))})^T y_i^{(j(i,x))} = \max_{1 \leq j \leq n_i}\left\{x^T y_i^{(j)} - \frac{1}{2}(y_i^{(j)})^T y_i^{(j)}\right\}$$

Step 2.   Find k which satisfies

$$x^T y_k^{(j_k)} - \frac{1}{2}(y_k^{(j_k)})^T y_k^{(j_k)} = \max_{1 \leq i \leq m} \left\{ x^T y_i^{(j_i)} - \frac{1}{2}(y_i^{(j_i)})^T y_i^{(j_i)} \right\}$$

where $j_i \equiv j(i,x)$ and stop.

A subroutine MCMP which incorporates algorithm 3.2.1 is given in the appendix.

3.2.3 Nearest-Neighbor Classification (NN)

Consider the case of m classes $\{C_i\}_{i=1}^m$ and a set of N sample patterns $\{y_i\}_{i=1}^N$ whose classification is *a priori* known. Let x denote an arbitrary incoming pattern. The *nearest neighbor* classification approach classifies x in the pattern class of its nearest neighbor in the set $\{y_i\}_{i=1}^N$, i.e. if

$$\|x - y_j\| = \min_{1 \leq i \leq N} \|x - y_i\| \tag{3.2.12}$$

then $x \in C_j$. This scheme which is basically another type of minimum-distance classification, can be modified by considering the k nearest neighbors to x and using a majority-rule type classifier.

■ **Example 3.2.3** Consider a two-class problem in R^2. Assume the following patterns to have *a priori* known classification as follows:

$$(1,1), (2,3), (2,1), (2,2) \in C_1$$

$$(4,0), (3,-1), (3,1) \in C_2$$

Using NN classification we see that the nearest neighbor to $x = (2.2,0)$ is $(2,1)$, and consequently $x \in C_1$. If we classify by the three nearest neighbors, we find them to be $(2,1)$ $(3,1)$, $(3,-1)$. Since two out of three patterns are in C_2 so is x. This is a simple case which demonstrates how two classifiers based *almost* on the same principle may lead to different results. The reason is of course that the particular x is located at a region for which classification is not at all clear and unique.

♠

The next algorithm is based on the nearest neighbor classification approach.

Algorithm 3.2.2.

(A minimum-distance (MD) nearest neighbor (NN) classifier: MD-NN).

Input: $n-$ the problem's dimension.

$N-$ the number of pre-classified patterns.

$m-$ the number of pattern classes.

(x_i, j_i) , $1 \le i \le N-N$ ordered pairs, where x_i is the $i-$th pre-classified pattern and $j_i -$ its class number $(1 \le j_i \le m$ for all $i)$.

$k-$ the order of NN classifier (i.e. the k closest neighbors to the incoming patterns are considered).

$x-$ an incoming pattern

Output: $l-$ the number of class into which x is classified.

Step 1.   Set

$$S = \left\{ (x_i, j_i) \right\}_{i=1}^{N}$$

Step 2.   Find $(y, j_0) \in S$ which satisfies

$$\|y - x\| = \min \|z - x\|, \quad (z, j) \in S$$

Step 3. If $k = 1$ set $l = j_0$ and stop; else initialize an

$m-$ dimensional vector IC:

$$IC(i') = 0, \; i' \neq j_0 ; IC(j_0) = 1$$

and set $S = S - \{(y, j_0)\}$.

Step 4. For $i_0 = 1, 2, \ldots, k - 1$ do steps 5-6.

Step 5. Find $(y, j_0) \in S$ such that

$$\|y - x\| = \min \|z - x\|, \quad (z, j) \in S$$

Step 6. Set $IC(j_0) = IC(j_0) + 1$ and $S = S - \{(y, j_0)\}$.

Step 7. Set $l = \max\{IC(i)\}, \; 1 \leq i \leq m$ and stop.

A subroutine MDNN which incorporates algorithm 3.2.2 is given in the appendix.

PROBLEMS

1. Consider a four-class single-prototype problem in R^2, with prototypes $(1,1)$, $(-1,-1)$, $(-1,1)$ and $(0,0)$. Sketch the four decision regions using the minimum-distance approach.
2. What are the decision regions in problem 1 if instead of four classes we consider two classes C_1 and C_2 just that $(1,1)$, $(0,0)$ are in C_1 and $(-1,-1)$, $(-1,1)$ in C_2.

3. In view of problems 1 and 2, derive a general conclusion with regard to single-prototype and multiprototype problems.

4. Let the patterns $(0,3)$, $(0,2)$, $(0,1)$, $(0,0)$, $(-1,0)$, $(-2,0)$ in R^2 belong to C_1, and $(1,3)$ $(1,1)$, $(1,0)$, $(0,-1)$ belong to C_2. Denote by $k-$ NN a classifier based on the minimum-distance approach and the majority rule, applied to the k nearest neighbors of an incoming pattern.

   (a) Classify the pattern $(1,4)$ using $1-$ NN, $3-$ NN and $5-$ NN schemes.

   (b) Explain the results.

5. Consider a two-class classification problem where a $1-$ NN classifier is applied over sample patterns of a set $S = \{y_1, y_2, \ldots, y_n\}$, whose classification in known. Let x be an incoming pattern. Is it reasonable to add x to S and apply the new set for further classification?

   Demonstrate your answer!

6. Consider a two-class classification problem where the patterns of C_1 and C_2 are equally likely to occur and let their regions R_1 and R_2 be such that for arbitrary $x_1, x_2 \in R_1$ and $y_1, y_2 \in R_2$ the inequalities

$$\|x_1 - x_2\| < \|x_1 - y_1\|, \ \|y_1 - y_2\| < \|x_1 - y_1\|$$

always hold. Let $\{z_i\}_{i=1}^N$ denote sample patterns for which a $k-$ NN classification is applied for incoming patterns. Compare the error probabilities of $1-$ NN and $k-$ NN classifications.

3.3 CLUSTERS AND CLUSTERING

Determining the prototypes or *cluster centers*, is a major task in designing classifiers which are based on the minimum-distance approach.   Given initial data (i.e. patterns), we will analyze several approaches for *clustering* it. Prior to introducing pattern-clustering algorithms, we must define some measure of *similarity* between patterns, by which we decide whether or not two patterns x and y are members of the same cluster.   A similarity measure $\delta(x,y)$ is usually defined, so that the principle

$$\lim \delta(x,y) = 0 \text{ as } x \to y \tag{3.3.1}$$

holds. This is the case for example, if the patterns are in R^n and if we define

$$\delta(x,y) = \|x-y\| \tag{3.3.2}$$

If x is a pattern which is expected to be normally distributed, the similarity is often defined as

$$\delta(x,\mu) = \|x-\mu\|_C \tag{3.3.3}$$

where μ is the population mean, C - its covariance matrix, and

$$\|x-\mu\|_C = (x-\mu)^T C^{-1}(x-\mu) \tag{3.3.4}$$

is the Mahalanobis distance.
      Once a measure of similarity is chosen, the next step is obtaining *clustering procedure* that will create the clusters and assign each given pattern to its cluster. Although a clustering algorithm may be completely based on heuristic ideas, i.e. rules of thumb, intuition etc., it usually includes optimizing some *performance index*. Such an index for patterns in R^n, is for example

$$I = \sum_{i=1}^{m} \sum_{x \in C_i} \|x-\mu_i\|^2 \tag{3.3.5}$$

where C_i, $1 \le i \le m$ denote the various clusters and μ_i, $1 \le i \le m$ are the clusters centers - usually defined as the arithmetic means, i.e.

$$\mu_i = \frac{1}{N_i} \sum_{j=1}^{N_i} x_j^{(i)}$$

(3.3.6)

where $x_j^{(i)}$, $1 \le j \le N_i$ are all the patterns in C_i. Unconditional minimization of I is definitely not our objective. Otherwise we can simply define each pattern as a new cluster and get $(N_1 + N_2 + ... + N_m)$ clusters with $I = 0$. Clearly, one would like two patterns x and y for which $\|x - y\|$ is less than some given *threshold*, to belong to the same cluster. At the same time it would be desirable to *also* decrease I. Another performance index is given by

$$I' = \sum_{i=1}^{m} \left(\frac{1}{N_i} \sum_{x,y \in C_i} \|x - y\|^2 \right)$$

(3.3.7)

Again, this is a quantity which we would like to minimize under certain constraints. If squares of distances between x and y of different clusters are considered instead, the goal is then to *maximize* the performance index, subjected to appropriate constraints.

3.3.1   Threshold Order-Dependent Clustering Algorithm

In this subsection we present an exceptionally simple clustering algorithm and demonstrate both its applicability and limitations. Let us consider a set of sample patterns in R^n

$$S = \{x_1, x_2, ..., x_N\}$$

(3.3.8)

which need to be clustered, i.e. we search for cluster centers around which the data clusters. The measure of similarity is the Euclidean norm, and some threshold quantity t which determines whether two patterns are assigned the same cluster, is prefixed.

Processing the data starts at x_1 and progresses through $x_2, x_3, \ldots$ until it ends at x_N. Initially there are no clusters and we choose $y_1 = x_1$ as the first cluster center. If $\left\| x_2 - y_1 \right\| < t$ we assign x_2 to the first cluster. Otherwise a new cluster centered at $y_2 = x_2$ is introduced. Assume that the clusters centered at $y_1, y_2, \ldots, y_k$ already exist and include the patterns $x_1, x_2, \ldots, x_l$ (obviously $k \leq l$). The next pattern to be processed is x_{l+1}. If

$$\left\| x_{l+1} - y_j \right\| \geq t, \ 1 \leq j \leq k \tag{3.3.9}$$

x_{l+1} cannot belong to any of the existing clusters and a new cluster centered at $y_{k+1} = x_{l+1}$ is created. Otherwise, we find j_0 between 1 and k for which

$$\left\| x_{l+1} - y_{j_0} \right\| = \min_j \left\| x_{l+1} - y_j \right\| \tag{3.3.10}$$

considering only those j's that satisfy $\left\| x_{l+1} - y_j \right\| < t$, and assign x_{l+1} to y_{j_0}.

■ **Example 3.3.1** Consider six patterns in R^2 as shown in Fig. 3.3.1. Let the threshold for similarity (defined by the Euclidean norm) be 1.5. Following the Threshold Order-Dependent (TOD) algorithm, we define x_1 as the first cluster center, i.e. $y_1 = x_1 = (1,1)^T$. Since $\left\| x_2 - x_1 \right\| = \sqrt{5} > 1.5$ we get $y_2 = x_2 = (2,3)$. The next pattern x_3 satisfies $\left\| x_3 - y_1 \right\| = 1 < 1.5$ and $\left\| x_3 - y_2 \right\| = 2 > 1.5$. Consequently, x_3 belongs to the cluster centered at y_1. The distances of x_4 from y_1 and y_2 are $\sqrt{13}$ and 2 respectively, i.e. $y_3 = x_4 = (4,3)$. The remaining patterns x_5 and x_6, are equally close to y_2 and y_3. Since both distances are $\sqrt{2}$ (< 1.5), the patterns are assigned to the former cluster around y_2.

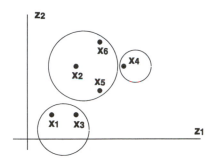

■ **Figure 3.3.1**   Clustering six ordered patterns.

♠

The TOD algorithm is not only simple and explicit (non-iterative) but also requests processing each pattern only once. Its disadvantages are being dependent on the threshold t, and even more - on the patterns' order.

■ **Example 3.3.2** Consider the previous example with the patterns reordered as in Fig. 3.3.2.

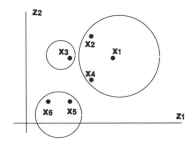

■ **Figure 3.3.2**   Classifying the reordered patterns.

The number of the clusters remains three, but the patterns' distribution among the clusters is different.

♠

Usually in order to obtain meaningful clustering of the given data using TOD, extensive experimentation is essential, using several thresholds and various arrangements of the data. However, this leads to additional computations which spoils the main attractive feature of the algorithm.

3.3.2   The Max-Min Distance Method

The Max-Min Distance (MMD) method is another clustering procedure based on the Euclidean norm concept. This algorithm first determines all the cluster centers. Consider the data set given by Eq. (3.3.8) and assume that at least two clusters are expected to exist. We prefix a threshold value t (see below) which at each step determines whether a new cluster should be created.

Let $y_1, y_2, \ldots, y_k$ be the existing cluster centers. Denote the arithmetic mean of the distances between the centers by a and let b be the data point most likely to be chosen as the center of a new cluster. If the quantity

$$s = \min \| b - y_i \|, \quad 1 \le i \le k \tag{3.3.11}$$

is less than ta then no new cluster center is created, and this part of the process terminates. Otherwise we choose $y_{k+1} = b$ and continue. After all the cluster centers have been found each remaining sample is assigned to its nearest cluster center. Finally, the cluster centers are adjusted so that each center is the arithmetic mean of the cluster's samples. The complete algorithm based on the max-min distance method is given next.

Algorithm 3.3.1.

(A maximum-minimum clustering procedure: MMD). Given a set of samples in R^n, whose distribution suggests the existence of at least two clusters, this algorithm determines all the reasonable cluster centers (based on some threshold parameter) and classifies the samples using a minimum distance classifier.

Input: $n-$ the problem's dimension.

              $m-$ the number of samples.

              $X = \{x_i\},\ 1 \le i \le m-$ the given samples in R^n.

              $t-$ a threshold value which determines whether a new cluster should be created.

Output: $k-$ the number of cluster centers found.

              $\{y_j\},\ 1 \le j \le k-$ the cluster centers.

              $\{m_j\},\ 1 \le j \le k-$ the cluster sizes.

              $\{l_{ij}\},\ 1 \le i \le m_j -$ the indices of the original samples which belong to the $j-$th cluster, $1 \le j \le k$.

Step 1.   Set $y_1 = x_1,\quad y_2 = x_{j_0},\quad l_{11} = 1,\quad l_{12} = j_0$ where

$$\left\| x_{j_0} - y_1 \right\| = \max_{2 \le i \le m} \left\| x_i - y_1 \right\|$$

Set $k = 2$, $a = \overline{\left\| y_i - y_j \right\|}$ (arithmetic mean), where $1 \le i, j \le k$, $i \ne j$ and $X' = X - \{y_1, y_2\}$.

Step 2.   Find $j_0,\ 1 \le j_0 \le k$ and $x_{i_0} \in X'$ such that

$$d = \left\| x_{i_0} - y_{j_0} \right\| = \max_{x_i \in x'} \min_{1 \le j \le k} \left\| x_i - y_j \right\|$$

If $d < ta$ (no more clusters) go to Step 4; otherwise go to Step 3.

Step 3.   Set $k \leftarrow k+1$, $y_{k+1} = x_{i_0}$, $l_{k1} = i_0$, $X' \leftarrow X' - \{y_{k+1}\}$ and go to Step 2.

Step 4.   Set $m_j = 1$, $1 \leq j \leq k$.

Step 5.   For each $x_i \in X'$ find $j: 1 \leq j \leq k$ for which

$$\|x_i - y_j\| = \min_{1 \leq j \leq k} \|x_i - y_j\|$$

and set $m_j \leftarrow m_j + 1$ and $l_{m_j j} = i$.

Step 6.   For $1 \leq j \leq k$ replace y_j by $(x_{l_{1j}} + x_{l_{2j}} + \ldots + x_{l_{m_j j}})/m_j$.

Step 7.   For $1 \leq j \leq k$ output $y_j, m_j, \{l_{ij}\}_{i=1}^{m_j}$ and stop.

A subroutine MMD which incorporates algorithm 3.3.1 is given in the appendix.

■   **Example 3.3.3**   Consider the data set in Fig. 3.3.3 with the threshold parameter $t = 0.7$. This is a 2-dimensional problem in the $z_1 - z_2$ plane. By definition $y_1 = x_1$ and $y_2 = x_{11}$. The max-min distance search provides x_7 which satisfies

$$3\sqrt{2} = \|x_7 - y_1\| = \max_i \min_j \|x_i - y_j\|, \ i \neq 1,11, \ 1 \leq j \leq 2$$

Here $a = \|y_1 - y_2\| = 6$, $ta = 0.42$ and $3\sqrt{2} > 0.42$ i.e. $y_3 = x_7$. The next implementation of the max-min distance search yields $x_4 (\text{or } x_2)$, for which

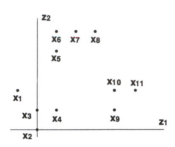

■ **Figure 3.3.3**   Clustering using max-min distance method.

$$\sqrt{5} = \|x_4 - y_1\| = \max_i \min_j \|x_i - y_j\|, \ i \neq 1,11,7, \ 1 \le j \le 3$$

Now $a = \left(6 + 3\sqrt{2} + 3\sqrt{2}\right)/3 = 4.828$, $ta = 3.380$ and $\sqrt{5} < 3.380$, i.e. the process terminates with three clusters. Any other arbitrary remaining sample is assigned to its nearest cluster center. The final clusters are therefore:

$$C_1 = \{x_1, x_2, x_3, x_4\}, \quad C_2 = \{x_{11}, x_9, x_{10}\}, \quad C_3 = \{x_7, x_5, x_6, x_8\}$$

and the final cluster centers:

$$y_1 = (0,1)^T, \quad y_2 = \left(\frac{13}{3}, \frac{5}{3}\right)^T, \quad y_3 = \left(\frac{7}{4}, \frac{19}{4}\right)^T$$

♠

While the MMD algorithm requires more computations than the TOD procedure, the result using MMD depends *only* on the first sample x_1. If we apply the TOD scheme, the outcome will depend on the complete ordering of the samples.

The common feature of the TOD and the MMD algorithms is that both procedures are almost completely heuristic and are highly motivated by intuition. The next algorithm although partially heuristic, already includes the process of minimizing a performance index.

3.3.3 c-Means Iterative Algorithm (CMI)

Given a data set $X = \{x_1, x_2, \ldots, x_m\}$ we assume the existence of c clusters whose centers are initially approximated by $y_1^{(0)}, y_2^{(0)}, \ldots, y_c^{(0)}$. The process of finding the final values of the cluster centers is iterative. At each step all the patterns are classified and each center is adjusted using a minimizing scheme of an associated performance index which replaces the cluster center by the arithmetic mean of the cluster's samples. The process terminates when there is no difference between two consecutive iterations.

Algorithm 3.3.2.

(A c-Means iterative procedure: CMI). Given samples in R^n which presumably group around c clusters and initial approximations to the cluster centers, this algorithm calculates the centers iteratively, minimizing at each iteration a set of performance indices.

Input: $n-$ the problem's dimension.

$m-$ the number of samples.

$c-$ the number of clusters.

$X = \{x_i\}_{i=1}^m$, $1 \le i \le m-$ the given samples in R^n.

$N-$ maximum number of iterations allowed.

Output: $\{y_j\}$, $1 \le j \le c -$ the final cluster centers.

$\{m_j\}$, $1 \le j \le c -$ the cluster sizes.

$\{l_{ij}\}$, $1 \le i \le m_j -$ the indices of the original samples which belong to the j cluster, $1 \le j \le c$.

$it -$ the number of iterations needed for convergence.

Step 1.   Initialization: set $y_{j0} = x_j$, $1 \le j \le c$ and it $= 0$.

Step 2.   Classify $\{x_i\}_{i=1}^{m}$ about the cluster centers $\{y_{j0}\}_{j=1}^{c}$ using the minimum distance classifier. For $1 \le j \le c$ denote by $\{x_{l_{ij}}\}_{i=1}^{m_j}$ the samples which cluster around y_{j0}.

Step 3.   For $1 \le j \le c$ obtain y_j which minimizes the performance index

$$I_j(z) = \sum_{i=1}^{m_j} \left\| z - x_{l_{ij}} \right\|^2, \; z \in R^n \tag{3.3.12}$$

Basic calculus implies

$$y_j = \left(\sum_{i=1}^{m_j} x_{l_{ij}} \right) / m_j \tag{3.3.13}$$

i.e. y_j is the arithmetic mean of $\{x_{l_{ij}}\}_{i=1}^{m_j}$. Set $it \leftarrow it + 1$.

Step 4.   If

$$y_j = y_{j0}, \; 1 \le j \le c \tag{3.3.14}$$

output $y_j, m_j, \{x_{l_{ij}}\}_{i=1}^{m_j}$, $1 \le j \le c$; it and stop. Otherwise, if $it > N$ output 'number of iterations exceeded';   else set $y_{j0} = y_j$ and go to Step 2.

A general optimal choice of c and y_{j0} as well as practical sufficient conditions for convergence of this algorithm are not known, except in obvious cases such as samples that are spread among disjoint cells which are sufficiently apart from each other.

A subroutine CMI which incorporates the c – means algorithm is given in the appendix.

■ **Example 3.3.4** Consider the samples in Fig. 3.3.4. Assume $c = 2$. The initial approximations for the two cluster centers are $y_{10} = x_1 = (2,3)^T$ and $y_{20} = x_2 = (1,2)^T$. The samples in the first cluster are x_1, x_4, x_5, x_6, x_7 while x_2, x_3 belong to the second one. The first iteration provides the new cluster centers $y_1 = (3.4,1.8)^T$, $y_2 = (1.0,1.5)^T$. Since convergence is not obtained, the samples are again classified with respect to the new cluster centers. Now x_5, x_6, x_7 are in the first cluster and x_1, x_2, x_3, x_4 are in the second.   The cluster centers are adjusted to $y_1 = (4.333,1.333)^T$, $y_2 = (1.5,2.0)^T$. The next classification yields the same partition of the samples, i.e. the same y_1 and y_2 and the process terminates after three iterations.

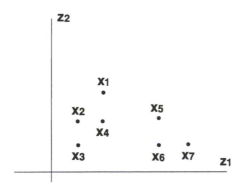

■ **Figure 3.3.4**   Applying c – means algorithm with $c = 2$.

In the next example more iterations are needed for convergence.

■ **Example 3.3.5** Consider the samples shown in Fig. 3.3.5 with the assumption $c = 4$. Convergence is obtained after nine iterations and the cluster centers are $y_1 = x_1$, $y_2 = x_5$, $y_3 = x_6$ and $y_4 = (1.333, 1.222)^T$.

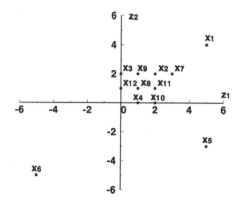

■ **Figure 3.3.5**   Applying the $c-$means algorithm with $c = 4$.

♠

The next algorithm is most commonly used in many applications. Like the $c-$means it determines the cluster centers iteratively as arithmetic means of their samples. In addition it incorporates several heuristic procedures which have been successfully implemented in an extensive number of applications. The user of this algorithm - ISODATA (Iterative Self-Organizing Analysis Techniques) must have a clear idea about the desired number of clusters. The final number of clusters will not exceed twice this value, or decrease below one half of this number.

3.4 THE ISODATA ALGORITHM

Consider the samples $X = \{x_1, x_2, \ldots, x_m\}$ with c initial cluster centers $y_1, y_2, \ldots, y_c$.

Algorithm 3.4.1.

(A general comprehensive iterative clustering algorithm: ISODATA)

Input: n – the problem's dimension.

m – the number of the given samples.

$X = \{x_i\}$, $1 \leq i \leq m$ – the m samples in R^n.

$Y = \{y_i\}$, $Z = \{z_i\}$, $1 \leq i \leq c$ – two identical sequences which contain the initial cluster centers.

k –   the desired number of clusters.

m_0 – minimum allowed size of a cluster.

σ_0 – standard deviation threshold (for splitting).

λ – splitting fraction: $0 < \lambda \leq 1$.

d_0 – lumping threshold.

l –   maximum number of pairs of clusters which may be lumped simultaneously.

ε –   a given tolerance.

N –   maximum number of iterations allowed.

S, L – vectors of size N. Initially

$$S(i) = L(i) = 2, \ 1 \leq i \leq N$$

After the i – th iteration, set $S(i) = 0$ or $L(i) = 0$ if splitting or lumping starts respectively. If splitting or lumping is completed   successfully,   set $S(i) = 1$ or $L(i) = 1$ respectively.

$NC-$ indicates a change in the set of cluster centers during the classification: Step 2 - Step 4.

Output: $Y = \{y_j\}$, $1 \le j \le c-$ the final cluster centers.

$it-$ the number of iterations needed for convergence.

Step 1.   Set $it = 0$; $S(i) = L(i) = 2$, $1 \le i \le N$.

Step 2.   Set $c' = c$, $z_j = y_j$ $1 \le j \le c$ and $NC = 1$.

Use the existing cluster centers and the minimum-distance principle to classify the samples, i.e.

$$x \in C_j \ iff \left\| x - y_j \right\| \le \left\| x - y_i \right\|, \ 1 \le i \le c, \ i \ne j \tag{3.4.1}$$

for all $x \in X$, where C_j is the cluster centered at y_j with m_j samples $\{x_{l_{ij}}\}_{i=1}^{m_j}$.

Step 3.   Each cluster center with fewer than m_0 samples is discarded. Its elements are distributed among the remaining clusters and we set $c \leftarrow c - 1$.

Step 4.   For $1 \le j \le c$ update the existing cluster centers by

$$y_j \leftarrow \frac{1}{m_j} \sum_{i=1}^{m_j} x_{l_{ij}} \tag{3.4.2}$$

If $c = c'$ and $\sum_{i=1}^{c} \left\| y_j - z_j \right\| < \varepsilon$ set $NC = 0$.

Step 5.   For $1 \le j \le c$ calculate the average distance of $x_{l_{ij}}$, $1 \le i \le m_j$ from y_j:

$$\overline{d}_j = \frac{1}{m_j} \sum_{i=1}^{m_j} \left\| x_{l_{ij}} - y_j \right\| \tag{3.4.3}$$

Step 6.   Calculate the global average distance $\overline{d}$ of all the m samples from their respective cluster centers, i.e.

$$\overline{d} = \frac{1}{m} \sum_{j=1}^{c} m_j \overline{d}_j \qquad (3.4.4)$$

This is the end of an iteration. Set $it \leftarrow it + 1$.

Step 7.   If $it = N$ go to Step 13. Otherwise

(a) If $c \leq \left[\dfrac{k+1}{2}\right]$ go to Step 8 (splitting a cluster).

(b) If $\left[\dfrac{k+1}{2}\right] < c < 2k$ and it is odd, go to Step 8.

(c) If $c \geq 2k$ go to Step 10 (lumping clusters).

(d) If $\left[\dfrac{k+1}{2}\right] < c < 2k$ and it is even, go to Step 10.

Step 8.   Trying to split. Set $S(it) = 0$. For every cluster denote the cluster center and the cluster samples by

$$\boldsymbol{y}_j = \left(y_j^{(1)}, y_j^{(2)}, \ldots, y_j^{(n)}\right)^T, \quad 1 \leq j \leq c \qquad (3.4.5)$$

$$\boldsymbol{x}_{l_{kj}} = \left(x_{l_{kj}}^{(1)}, x_{l_{kj}}^{(2)}, \ldots, x_{l_{kj}}^{(n)}\right)^T, \quad 1 \leq j \leq c, \ 1 \leq k \leq m_j \qquad (3.4.6)$$

respectively. Calculate the standard deviation vectors

$$\boldsymbol{\sigma}_j = \left(\sigma_j^{(1)}, \sigma_j^{(2)}, \ldots, \sigma_j^{(n)}\right)^T, \quad 1 \leq j \leq c \qquad (3.4.7)$$

where

$$\sigma_j^{(i)} = \left(\frac{\sum_{k=1}^{m_j}\left(x_{l_{kj}}^{(i)} - y_j^{(i)}\right)^2}{m_j}\right)^{1/2}, \quad 1 \leq j \leq c, \ 1 \leq i \leq n \qquad (3.4.8)$$

Each $\sigma_j^{(i)}$ is the standard deviation of the j-th cluster population along the i-th coordinate. Denote $\sigma_j^{(i_0)} = \max \sigma_j^{(i)}$, $1 \le i \le n$ (clearly i_0 depends on j).

Step 9.   For $j: 1 \le j \le c$ if $\sigma_j^{(i_0)} \le \sigma_0$ do not split the j-th cluster; otherwise split it, provided that *at least* one of the relations

$$c \le \left[\frac{k+1}{2} \right] \tag{3.4.9}$$

$$\bar{d}_j > \bar{d} \text{ and } m_j \ge 2m_0 \tag{3.4.10}$$

holds. Splitting the j-th cluster is done as follows. The cluster center y_j is deleted while two new cluster centers y_{j+}, y_{j-} defined as

$$y_{j+} = \left(y_j^{(1)}, \ldots, y_j^{(i_0-1)}, y_j^{(i_0)} + \lambda\sigma_j^{(i_0)}, y_j^{(i_0+1)}, \ldots, y_j^{(n)} \right) \tag{3.4.11}$$

$$y_{j-} = \left(y_j^{(1)}, \ldots, y_j^{(i_0-1)}, y_j^{(i_0)} - \lambda\sigma_j^{(i_0)}, y_j^{(i_0+1)}, \ldots, y_j^{(n)} \right) \tag{3.4.12}$$

are created, and we set $c \leftarrow c+1$. Thus, y_j is splitted along the i_0-th coordinate. The splitting is controlled by the parameter λ which ensures a noticeable but not dramatic change in the cluster centers arrangement. If splitting occurred, set $S(it)=1$ and go to Step 2. Otherwise:

1.   If $it>1$, $L(it-1)=0$ and $NC=0$ go to Step 12.
2.   If $it>1$, $L(it-1)=0$ and $NC=1$ go to Step 2.
3.   If $it>1$, $L(it-1)\ne0$ continue.
4.   If $it=1$ continue.

Step 10.   Lumping. Set $L(it)=0$. If $c<2$, $S(it)=0$ and $NC=0$, go to Step 12. If $c<2$ $S(it)=0$ and $NC=1$, go to Step 2. If

$c < 2$ and $S(it) = 2$, go to Step 2; otherwise calculate all the distances between arbitrary two cluster centers, i.e.

$$d_{ij} = \|y_i - y_j\|, 1 \le i \le c-1, i+1 \le j \le c \qquad (3.4.13)$$

Rearrange $\{d_{ij}\}$ as a monotonic increasing sequence and denote by l' the number of $d_{ij}'s$ which do not exceed d_0. Consider now the first $l^* = \min(l, l')$ numbers of this sequence which satisfy

$$d_{i_1 j_1} \le d_{i_2 j_2} \le \ldots \le d_{i_{l^*} j_{l^*}} \le d_0 \qquad (3.4.14)$$

If $l^* = 0$ no lumping occurs: if $S(it) = 2$ go to Step 2 and if $S(it) = 0$ go to Step 12. If $l^* \ne 0$ set $L(it) = 1$ and continue.

Step 11. The lumping starts with the pair of cluster centers (i_1, j_1) and terminates with (i_{l^*}, j_{l^*}). Each two cluster centers are lumped together and if a given pair (i_r, j_r) is such that either the $i_r - th$ or the $j_r - th$ cluster center had already been lumped, this pair is ignored. The lumping is done by replacing the $i_r - th$ and the $j_r - th$ cluster centers by

$$y_{(i_r, j_r)} = \frac{m_{i_r} y_{i_r} + m_{j_r} y_{j_r}}{m_{i_r} + m_{j_r}} \qquad (3.4.15)$$

i.e. by their center of gravity based on their current populations. Since y_{i_r} and y_{j_r} are deleted we also set $c \leftarrow c-1$. When the lumping is completed go to Step 2.

Step 12. Output $\{y_j\}$, $1 \le j \le c$; it and stop.

Step 13. Output y_j, $1 \le j \le c$; 'number of iterations exceeded' and stop.

It is needless to say that a successful implementation of ISODATA on general pattern set, requires extensive experimentation in order to obtain the appropriate values for parameters such as σ_0, λ, d_0. The next example for which ISODATA is applied, is given in detail.

■ **Example 3.4.1** Consider the samples (+) given in Fig. 3.4.1, and choose $c = 5$, $k = 3$, $m_0 = 2$, $\sigma_0 = 1.5$, $\lambda = 0.5$, $d_0 = 2.5$, $l = 2$, $N = 10$, $Y = \{(0,0)^T, (4,1)^T, (7,2)^T, (2,3)^T, (3,5)^T\}$.

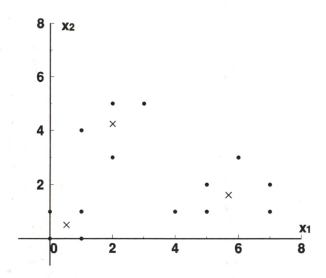

■ **Figure 3.4.1**   ISODATA - No. of desired clusters = 3.

Step 1. $it = 0$, $S(i) = L(i) = 2$, $1 \le i \le 10$.

Step 2. Clustering is performed, using Eq. (3.4.1):

$$
\begin{array}{ccccc}
C_1 & C_2 & C_3 & C_4 & C_5 \\
(0,0)^T & (4,1)^T & (7,1)^T & (2,3)^T & (2,5)^T \\
(1,0)^T & (5,1)^T & (7,2)^T & (1,4)^T & (3,5)^T \\
(1,1)^T & (5,2)^T & (6,3)^T & & \\
(0,1)^T & & & &
\end{array}
$$

Step 3. Since $m_j \geq m_0 = 2$ no cluster center is deleted at this point.

Step 4. Updating the cluster centers by replacing them with the clusters arithmetic means yields

$$Y = \left\{(0.5,0.5)^T, (4.667,1.333)^T, (6.667,2)^T, (1.5,3.5)^T, (2.5,5)^T\right\}$$

Step 5. Using Eq. (3.4.3) we get for each cluster the average distance of its samples from the cluster center:

$$\bar{d}_1 = 0.707, \bar{d}_2 = 0.654, \bar{d}_3 = 0.863, \bar{d}_4 = 0.707, \bar{d}_5 = 0.500$$

Step 6. The global average is

$$\bar{d} = \left(4\bar{d}_1 + 3\bar{d}_2 + 3\bar{d}_3 + 2\bar{d}_4 + 2\bar{d}_5\right)/14 = 0.700$$

and a full iteration is completed, i.e. $it = 1$.

Step 7. Since $it < N = 10$ and $2 = \left[\dfrac{k+1}{2}\right] < c < 2k = 6$ we go to Step 8 and try splitting.

Step 8. Set $S(1) = 0$. We calculate the standard deviation vectors

$$
\sigma_1 = \begin{pmatrix} 0.500 \\ 0.500 \end{pmatrix}, \quad
\sigma_2 = \begin{pmatrix} 0.471 \\ 0.471 \end{pmatrix}, \quad
\sigma_3 = \begin{pmatrix} 0.471 \\ 0.816 \end{pmatrix}, \quad
\sigma_4 = \begin{pmatrix} 0.500 \\ 0.500 \end{pmatrix}, \quad
\sigma_5 = \begin{pmatrix} 0.500 \\ 0.000 \end{pmatrix}
$$

Step 9. Clearly $\sigma_j^{(i)} \leq \sigma_0 = 1.5$ for arbitrary i, j and we conclude that there is no splitting. Since $it = 1$ we continue to Step 10.

Step 10.   Set $L(1) = 0$.   Since $c \geq 2$ lumping is possible.   We first calculate d_{ij} (Table 3.4.1) using Eq. (3.4.13).

■ **Table 3.4.1** Calculating d_{ij}.

i j:	2	3	4	5
1	4.249	6.346	3.162	4.924
2		2.108	3.837	4.259
3			5.380	5.134
4				1.803

Since $d_0 = 2.5$ we get $l' = 2$ and $l^* = \min(1, l') = 2$. Since $l^* \neq 0$ we set $L(1) = 1$. By virtue of

$$d_{45} \leq d_{23} \leq d_0$$

we first lump the cluster centers 4,5 and then 2,3.

Step 11.   Cluster centers 4 and 5 are lumped and replaced by

$$y_{(4,5)} = \frac{2y_4 + 2y_5}{4} = \begin{pmatrix} 2.00 \\ 4.25 \end{pmatrix}$$

Cluster centers 2 and 3 are lumped and replaced by

$$y_{(2,3)} = \frac{3y_2 + 3y_3}{6} = \begin{pmatrix} 5.667 \\ 1.667 \end{pmatrix}$$

The number of cluster centers is reduced to $c = 3$. We go to Step 2.

Step 2.   Cluster the samples around $y_1 = (0.5, 0.5)^T$, $y_2 = (5.667, 1.667)^T$ and $y_3 = (2, 4.25)^T$:

$$
\begin{array}{ccc}
C_1 & C_2 & C_3 \\
(0,0)^T & (4,1)^T & (2,3)^T \\
(1,0)^T & (5,1)^T & (1,4)^T \\
(1,1)^T & (5,2)^T & (2,5)^T \\
(0,1)^T & (7,1)^T & (3,5)^T \\
 & (7,2)^T & \\
 & (6,2)^T & \\
\end{array}
$$

Step 3.   No cluster center is deleted.

Step 4.   Cluster centers are updated but remain the same.

Step 5.   The new averages are $\bar{d}_1 = 0.707$, $\bar{d}_2 = 1.287$, $\bar{d}_3 = 1.070$

Step 6.   The new global average is $\bar{d} = 1.059$. Set $it = 2$.

Step 7.   Since $\left[\dfrac{k+1}{2}\right] < c < 2k$ and it is even we go to Step 10.

Step 10.   Since all d_{ij}, $1 \le i \le 2$, $i+1 \le j \le 3$ are greater than d_0, there is no lumping. We also have $S(2) = 2$ and therefore go to Step 2. (So far $S(1) = 0$, $L(1) = 1$, $S(2) = 2$, $L(2) = 0$).

Steps 2-6.   No change; Set $it = 3$.

Step 7.   Since $\left[\dfrac{k+1}{2}\right] < c < 2k$ and it is odd, we go to Step 8.

Step 8.   Set $S(3) = 0$. The standard deviation vectors are

$$\sigma_1 = \begin{pmatrix} 0.5 \\ 0.5 \end{pmatrix} \quad , \quad \sigma_2 = \begin{pmatrix} 1.106 \\ 0.745 \end{pmatrix} \quad , \quad \sigma_5 = \begin{pmatrix} 0.707 \\ 0.829 \end{pmatrix}$$

Step 9.   Since $\sigma_j^{(i)} \leq \sigma_0 = 1.5$ for all i, j there is no splitting.   But $L(2) = 0$ and therefore we go to Step 12.

Step 12.   The final cluster centers are (* in Fig. 3.4.1)

$$y_1 = \begin{pmatrix} 0.5 \\ 0.5 \end{pmatrix} \quad , \quad y_2 = \begin{pmatrix} 5.667 \\ 1.667 \end{pmatrix} \quad , \quad y_3 = \begin{pmatrix} 2.00 \\ 4.25 \end{pmatrix}$$

♠

and the number of iterations is $it = 2$.

A change in the problem's parameters may well result in a different arrangement of the cluster centers.

■ **Example 3.4.2**   In the previous example make the following changes: $c = 3$, $k = 3$, $\sigma_0 = 0.8$, $d_0 = 1$, $Y = \{(0,0)^T, (4,1)^T, (3,5)^T\}$.   After the first iteration two cluster centers are splitted and the new set of cluster centers (modified by Eq. (3.4.2)) is

$$Y = \{(0.5.05)^T, (6.667,2)^T, (2.5,5)^T, (4.667,1.333)^T, (1.5,3.5)^T\}$$

After the second iteration no lumping occurs and after the third iteration there is no splitting. The clustering thus terminates with 5 cluster centers.

♠

It should be noted that using ISODATA with inappropriate parameters may lead to oscillations. For example, a wrong choice of λ, σ_0, d_0 may cause an infinite sequence of alternate splitting and lumping.   This anomaly is likely to happen whenever $2\lambda\sigma_0 < d_0$. Indeed, consider a splitting where the distance between the new cluster centers is $2\lambda\sigma_j^{(i_0)}$ (Eqs. (3.4.11-12)). If we assume $\sigma_j^{(i_0)} \sim \sigma_0$ and in addition, that modifying the new centers using Eq. (3.4.2) causes a minor change in their locations, then unless

$$2\lambda\sigma_0 > d_0 \qquad (3.4.16)$$

lumping which brings us to the initial state, must occur.

■ **Example 3.4.3** In Example 3.4.1 make the following changes: $\sigma_0 = 0.8$, $d_0 = 2$. Splitting and lumping occur alternatively and the system oscillates between

$$Y_1 = \left\{ (0.5,0.5)^T, (4.667,1.333)^T, (6.667,2)^T, (2.5,5)^T, (1.5,3.5)^T \right\}$$

after each splitting, and

$$Y_2 = \left\{ (0.5,0.5)^T, (4.667,1.333)^T, (6.667,2)^T, (2,4.25)^T \right\}$$

after each lumping.

♠

In the next example we cluster 100 samples using several different sets of cluster centers.

■ **Example 3.4.4** Consider the samples in Fig. 3.4.2. The prefixed parameters are: $n = 2$, $m = 100$, $k = 4$, $m_0 = 6$, $\sigma_0 = 1.05$, $d_0 = 1.5$, $l = 1$, $N = 20$, $\varepsilon = 10^{-6}$ and $\lambda = 0.5$. Two sets of initial cluster centers are taken:

$$(a) \ y_1 = \begin{pmatrix} 2 \\ 1 \end{pmatrix}, \quad y_2 = \begin{pmatrix} 1 \\ 5 \end{pmatrix}, \quad y_3 = \begin{pmatrix} 6 \\ 1 \end{pmatrix}$$

$$(b) \ y_1 = \begin{pmatrix} 2 \\ 3 \end{pmatrix}, \quad y_2 = \begin{pmatrix} 5 \\ 3 \end{pmatrix}, \quad y_3 = \begin{pmatrix} 8 \\ 8 \end{pmatrix}$$

Only the first initial set is based on preliminary observation of the samples. The second set is a pure random choice. In either case only seven iterations are needed for convergence. The final cluster centers are

$$y_1 = \begin{pmatrix} 1.57 \\ 1.40 \end{pmatrix}, \quad y_2 = \begin{pmatrix} 1.17 \\ 5.37 \end{pmatrix}, \quad y_3 = \begin{pmatrix} 7.93 \\ 2.06 \end{pmatrix}, \quad y_4 = \begin{pmatrix} 5.85 \\ 4.93 \end{pmatrix}, \quad y_5 = \begin{pmatrix} 4.58 \\ 1.31 \end{pmatrix}$$

and the associated clusters have 41, 23, 7, 9 and 20 samples respectively.

Other choices of initial cluster centers, may converge to different cluster centers or oscillate. The initial cluster centers of (a) are denoted by ■, and the final cluster centers are denoted by ▲.

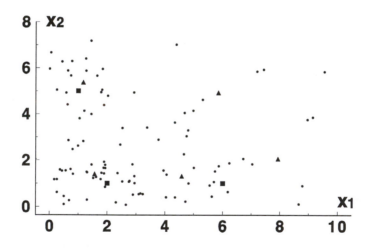

■ **Figure 3.4.2**   ISODATA applied on 100 samples.

The version of ISODATA given here is relatively simple. A more advanced procedure should include the option of deleting patterns which represent noise and the option of constantly tuning parameters such as σ_0, d_0, λ, m_0, i.e. re-initialization whenever necessary.

PROBLEMS

1. Use the TOD algorithm with the Euclidean norm as a measure of similarity to cluster the patterns

$$S = \left\{ (0,0)^T, (1,0,)^T, (1,1)^T, (5,3)^T, (4,4)^T, (0,6)^T, (0,5)^T, (2,2)^T, (3,3)^T \right\}$$

given a threshold parameter (a) $t = 1.2$ (b) $t = 2.1$ (c) $t = 4.3$.

2. Solve problem 1 after exchanging the locations of $(0,0)^T$ and $(2,2)^T$.

3. For $x = (x_1, x_2, \ldots, x_n)^T$ and $y = (y_1, y_2, \ldots, y_n)^T$ in R^n define a measure of similarity

$$\delta(x, y) = \max_{1 \le i \le n} | x_i - y_i | \qquad (3.4.17)$$

and use it instead of the Euclidean norm to solve problem 1.

4. (a) Modify the TOD algorithm as follows: Replace y_j in Eqs. (3.3.9-10) by $\bar{y}_j$ – the updated arithmetic mean of the samples in the j- th cluster.

    (b) Use the modified algorithm to cluster the samples $(1,0)^T$, $(1,1)^T$, $(0,0)^T$, $(3,1)^T$, $(5,2)^T$, $(3,3)^T$, $(5,3)^T$, $(2,4)^T$, $(3,5)^T$, $(1,4)^T$, $(0,3)^T$, $(2,0)^T$. Use the threshold parameter $t = 1.2$.

    (c) Use the original TOD algorithm to cluster the same data and the same threshold parameter.

5. Apply the MMD method to cluster the data of problem 4, using $t = 1.2$.

6. Repeat and solve problem 5, using the similarity measure defined by Eq. (3.4.17).

7. (a)   Using TOD or MMD obtain a sufficient condition for two measures of similarity $\delta_1(x,y)$ and $\delta_2(x,y)$ to provide identical sets of cluster centers for arbitrary data.

(b) In view of part (a) discuss the particular case

$$\delta_1(x, y) = \|x - y\|, \quad \delta_2(x, y) = \max_{1 \le i \le n} |x_i - y_i|$$

8. Apply the CMI algorithm to cluster the samples (`*`) in Fig. 3.4.3. Assume four clusters.

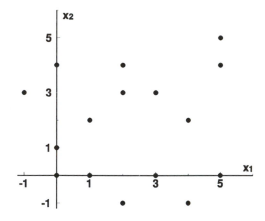

■   **Figure 3.4.3**   Clustering 16 samples using CMI.

9. Solve Problem 8 using the MMD method with $x_1 = (3,0)^T$ for
   (a) $t = 1.2$ (b) $t = 1.8$. Compare with the results of Problem 8.

10. Use a random number generator to provide random numbers $r_i, s_i, 1 \le i \le 100$ within the interval $[-1,1]$. Define the sample patterns $x_i = (x_{i1}, x_{i2})^T, 1 \le i \le 100$ as

$$x_{i1} = 0.4 + (0.6r_i)^3, \quad x_{i2} = 0.5 + (0.7s_i)^3, \quad 1 \le i \le 30$$

$$x_{i1} = 0.6 + (0.5r_i)^3, \quad x_{i2} = 0.3 + (0.8s_i)^3, \quad 31 \le i \le 58$$

$$\text{(3.4.18)}$$

$$x_{i1} = 0.2 + (0.6r_i)^3, \quad x_{i2} = 0.8 + (0.4s_i)^3, \quad 59 \le i \le 82$$

$$x_{i1} = 0.7 + (0.5r_i)^3, \quad x_{i2} = 0.7 + (0.5s_i)^3, \quad 83 \le i \le 100$$

and apply ISODATA to cluster them using $c = 4$, $k = 4$, $m_0 = 5$, $\sigma_0 = 0.1$, $d_0 = 0.2$, $l = 1$, $\lambda = 0.5$. Solve the problem with two choices of initial cluster centers:

(a) $y_1 = (0.4, 0.5)^T$, $y_2 = (0.6, 0.3)^T$, $y_3 = (0.2, 0.8)^T$, $y_4 = (0.7, 0.7)^T$

(b) $y_1 = (0,0)^T$, $y_2 = (1,0)^T$, $y_3 = (1,1)^T$, $y_4 = (0,1)^T$

11. Solve Problem 10 using a single initial cluster center $y_1 = (0.5, 0.5)^T$.

12. Solve Problem 10 using $m_0 = 10, 15$.

13. (a) Solve Problem 10 after replacing all the powers in Eq. (3.4.18) from 3 to 5.

(b) Compare the results with those of Problem 10.

3.5   CLUSTERING AND PATTERN RECOGNITION

The results of a clustering process are usually applied in pattern recognition for two objectives:

1. Obtaining features which are related to the geometric structure of the given sample patterns.

2. Designing decision functions for future classification in a pattern recognition problem.

3.5.1 Evaluating the Clustering Results

When the pattern space is 4-dimensional or of higher dimensionality, getting a visual representation of the samples and the cluster centers is impossible. In this case the only way to interpret the numerical results is to use information such as the distances between the cluster centers, the number of samples in each cluster and the standard deviation vectors of the various clusters. These quantities are usually sufficient for determining the general structure and features of the given samples as may be seen from the next example.

■ **Example 3.5.1** Consider a set of 200 samples which is clustered using ISODATA. The samples are in R^4, so that no graphic illustration is possible. The *a priori* knowledge is that the number of expected clusters $\{C_i\}$, is between five and seven and that 'noise samples' may occur. Let the outcome of the clustering consist of seven final cluster centers whose pairwise distances and associated populations are given in Table 3.5.1.

■ **Table 3.5.1**   Populations and distances between cluster centers.

m_j	i	$j:$	1	2	3	4	5	6	7
40	1			3.5	5.6	3.7	25.1	17.3	7.8
23	2				4.8	5.8	26.3	14.5	6.0
48	3					5.0	24.0	12.7	6.3
18	4						22.2	13.8	4.9
26	5							33.6	22.4
3	6								15.1
42	7								

The other useful information are the seven $4-$dimensional standard deviation vectors, given in Table 3.5.2.

■ **Table 3.5.2**   The standard deviation vectors.

i	σ_{x_1}	σ_{x_2}	σ_{x_3}	σ_{x_4}
1	1.2	1.5	2.1	0.8
2	1.3	1.4	1.2	1.4
3	2.0	1.3	1.7	1.1
4	0.9	1.1	2.2	1.7
5	0.3	0.4	2.3	0.6
6	2.5	4.2	1.7	2.3
7	2.2	1.9	1.1	3.5

The final number of clusters is in agreement with our preliminary expectation (based upon sample-related knowledge). However, the cluster C_6 has only three samples and a standard deviation vector with relatively large components. This indicates that these samples are likely to be noise samples and the whole cluster should be deleted. The remaining clusters are too populated to be treated as 'noise clusters.' Table 3.5.2 illustrates that C_i, $1 \leq i \leq 5$ have standard deviation vectors with relatively small components and should not be splitted. The vector associated with C_7 has larger components and further investigation may indicate that splitting is desirable. Since none of the pairwise distances is small, no lumping is necessary.

Other features are easily obtained from the tables:

1. C_1, C_3, C_7 are major clusters while C_2, C_4, C_5 are minors.

2.   The clusters $C_1 - C_4$ and C_7 form a group of clusters which are relatively close to each other, while C_5 is far from all of them. However, we may not consider defining one large cluster which includes C_i, $1 \leq i \leq 4$ and C_7 since it contradicts the assumption of having 'about' 5-7 clusters.

3.   The domain of C_2 is 'close' to a sphere (since σ_{x_i}, $1 \leq i \leq 4$ are almost identical).

3.5.2 Clustering as Unsupervised Learning

The clustering of given data of unknown characteristics is a problem in *unsupervised pattern recognition*. Originally, we have a set of sample patterns with no information to indicate the number and locations of classes in this set. The *unsupervised learning problem* related to these patterns can be defined as determining the various classes to which the given patterns belong. This can be done for example by using clustering algorithms. Naturally, the conclusions derived by these algorithms will have to be backed by intuition and a significant quantity of experimentation. Implementation of such algorithms on the given samples provides cluster centers and cluster domains for the data. Once determined, the cluster domains regarded as 'classes,' can be applied to obtain decision functions using various *training algorithms*. An alternative approach is to design a minimum-distance classifier based on the cluster centers which were already established in the preliminary unsupervised learning, and use it for future classification. The efficiency and applicability of such classifier depends on the reliability of the cluster centers and cluster domains obtained at the initial phase.

4 CLASSIFICATION USING STATISTICAL APPROACH

4.1 INTRODUCTION

In this chapter we will present a statistical approach to the problem of pattern classification. It is mainly based on Bayes formula from probability theory and assumes that all the relevant probability values are known. We open our discussion with a simple example. Given a quantity of pencils we are asked to classify them into two categories: C_1 - pencils made of lead, C_2 - pencils made of graphite. The *a priori* probabilities of a random pencil to belong to C_1 and C_2 are $p(C_1)$ and $p(C_2)$ respectively. If all the pencils share the same color and if we may not perform any chemical tests on the pencils, then the only way to classify the next pencil would be using the following decision rule:

$$If \ \ p(C_1) > p(C_2) \ then \ pencil \ in \ C_1$$

$$If \ \ p(C_2) > p(C_1) \ then \ pencil \ in \ C_2 \tag{4.1.1}$$

One should realize that if for example $p(C_1) > p(C_2)$ then *all* the pencils will be classified of C_1 although some of them obviously belong to C_2. The decision rule given by Eq. (4.1.1) could be accepted whenever $p(C_1) \gg p(C_2)$ or $p(C_2) \gg p(C_1)$.   However, if for example $p(C_1) = 0.51$ and $p(C_2) = 0.49$ the error probability of this rule is 0.49, i.e. an average of 49 out of 100 pencils are misclassified.

We now assume that each pencil is either 'yellow' or 'white' and let this value be assigned to an associated logic variable x. Let $p(x|C_i)$ denote the conditional probability distribution of x, if the pencil is already known to be in C_i. Then, the probability that the pencil is in C_i, provided that x occurred ('yellow' or 'white') can be calculated by Bayes formula as

$$p(C_i \mid x) = \frac{p(C_i)p(x \mid C_i)}{p(x)}, \ i = 1,2 \tag{4.1.2}$$

where

$$p(x) = \sum_{i=1}^{2} p(C_i)p(x \mid C_i) \tag{4.1.3}$$

is the *a priori* probability distribution of x. Thus, by observing the pencils color, i.e. by knowing the value of x and consequently the numbers $p(x|C_i)$, $i = 1,2$ we obtain the *a posteriori* probability $p(C_i|x)$, which is the probability of the next pencil to belong to C_i once its color is known.

Motivated by Eq. (4.1.2) we may now propose a new decision rule for classification, namely

$$\text{If } p(C_1|x) > p(C_2|x) \text{ then pencil in } C_1$$

$$\tag{4.1.4}$$

$$\text{If } p(C_2|x) > p(C_1|x) \text{ then pencil in } C_2$$

Which of the two classifiers should we use? Naturally, the second one, given by Eq. (4.1.4) and known as the Bayes classifier has the advantage that our decision is based on additional information, namely the color of the pencil and its conditional probability distributions.   However, an *objective* choice can be made only by comparing the two error probabilities. Thus, one must find whether the average error probability associated with Bayes classifier, does not exceed the error probability of the previous classifier (Eq. (4.1.1)) given by $\min\{p(C_i)\}$, $1 \le i \le 2$. The question is therefore, whether the inequality

$$p(Y) \cdot \min_{1 \le i \le 2}\{p(C_i \mid Y)\} + p(W) \cdot \min_{1 \le i \le 2}\{p(C_i \mid W)\} \le \min_{1 \le i \le 2}\{p(C_i)\} \qquad (4.1.5)$$

always holds (Y and W denote 'yellow' and 'white' respectively).

■ **Lemma 4.1.1** For all real a,b,c,d the inequality

$$\min\{a,b\} + \min\{c,d\} \le \min\{a+c,b+d\}$$

holds.

Proof.

Since $a \ge \min\{a, b\}$ and $c \ge \min\{c, d\}$ we have $a+c \ge \min\{a,b\}+ \min\{c,d\}$. Similarly $b+d \ge \min\{a,b\}+ \min\{c,d\}$ which completes the proof.

□

■ **Corollary 4.1.1** Bayes classifier is superior to the *a priori* probability classifier.

Proof.

By using Eq. (4.1.2) and Lemma 4.1.1., the left-hand side of Eq. (4.1.5) can be rewritten as

$$\min_{1\le i\le 2}\{p(C_i)p(Y|C_i)\}+\min_{1\le i\le 2}\{p(C_i)p(W|C_i)\}\le\min_{1\le i\le 2}\{p(C_i)[p(Y|C_i)+p(W|C_i)]\}$$

and since $p(Y\mid C_i)+p(W\mid C_i)=1$, $1\le i\le 2$, Eq. (4.1.5) holds.

□

■ **Example 4.1.1** Let $p(C_1)=\dfrac{1}{3}$, $p(C_2)=\dfrac{2}{3}$, $p(Y|C_1)=\dfrac{1}{5}$,

$p(W\mid C_1)=\dfrac{4}{5}$, $p(Y|C_2)=\dfrac{2}{3}$, $p(W\mid C_2)=\dfrac{1}{3}$. Then

$$p(Y)=p(C_1)p(Y\mid C_1)+p(C_2)p(Y\mid C_2)=\frac{1}{3}\cdot\frac{1}{5}+\frac{2}{3}\cdot\frac{2}{3}=\frac{23}{45}$$

$$p(W)=p(C_1)p(W\mid C_1)+p(C_2)p(W\mid C_2)=\frac{1}{3}\cdot\frac{4}{5}+\frac{2}{3}\cdot\frac{1}{3}=\frac{22}{45}$$

By using Bayes formula we get

$$p(C_1\mid Y)=\frac{p(C_1)p(Y\mid C_1)}{p(Y)}=\frac{(1/3)\cdot(1/5)}{(23/45)}=\frac{3}{23}$$

$$p(C_1\mid W)=\frac{p(C_1)p(W\mid C_1)}{p(W)}=\frac{(1/3)\cdot(4/5)}{(22/45)}=\frac{6}{11}$$

and consequently $p(C_2\mid Y)=1-p(C_1\mid Y)=20/23$ and $p(C_2\mid W)=1-p(C_1\mid W)=5/11$. Bayes classifier therefore classifies a yellow pencil in C_2 (graphite) with an error probability 3/23 and a white pencil in C_1 (lead) with an error probability 5/11. The total error probability is (Eq. (4.1.5))

$$\frac{23}{45}\cdot\frac{3}{23}+\frac{22}{45}\cdot\frac{5}{11}=\frac{13}{45}<\frac{1}{3}=\min_{1\le i\le 2}\{p(C_i)\}$$

♠

Our next step is to replace the discrete logic variable by a continuous observation x which is meaningful for both pattern classes C_1 and C_2. In other words, a *feature* which is meaningful for both C_1 and C_2 is represented by a continuous random variable x whose conditional probabilities are denoted by $p(x|C_1)$ and $p(x|C_2)$. The equations derived for the discrete Bayes model, i.e. Eqs. (4.1.2 - 4), hold here as well. The error probability e_p of the continuous Bayes classifier satisfies (assuming $-\infty < x < \infty$)

$$e_p = \int_{-\infty}^{\infty} p(x) \cdot \min_{1 \le i \le 2}\{p(C_i \mid x)\}\, dx = \int_{-\infty}^{\infty} \min_{1 \le i \le 2}\{p(x)p(C_i \mid x\}\, dx$$

$$= \int_{-\infty}^{\infty} \min_{1 \le i \le 2}\{p(x \mid C_i)p(C_i)\}\, dx \le \min_{1 \le i \le 2}\{\int_{-\infty}^{\infty} p(x \mid C_i)p(C_i)dx\}$$

$$= \min_{1 \le i \le 2}\{p(C_i)\int_{-\infty}^{\infty} p(x \mid C_i)dx\} = \min_{1 \le i \le 2}\{p(C_i)\} \qquad (4.1.6)$$

i.e. the continuous Bayes classifier outperforms the *a priori* probability classifier.

■   **Example 4.1.2** Consider the previous example, but instead of two colors we assume all the pencils to be yellow of various shade varying from 0 to 2. The conditional probability distributions $p(x|C_1)$ and $p(x|C_2)$ of the shade x are given in Fig. 4.1.1.

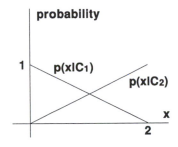

■   **Figure 4.1.1**   Conditional probabilities.

Using Eq. (4.1.3) we get $p(x) = \dfrac{1}{3} \cdot \dfrac{2-x}{2} + \dfrac{2}{3} \cdot \dfrac{x}{2} = \dfrac{2+x}{6}$ and consequently the *a posteriori* probabilities

$$p(C_1|x) = \frac{\left(\dfrac{1}{3}\right)\left(\dfrac{2-x}{2}\right)}{\left(\dfrac{2+x}{6}\right)} = \frac{2-x}{2+x} , \quad p(C_2|x) = \frac{\left(\dfrac{2}{3}\right)\left(\dfrac{x}{2}\right)}{\left(\dfrac{2+x}{6}\right)} = \frac{2x}{2+x}$$

which are shown in Fig. 4.1.2 and present the Bayes classifier in this case.

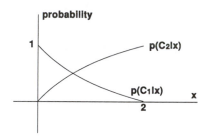

■ **Figure 4.1.2**   Bayes classifier: a posteriori probabilities.

The simplified classifier based only on the *a priori* probabilities can be portrayed by two parallel straight lines (Fig. 4.1.3) which imply that classification does not depend on x: each incoming pencil is classified in C_2.

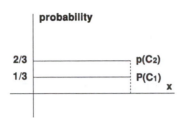

■ **Figure 4.1.3**   Simplified classifier: a priori probabilities.

PROBLEMS

1. In Example 4.1.1 take the same *a priori* probabilities but assume $p(x\,|\,C_i) = \dfrac{1}{2}$ for $x = Y, W$ and $1 \le i \le 2$. Is the classification improved by using Bayes classifier? Why?

2. Let C_1 and C_2 be as in Example 4.1.1 with $p(C_1) = \dfrac{1}{3}$, $p(C_2) = \dfrac{2}{3}$, and assume that each pencil is either yellow (Y), white (W) or red (R) with conditional probabilities given by

	Y	W	R
C_1	3/5	3/4	1/4
C_2	3/5	1/4	3/4

Construct the discrete Bayes classifier for this case.

3. In Example 4.1.2 assume $p(C_1) = \dfrac{1}{2}$, $p(C_2) = \dfrac{1}{2}$ and let x (the shade of yellow) vary between 0 and π, having the conditional probability distributions $p(x|C_1) = \dfrac{\sin x}{2}$ and $p(x|C_2) = \dfrac{2(\pi - x)}{\pi^2}$.

   (a) Construct the continuous Bayes classifier.
   (b) For what values of x the pencil is classified in C_1?
   (c) Why is Bayes classifier useful in this particular case?

4. Solve parts (a) and (b) of problem 3 if $p(C_1) = \dfrac{1}{3}$ and $p(C_2) = \dfrac{2}{3}$.

4.2   A GENERAL BAYES CLASSIFIER

We will now extend and generalize the ideas introduced in the previous section. Let us consider a finite set of pattern classes $\{C_1, C_2, ..., C_m\}$ and a *feature vector* x in R^n. Each component of this vector is a *meaningful* scalar feature of C_i, $1 \le i \le m$. The feature vector is a vector random variable with given conditional probability distributions $p(x|C_i)$, $1 \le i \le m$. If we denote by $p(C_i)$ the *a priori* probability of an incoming pattern to belong to C_i, then the *a posteriori* probability of this pattern with an attached feature vector x to belong to C_i is given by Bayes formula as

$$p(C_i | x) = \frac{p(C_i)p(x|C_i)}{p(x)}, \quad 1 \le i \le m \tag{4.2.1}$$

where

$$p(x) = \sum_{i=1}^{m} p(C_i)p(x|C_i) \tag{4.2.2}$$

is the probability distribution of x.

Throughout Section 4.1 we classified an incoming pattern by using either the *a priori* probability classifier or the Bayes classifier. In both cases, the pattern was classified either in class C_1 or in class C_2. Let us consider again two pattern classes and a particular feature vector x for which

$$p(C_1 \mid x) \sim p(C_2 \mid x)$$

In this case one could decide to take a third option: *not to classify* x. For example, if a 'loss' (or 'penalty') is attached to each misclassification, it could be rewarding to choose the following strategy:

$$\text{If } p(C_1 \mid x) \sim p(C_2 \mid x) \qquad \text{do not classify.}$$
$$\textit{Otherwise}: \quad \text{If } p(C_1 \mid x) > p(C_2 \mid x) \qquad \text{choose } C_1.$$
$$\text{If } p(C_1 \mid x) < p(C_2 \mid x) \qquad \text{choose } C_2.$$

Thus, for each feature vector x we take one of three possible *actions*.

In general, a finite set of actions $\{a_1, a_2, \ldots, a_k\}$ is attached to a given set of pattern classes $\{C_1, C_2, \ldots, C_m\}$ with a feature vector x. For each possible action a_i, $1 \le i \le k$ taken for an incoming pattern, we denote by $l(a_i \mid C_j)$ the *loss* for choosing a_i when x is known to be in C_j. For example, let $k = m + 1$ and define

$$a_i \triangleq \text{choose } C_i, \quad 1 \le i \le m$$
$$a_k \triangleq \text{do not classify}$$

A possible table of losses is

$$l(a_i \mid C_j) = 1 \quad, \quad 1 \le i, j \le m \ , \ i \ne j$$
$$l(a_i \mid C_i) = 0 \quad, \quad 1 \le i \le m$$
$$l(a_k \mid C_i) = 1/2 \ , \quad 1 \le i \le m$$

This table clearly suggests that a decision not to classify is less costly than a misclassification.

For a given feature vector x, we will define the *conditional risk* associated with the particular action a_i as

$$r(a_i \mid x) = \sum_{j=1}^{m} l(a_i \mid C_j) p(C_j \mid x) \qquad (4.2.3)$$

We also define a *decision rule* as a function $a(x)$ which assigns one of actions $\{a_i\}_{i=1}^{k}$ to any given feature vector x. Obviously, we are interested in a decision rule which will minimize the *total risk*

$$R = \int_{R^n} r(a(x) \mid x) p(x) dx \qquad (4.2.4)$$

where $dx = dx_1 dx_2 \ldots dx_n$. This is achieved by applying the general *Bayes decision rule* which can be stated as follows:

Given a feature vector x, define

$$a(x) = a_{i(x)} \qquad (4.2.5)$$

where

$$a_{i(x)} = \min\{r(a_j \mid x)\}, \ 1 \le j \le k \qquad (4.2.6)$$

No decision rule can outperform Bayes decision rule, since $r(a(x)|x)$ of Eq. (4.2.4) is minimized for each individual x while $p(x)$ is a prefixed function. The minimum risk associated with Bayes decision rule is called *Bayes risk*.

■ **Example 4.2.1**   Consider   a   2-class   problem   with $p(C_1) = 2/3$, $p(C_2) = 1/3$; a scalar feature x and three possible actions a_1, a_2, a_3 defined as: $a_1 -$ choose C_1, $a_2 -$ choose C_2, $a_3 -$ do not classify. Let the *loss matrix* (i.e. the values $l(a_i|C_j)$) be

$$
\begin{array}{cccc}
 & a_1 & a_2 & a_3 \\
C_1 & 0 & 1 & 1/4 \\
C_2 & 1 & 0 & 1/4
\end{array}
$$

and let the conditional probability distributions of x be

$$
p(x|C_1) = \frac{2-x}{2} , \quad p(x|C_2) = \frac{1}{2} ; \quad 0 \le x \le 2
$$

The probability distribution of x is therefore

$$
p(x) = \frac{2}{3} \cdot \frac{2-x}{2} + \frac{1}{3} \cdot \frac{1}{2} = \frac{5-2x}{6}
$$

and consequently

$$
p(C_1|x) = \frac{\left(\dfrac{2}{3}\right)\left(\dfrac{2-x}{2}\right)}{\left(\dfrac{5-2x}{6}\right)} = \frac{4-2x}{5-2x}
$$

$$
p(C_2|x) = \frac{\left(\dfrac{1}{3}\right)\left(\dfrac{1}{2}\right)}{\left(\dfrac{5-2x}{6}\right)} = \frac{1}{5-2x}
$$

This leads to conditional risks

$$
r_1(x) = r(a_1|x) = 0 \cdot p(C_1|x) + 1 \cdot p(C_2|x) = \frac{1}{5-2x}
$$

$$
r_2(x) = r(a_2|x) = 1 \cdot p(C_1|x) + 0 \cdot p(C_2|x) = \frac{4-2x}{5-2x}
$$

$$
r_3(x) = r(a_3|x) = \frac{1}{4} \cdot p(C_1|x) + \frac{1}{4} \cdot p(C_2|x) = \frac{1}{4}
$$

Bayes decision rule assigns to each x the action with the minimum conditional risk. The conditional risks are sketched in Fig. 4.2.1 and the optimal decision rule is therefore

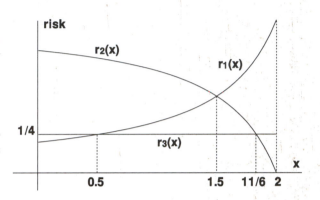

■ **Figure 4.2.1** Conditional risks.

$$0 \leq x \leq 0.5 \quad \Rightarrow \text{action } a_1 \Rightarrow \text{choose } C_1$$
$$0.5 \leq x \leq 11/6 \quad \Rightarrow \text{action } a_3 \Rightarrow \text{do not classify}$$
$$11/6 \leq x \leq 2 \quad \Rightarrow \text{action } a_2 \Rightarrow \text{choose } C_2$$

In this particular case the action 'do not classify' is optimal whenever x is between 1/2 and 11/6. Considering the probability distribution of x, this strategy should occur for approximately 60% of the incoming patterns. Finally, the minimum total risk is given by

$$\int_0^2 \min\{r_1(x), r_2(x), r_3(x)\} p(x) dx = \int_0^{1/2} r_1(x) p(x) dx$$
$$+ \int_{1/2}^{11/6} r_3(x) p(x) dx + \int_{11/6}^2 r_2(x) p(x) dx = \frac{1}{12} + \frac{4}{27} + \frac{1}{216} \sim 0.236$$

If instead of using Bayes classifier we choose to take a_1 for all x, the total risk is

$$\int_0^2 r_1(x) p(x) dx = \frac{1}{3} > 0.236$$

♠

■ **Example 4.2.2** In the previous example, assume that $l(a_3|C_1)$ and $l(a_3|C_2)$ are free parameters, α and β respectively, while the remaining data is the same. In order for the Bayes decision rule to force classification for any given x, we must have

$$\alpha p(C_1|x) + \beta p(C_2|x) \geq \min\{r_1(x), r_2(x)\}$$

In the particular case $\alpha = \beta$ this happens (Fig. 4.2.1) only if $\alpha \geq \dfrac{1}{2}$.

♠

A simple case study is a 2-class classification problem with two actions: a_1 − choose C_1 and a_2 − choose C_2. Denote $l(a_i|C_j)$ by l_{ij} and consider the conditional risks

$$r(a_1|x) = l_{11}p(C_1|x) + l_{12}p(C_2|x)$$

$$r(a_2|x) = l_{21}p(C_1|x) + l_{22}p(C_2|x)$$

Given a pattern with an associated feature vector x, we take action a_1 only if $r(a_1|x) < r(a_2|x)$, i.e.

$$l_{11}p(C_1|x) + l_{12}p(C_2|x) < l_{21}p(C_1|x) + l_{22}p(C_2|x)$$

which implies

$$(l_{21} - l_{11})p(C_1|x) > (l_{12} - l_{22})p(C_2|x)$$

By applying Eq. (4.2.1) we get

$$(l_{21} - l_{11})p(C_1)p(x|C_1) > (l_{12} - l_{22})p(C_2)p(x|C_2)$$

Naturally, one expects the loss in the case of a misclassification to be greater than the loss associated with a correct decision, i.e. $l_{21} > l_{11}$ and $l_{12} > l_{22}$. Therefore

$$s_{12}(\mathbf{x}) = \frac{p(\mathbf{x}|C_1)}{p(\mathbf{x}|C_2)} > \frac{(l_{12} - l_{22})p(C_2)}{(l_{21} - l_{11})p(C_1)} \tag{4.2.7}$$

The conditional probability distribution $p(\mathbf{x}|C_i)$ is often called the *likelihood function* of C_i with respect to $\mathbf{x}$ and $s_{12}(\mathbf{x})$ is the *likelihood ratio*. Thus, Bayes decision rule classifies a given pattern $\mathbf{x}$ in C_1 provided that the likelihood ratio calculated at $\mathbf{x}$ exceeds the threshold value

$$\lambda = \frac{(l_{12} - l_{22})p(C_2)}{(l_{21} - l_{11})p(C_1)} \tag{4.2.8}$$

Otherwise, $\mathbf{x}$ is classified in C_2. If $s_{12}(\mathbf{x}) = \lambda$ any arbitrary decision may be taken.

■ **Example 4.2.3** Consider a 2-class problem with $p(C_1) = \frac{2}{5}$, $p(C_2) = \frac{3}{5}$; a scalar feature x and the two actions a_1 and a_2 defined as in Example 4.2.1. If the loss matrix is

$$
\begin{array}{ccc}
 & a_1 & a_2 \\
C_1 & 1/4 & 1 \\
C_2 & 1/2 & 1/8
\end{array}
$$

the threshold value of Eq. (4.2.8) is

$$\lambda = \frac{(1/2 - 1/8) \cdot (3/5)}{(1 - 1/4) \cdot (2/5)} = \frac{3}{4}$$

Let the likelihood functions of C_1, C_2 be

$$p(x|C_1) = \frac{2-x}{2}, \quad p(x|C_2) = \frac{3x^2}{8}; \quad 0 \le x \le 2$$

Then, the likelihood ratio given by Eq. (4.2.7) is

$$S_{12}(x) = \frac{\left(\dfrac{2-x}{2}\right)}{\left(\dfrac{3x^2}{8}\right)} = \frac{4(2-x)}{3x^2} , \quad 0 \le x \le 2$$

and a pattern will be classified in C_1 if and only if

$$\frac{4(2-x)}{3x^2} > \frac{3}{4}$$

This inequality holds for $-2.9735 < x < 1.1957$, but since a relevant x must satisfy $0 \le x \le 2$ we get that the pattern is in C_1 for all x: $0 \le x < 1.1957$.

♠

In the next example we treat a problem with a feature vector x in R^2.

■ **Example 4.2.4** Consider a classification for which $p(C_1) = 1/3$, $p(C_2) = 2/3$ with a feature vector $x = (x_1, x_2)^T$, $0 \le x_1, x_2 \le 1$. Let the conditional probabilities be

$$p(x|C_1) = 4x_1 x_2 , \quad p(x|C_2) = x_1 + x_2 ; \quad 0 \le x_1, x_2 \le 1$$

(Note that the integrals of $p(x|C_i)$, $1 \le i \le 2$ over the unit square, must be equal to 1). Assume the actions and the loss matrix of Example 4.2.3. Then, a_1 is fired if and only if

$$S_{12}(x) = \frac{4x_1 x_2}{x_1 + x_2} > \frac{(1/2 - 1/8) \cdot (2/3)}{(1 - 1/4) \cdot (1/3)} = 1$$

i.e. whenever $4x_1 x_2 > x_1 + x_2$. This inequality is valid only if x is inside the shaded area in Fig. 4.3.2 which is the area bounded by the hyperbola $1/x_1 + 1/x_2 = 4$ and the straight lines $x_1 = 1$, $x_2 = 1$.

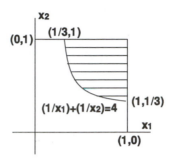

■ **Figure 4.2.2**   Decision region of C_1.

At the end of this section we will consider an $n-$ dimensional multiclass problem with the unit matrix as a loss matrix, and obtain the Bayes decision rule as an implementation of the decision functions

$$d_i(x) = p(x|C_i)p(C_i)$$

as in Eq. (2.2.6)

In most applications l_{ij} is taken as 0 if the decision is correct (i.e. $i = j$) and as 1 for an incorrect decision (i.e. $i \neq j$). Let the action a_i be 'assigning x to C_i' for all $1 \leq i \leq m$. Then

$$r(a_i \mid x) = \sum_{j=1}^{m} l_{ij} p(C_j \mid x) = [1/p(x)]\sum_{j=1}^{m} l_{ij} p(C_j)p(x \mid C_j)$$

$$= 1 - \frac{p(C_i)p(x \mid C_i)}{p(x)} \qquad (4.2.9)$$

for all $1 \le i \le m$, and x is classified by Bayes rule in C_i, if

$$1 - \frac{p(C_i)p(x \mid C_i)}{p(x)} < 1 - \frac{p(C_j)p(x \mid C_j)}{p(x)}$$

for all $j \ne i$, i.e. if

$$p(C_i)p(x|C_i) > p(C_j)p(x|C_j) \qquad (4.2.10)$$

for all $j \ne i$. Clearly, this is Eq. (2.2.6) implemented in its general form (i.e. not necessarily for *linear* decision function) for

$$d_i(x) = p(C_i)p(x|C_i), \quad 1 \le i \le m \qquad (4.2.11)$$

In the next section we will discuss in detail a particular case, when the conditional probabilities $p(x|C_i)$ are multivariate normal.

PROBLEMS

1. In a single feature 2-class problem with actions of Example 4.2.1, let $p(C_1) = 1/4$, $p(C_2) = 3/4$. Calculate Bayes risk for the loss matrix

	a_1	a_2	a_3
C_1	0	1	1/4
C_2	1	0	1/2

    and conditional probabilities

    $$p(x|C_1) = 1, \quad p(x|C_2) = 2(1 - x) ; \quad 0 \le x \le 1$$

2. Repeat and solve Problem 1 for a loss matrix

	a_1	a_2	a_3
C_1	1/4	3/4	1/2
C_2	3/4	1/4	1/2

and conditional probabilities

$$p(x|C_1) = 2x, \quad p(x|C_2) = \frac{4}{3} - x^2; \ 0 \le x \le 1$$

3. Consider a 2-feature 2-class classification with the actions a_1, a_2, a_3 as previously defined in Example 4.2.1. Assume $P(C_1) = \frac{1}{3}$, $P(C_2) = \frac{2}{3}$, a loss matrix

	a_1	a_2	a_3
C_1	1/4	1	1/3
C_2	1	1/2	2/3

and conditional probabilities

$$p(x|C_1) = x_1 + x_2, \quad p(x|C_2) = 2x_1; \ 0 \le x_1, x_2 \le 1$$

Construct the Bayes decision rule and obtain the Bayes risk.

4. In Problem 3 take $l(a_3|C_1) = l(a_3|C_2) = \alpha$ while the remaining data is unchanged. What is the minimum α for what a_3 is never fired. What is Bayes risk for this α?

5. For a one dimensional 2-class problem let $p(C_1) = p(C_2) = 1/2$. Assume two actions as in Example 4.2.3 with a loss matrix

	a_1	a_2
C_1	1/4	1/2
C_2	1	1/3

and likelihood functions

$$p(x|C_1) = \frac{3x^2}{8}, \quad p(x|C_2) = 3x(1 - \frac{x}{2}); \ 0 \le x \le 2$$

Find the likelihood ratio $s_{12}(x)$, the associated threshold value and the values of x for which an incoming pattern will be classified in C_2.

6. Replace the loss matrix in Problem 5 by

$$
\begin{array}{cc}
 & a_1 \quad a_2 \\
C_1 & 1/4 \quad \beta \\
C_2 & \alpha \quad 1/3
\end{array}
$$

(a) Present the Bayes decision rule.

(b) Calculate the Bayes risk $R(\alpha, \beta)$ and find nonnegative α, β for which $R(\alpha, \beta)$ is minimum.

7. For a one dimensional 2-class problem with two actions a_1, a_2 (as in Example 4.2.3) we have $p(C_1) = 3/5$, $p(C_2) = 2/5$; conditional probabilities

$$
p(x \mid C_1) = e^{-x}, 0 \le x < \infty
$$

$$
p(x \mid C_2) =
\begin{cases}
1/2 & , \ 0 \le x \le 1 \\
e^{-2(x-1)}/2 & , \ 1 < x < \infty
\end{cases}
$$

and a loss matrix

$$
\begin{array}{cc}
 & a_1 \quad a_2 \\
C_1 & 1/4 \quad 1 \\
C_2 & 1 \quad 1/4
\end{array}
$$

(a) Find the likelihood ratio $s_{12}(x)$ and it s associated threshold value.
(b) Calculate the Bayes risk.
(c) Using the Bayes classifier, how often (%) a pattern is classified in C_1?

4.3   NORMALLY DISTRIBUTED PATTERNS

The multivariate normal density function has received considerable attention due to:

(a) Its capability to portray a suitable model for many applications. (b) Being mathematically tractable.

4.3.1   The Univariate Normal Distribution

The scalar normal distribution function given by

$$p(x) = \frac{1}{\sqrt{2\pi}\sigma} \exp[-\frac{(x-\mu)^2}{2\sigma^2}], \quad -\infty < x < \infty \tag{4.3.1}$$

is characterized by two parameters, its *mean*

$$\mu = E[x] = \int_{-\infty}^{\infty} xp(x)dx \tag{4.3.2}$$

and *variance*

$$\sigma^2 = E[(x-\mu)^2] = \int_{-\infty}^{\infty} (x-\mu)^2 p(x)dx \tag{4.3.3}$$

and is frequently denoted by $N(\mu,\sigma^2)$. Simple calculation shows that normally distributed patterns cluster about the mean μ in a way that approximately 68.3%   of them fall within the interval $[\mu-\sigma,\mu+\sigma]$, 95.5% within $[\mu-2\sigma,\mu+2\sigma]$ and 99.75 within $[\mu-3\sigma,\mu+3\sigma]$.

4.3.2 The Multivariate Normal Distribution

A generalization of the univariate normal distribution in R^n is given by the multivariate normal distribution function, defined as

$$p(x) = \frac{1}{(2\pi)^{n/2} |C|^{1/2}} \exp[-\frac{1}{2}(x-\mu)^T C^{-1}(x-\mu)], \, x \in R^n \qquad (4.3.4)$$

where μ is a given vector in R^n and C - an $n \times n$ symmetric positive definite matrix, with inverse C^{-1} and determinant $|C|$. Under these conditions it can be shown that $p(x)$ is a multivariate probability distribution function with mean μ and covariance matrix C, i.e.

$$\mu = E[x] = \int_{R^n} xp(x)dx \qquad (4.3.5)$$

$$C = E[(x-\mu)(x-\mu)^T] = \int_{R^n} (x-\mu)(x-\mu)^T p(x)dx \qquad (4.3.6)$$

where $dx = dx_1 dx_2 \ldots dx_n$. The elements of μ are

$$\mu_i = \int_{R^n} x_i p(x)dx \qquad (4.3.7)$$

while those of C are

$$\sigma_{ij} = \int_{R^n} (x_i - \mu_i)(x_j - \mu_j)p(x)dx \qquad (4.3.8)$$

■ **Example 4.3.1** Consider the bivariate normal distribution with its parameters

$$\mu = \begin{pmatrix} 0 \\ 0 \end{pmatrix} \qquad C = \begin{pmatrix} 2 & 0 \\ 0 & 1 \end{pmatrix}$$

In this case

$$C^{-1} = \begin{pmatrix} 1/2 & 0 \\ 0 & 1 \end{pmatrix}, \, |C| = 2$$

and the distribution function is

$$p(x) = \frac{1}{2\pi\sqrt{2}} \exp\left(-\frac{x_1^2}{4} - \frac{x_2^2}{2}\right)$$

The first element of μ is

$$\mu_1 = \frac{1}{2\pi\sqrt{2}} \int_{-\infty}^{\infty} \int_{-\infty}^{\infty} x_1 \exp\left(-\frac{x_1^2}{4} - \frac{x_2^2}{2}\right) dx_1 dx_2$$

and since x_1 is an odd function we get $\mu_1 = 0$ and similarly $\mu_2 = 0$, i.e. $\mu = 0$. Once μ is known the covariance matrix of $p(x)$ can be calculated. In particular

$$\sigma_{11} = \frac{1}{2\pi\sqrt{2}} \int_{-\infty}^{\infty} \int_{-\infty}^{\infty} x_1^2 \exp\left(-\frac{x_1^2}{4} - \frac{x_2^2}{2}\right) dx_1 dx_2$$

$$= \frac{1}{\sqrt{2\pi}} \int_{-\infty}^{\infty} \exp\left(-\frac{x_2^2}{2}\right) dx_2 \cdot \frac{1}{\sqrt{4\pi}} \int_{-\infty}^{\infty} x_1^2 \exp\left(-\frac{x_1^2}{4}\right) dx_1$$

The first integral clearly equals to 1. By using integration by parts, the second integral is replaced by

$$-\frac{1}{\sqrt{4\pi}} 2x_1 \exp\left(-\frac{x_1^2}{4}\right) \Big|_{-\infty}^{\infty} + \frac{1}{\sqrt{4\pi}} \int_{-\infty}^{\infty} 2\exp\left(-\frac{x_1^2}{4}\right) dx_1$$

The first part obviously vanishes and by substituting $t = \dfrac{x_1}{\sqrt{2}}$, the second part becomes

$$\frac{\sqrt{2}}{\sqrt{4\pi}} \int_{-\infty}^{\infty} 2\exp\left(-\frac{t^2}{2}\right) dt = 2\left[\frac{1}{\sqrt{2\pi}} \int_{-\infty}^{\infty} \exp\left(-\frac{t^2}{2}\right) dt\right] = 2$$

Therefore, $\sigma_{11} = 2$ as expected.

♠

The multivariate normal distribution is determined by $n + \frac{1}{2}n(n+1)$ parameters which are μ_i, $1 \le i \le n$ and σ_{ij}, $1 \le i, j \le n$; $i \le j$. Patterns which are known to be normally distributed create a cluster with center at μ. The shape of this cluster is determined by the covariance matrix C. Since C is symmetric positive definite matrix, so is C^{-1} and the equation

$$(x - \mu)^T C^{-1}(x - \mu) = \text{const}$$

is a hyperellipsoid. Thus, the points in R^n with constant probability density are hyperellipsoids whose principal axes are determined by the eigenvectors of C and their lengths - by its eigenvalues.

4.3.3 A Multiclass Multivariate Normal Distribution Problem

Consider a multiclass pattern recognition problem with pattern classes $C_1, C_2, \ldots, C_m$ in R^n, associated with conditional probability distributions

$$p(x \mid C_i) = \frac{1}{(2\pi)^{n/2} |C_i|^{1/2}} \exp\left[-\frac{1}{2}(x - \mu_i)^T C_i^{-1}(x - \mu_i)\right], x \in R^n \quad (4.3.9)$$

for all $1 \le i \le m$. We assume an identity loss matrix and consequently get the decision functions of Eq. (4.2.11) implemented as in Eq. (2.2.6). For all practical purposes one can use $\ln[d_i(x)]$, $1 \le i \le m$ instead of $d_i(x)$, $1 \le i \le m$. Indeed, $\ln(t)$ is a monotonic increasing function of t, i.e.

$$d_i(x) > d_j(x) \quad \text{if and only if} \quad \ln[d_i(x) > \ln[d_j(x)] \quad (4.3.10)$$

Since $p(x|C_i)$ and therefore $d_i(x)$ includes an exponential function in its expression, it is convenient to redefine the decision functions as

$$d_i(x) = \ln\left[p(x|C_i)p(C_i)\right] = \ln\left[p(x|C_i)\right] + \ln(p(C_i)), \quad 1 \le i \le m \quad (4.3.11)$$

By substituting the right-hand side of Eq. (4.3.9) in Eq. (4.3.11) we get

$$d_i(x) = -\frac{n}{2}\ln(2\pi) - \frac{1}{2}\ln|C_i| - \frac{1}{2}(x-\mu_i)^T C_i^{-1}(x-\mu_i) + \ln(p(C_i))$$

and since the $i-$independent constant $(-\frac{n}{2}\ln(2\pi))$ can be removed, the decision functions may be taken as

$$d_i(x) = -\frac{1}{2}\ln|C_i| + \ln(p(C_i)) - \frac{1}{2}(x-\mu_i)^T C_i^{-1}(x-\mu_i) \quad (4.3.12)$$

Thus, if the loss matrix is the identity matrix and the patterns are normally distributed, no decision functions will produce better results than the quadratic surfaces given by Eq. (4.3.12).

Quite frequently all the covariance matrices C_i are equal, i.e.

$$C_i = C, \quad 1 \le i \le m$$

and by removing the new $i-$independent terms one can simplify the decision functions and get

$$d_i(x) = \ln(p(C_i)) + x^T C^{-1}\mu_i - \frac{1}{2}\mu_i^T C^{-1}\mu_i, \quad 1 \le i \le m \quad (4.3.13)$$

i.e., linear decision functions (hyperplanes). If we further assume that all the components of x are independent, i.e. $\sigma_{jk} = 0$, $j \ne k$ and that $\sigma_j^2 = 1$, $1 \le j \le n$ then C is the identity matrix of order n and if also $p(C_i) = 1/m$, $1 \le i \le m$ we can remove the constant $\ln(1/m)$ from Eq. (4.3.13) and get

$$d_i(x) = x^T \mu_i - \frac{1}{2}\mu_i^T \mu_i, \quad 1 \le i \le m \quad (4.3.14)$$

which is identical to Eq. (3.2.4) that was derived for classification using the minimum-distance classifier in the case of single prototypes.

The decision boundaries obtained from Eq. (4.3.13) are

$$d_{ij}(x) = d_i(x) - d_j(x) = \ln(p(C_i)) - \ln(p(C_j)) + x^T C^{-1}(\mu_i - \mu_j)$$
$$-\frac{1}{2}\mu_i^T C^{-1}\mu_i + \frac{1}{2}\mu_j^T C^{-1}\mu_j, 1 \le i, j \le m \tag{4.3.15}$$

i.e. hyperplanes. If the covariance matrices C_i are not the same, the decision boundaries are quadratic surfaces.

■ **Example 4.3.2** Consider a 2-D 3-class normal distribution problem with covariance matrices

$$C_1 = C_2 = \begin{pmatrix} 1 & 0 \\ 0 & 2 \end{pmatrix}, \ C_3 = \begin{pmatrix} 1 & 0 \\ 0 & 1 \end{pmatrix}$$

mean vectors

$$\mu_1 = \begin{pmatrix} 1 \\ 0 \end{pmatrix}, \ \mu_2 = \begin{pmatrix} 0 \\ 1 \end{pmatrix}, \ \mu_3 = \begin{pmatrix} 2 \\ 2 \end{pmatrix}$$

and $p(C_1) = p(C_2) = 1/4$, $p(C_3) = 1/2$. Thus,

$$|C_1| = |C_2| = 2, \ \frac{1}{2}\ln|C_1| = \frac{1}{2}\ln|C_2| = \frac{1}{2}\ln 2; \ |C_3| = 1, \ \frac{1}{2}\ln|C_3| = 0$$

$$C_1^{-1} = C_2^{-1} = \begin{pmatrix} 1 & 0 \\ 0 & 1/2 \end{pmatrix}, \ C_3^{-1} = \begin{pmatrix} 1 & 0 \\ 0 & 1 \end{pmatrix}$$

and the decision functions obtained by Eq. (4.3.12) are

$$d_1(\boldsymbol{x}) = -\frac{1}{2}\ln 2 - \ln 4 - \frac{1}{2}(x_1 - 1, x_2)\begin{pmatrix} 1 & 0 \\ 0 & 1/2 \end{pmatrix}\begin{pmatrix} x_1 - 1 \\ x_2 \end{pmatrix}$$

$$= -2.5\ln 2 - \frac{1}{2}\left[(x_1 - 1)^2 + \frac{1}{2}x_2^2\right]$$

$$d_2(\boldsymbol{x}) = -2.5\ln 2 - \frac{1}{2}\left[x_i^2 + \frac{1}{2}(x_2 - 1)^2\right]$$

$$d_3(\boldsymbol{x}) = -\ln 2 - \frac{1}{2}(x_1 - 2, x_2 - 2)\begin{pmatrix} 1 & 0 \\ 0 & 1 \end{pmatrix}\begin{pmatrix} x_1 - 2 \\ x_2 - 2 \end{pmatrix}$$

$$= -\ln 2 - \frac{1}{2}\left[(x_1 - 2)^2 + (x_2 - 2)^2\right]$$

The decision boundaries are the straight line

$$d_{12}(\boldsymbol{x}) = d_1(\boldsymbol{x}) - d_2(\boldsymbol{x}) = x_1 - \frac{x_2}{2} - \frac{1}{4} = 0$$

between C_1 and C_2, and the parabolas

$$d_{13}(\boldsymbol{x}) = d_1(\boldsymbol{x}) - d_3(\boldsymbol{x}) = \frac{x_2^2}{4} - 2x_2 - x_1 + \frac{7 - 3\ln 2}{2} = 0$$

$$d_{23}(\boldsymbol{x}) = d_2(\boldsymbol{x}) - d_3(\boldsymbol{x}) = \frac{x_1^2}{4} - 2x_1 - x_2 + \frac{7 - 3\ln 2}{2} = 0$$

between C_1, C_3 and between C_2, C_3 respectively.

♠

4.3.4   Error Probabilities

We will now discuss the error probability associated with the Bayes classifier for normally distributed patterns.

Consider a 2-class pattern recognition problem where the patterns of both classes share the same covariance matrix.   Let the multivariate normal densities be

$$p(x \mid C_i) = \frac{1}{(2\pi)^{n/2} \mid C \mid^{1/2}} \exp\left[-\frac{1}{2}(x - \mu_i)^T C^{-1}(x - \mu_i)\right], 1 \leq i \leq 2 \quad (4.3.16)$$

As previously stated we can simplify the discussion and replace the likelihood ratio $s_{12}(x)$ by

$$t_{12}(x) = \ln\left[s_{12}(x)\right] = \ln\left[p(x \mid C_1)\right] - \ln\left[p(x \mid C_2)\right] \quad (4.3.17)$$

By virtue of Eq. (4.3.16) we obtain

$$t_{12}(x) = \frac{1}{2}(x - \mu_2)^T C^{-1}(x - \mu_2) - \frac{1}{2}(x - \mu_1)^T C^{-1}(x - \mu_1) \quad (4.3.18)$$

and since C^{-1} is symmetric this leads to

$$t_{12}(x) = x^T C^{-1}(\mu_1 - \mu_2) - \frac{1}{2}(\mu_1 + \mu_2)^T C^{-1}(\mu_1 - \mu_2) \quad (4.3.19)$$

A commonly used 2x2 loss matrix is

$$\begin{pmatrix} s_{11} & s_{12} \\ s_{21} & s_{22} \end{pmatrix} = \begin{pmatrix} 0 & 1 \\ 1 & 0 \end{pmatrix} \quad (4.3.20)$$

for which the threshold value of Eq. (4.2.8) is

$$\lambda = \frac{p(C_2)}{p(C_1)} \quad (4.3.21)$$

Thus, in order to get minimum probability for misclassification one should classify $x \in C_1$ if and only if

$$t_{12}(x) > \ln\left[\frac{p(C_2)}{p(C_1)}\right] \tag{4.3.22}$$

and classify $x \in C_2$ otherwise. Since x is normally distributed and since $t_{12}(x)$ is a linear combination of the components of x, it must also be normally distributed. The expected value of $t_{12}(x)$ with respect to C_1 is (Eq. (4.3.9))

$$E_1(t_{12}(x)) = \mu_1 C^{-1}(\mu_1 - \mu_2) - \frac{1}{2}(\mu_1 + \mu_2)^T C^{-1}(\mu_1 - \mu_2)$$

$$= \frac{1}{2}(\mu_1 - \mu_2)^T C^{-1}(\mu_1 - \mu_2) = \bar{t}_{12}(x) \tag{4.3.23}$$

The scalar

$$D_{12} = (\mu_1 - \mu_2)^T C^{-1}(\mu_1 - \mu_2) \tag{4.3.24}$$

is called the *Mahalanobis distance* between the distributions $p(x|C_1)$ and $p(x|C_2)$

By definition, the variance of $t_{12}(x)$ with respect to C_1 is

$$V_1(t_{12}) = E_1[(t_{12} - \bar{t}_{12})^2] \tag{4.3.25}$$

From Eqs. (4.3.19) and (4.3.23) we get

$$t_{12} - \bar{t}_{12} = [x^T - \frac{1}{2}(\mu_1 + \mu_2)^T - \frac{1}{2}(\mu_1 - \mu_2)^T]C^{-1}(\mu_1 - \mu_2)$$

$$= (x - \mu_1)^T C^{-1}(\mu_1 - \mu_2) \tag{4.3.26}$$

which implies

$$E_1[(t_{12} - \bar{t}_{12})^2] = E_1[(\mu_1 - \mu_2)^T C^{-1}(x - \mu_1)(x^T - \mu_1^T)C^{-1}(\mu_1 - \mu_2)] \tag{4.3.27}$$

By virtue of Eq. (4.3.6) we therefore have

$$E_1[(t_{12} - \bar{t}_{12})^2] = (\mu_1 - \mu_2)^T C^{-1} CC^{-1} (\mu_1 - \mu_2)$$

$$= (\mu_1 - \mu_2)^T C^{-1} (\mu_1 - \mu_2) = D_{12} \qquad (4.3.28)$$

Thus, $t_{12}(x)$, $x \in C_1$ is distributed normally with mean $\dfrac{D_{12}}{2}$ and variance D_{12}. Similarly, $t_{12}(x)$, $x \in C_2$ has a normal distribution with mean $-\dfrac{D_{12}}{2}$ and variance D_{12}. Consequently

$$p(t_{12} > \alpha \mid C_2) = \frac{1}{\sqrt{2\pi D_{12}}} \int_\alpha^\infty \exp\left[-\frac{(t_{12} + D_{12}/2)^2}{2D_{12}}\right] dt_{12}$$

$$= 1 - erf\left(\frac{\alpha + D_{12}/2}{\sqrt{D_{12}}}\right) \qquad (4.3.29)$$

$$p(t_{12} < \alpha \mid C_1) = \frac{1}{\sqrt{2\pi D_{12}}} \int_{-\infty}^\alpha \exp\left[-\frac{(t_{12} - D_{12}/2)^2}{2D_{12}}\right] dt_{12}$$

$$= erf\left(\frac{\alpha - D_{12}/2}{\sqrt{D_{12}}}\right) \qquad (4.3.30)$$

where

$$erf(x) = \frac{1}{\sqrt{2\pi}} \int_{-\infty}^x \exp(-t^2/2)\, dt \qquad (4.3.31)$$

The error probability to misclassify an arbitrary x is

$$p(error) = p(C_1)p[(t_{12}(x) < \alpha_0|C_1)] + p(C_2)p[(t_{12}(x) > \alpha_0|C_2)]$$

$$= p(C_1)erf\left(\frac{\alpha_0 - D_{12}/2}{\sqrt{D_{12}}}\right) + p(C_2)\left[1 - erf\left(\frac{\alpha_0 + D_{12}/2}{\sqrt{D_{12}}}\right)\right] \qquad (4.3.32)$$

where

$$\alpha_0 = \ln\left[\frac{p(C_2)}{p(C_1)}\right] \qquad (4.3.33)$$

In the particular case $p(C_1) = p(C_2) = \dfrac{1}{2}$ we get $\alpha_0 = 0$, i.e.

$$p(error) = \frac{1}{2}\left[erf\left(-\sqrt{D_{12}}/2\right) + 1 - erf\left(\sqrt{D_{12}}/2\right)\right]$$

which yields

$$p(error) = \frac{1}{\sqrt{2\pi}}\int_{\sqrt{D_{12}}/2}^{\infty} \exp\left(-t^2/2\right)dt \qquad (4.3.34)$$

The quantity D_{12} is the Mahalanobis distance between the distributions $p(x|C_1)$ and $p(x|C_2)$. When this distance increases the error probability decreases, and converges to zero if $D_{12} \to \infty$.

PROBLEMS

1. Consider a 2-D 2-class classification problem, where the patterns of either class are normally distributed with the same covariance matrix

$$C = \begin{pmatrix} 2 & 1 \\ 1 & 2 \end{pmatrix}$$

The mean vectors of classes C_1 and C_2 are

$$\mu_1 = \begin{pmatrix} 1 \\ 1 \end{pmatrix}, \mu_2 = \begin{pmatrix} 2 \\ 1 \end{pmatrix}$$

respectively and $p(C_1) = p(C_2) = 1/2$. Get the decision boundary between the two classes.

2. Find the decision boundaries for the following 2-D 3-class classification problem with normally distributed patterns:

$$C_1 = \begin{pmatrix} 1 & 0 \\ 0 & 1 \end{pmatrix}, C_2 = \begin{pmatrix} 2 & 0 \\ 0 & 1 \end{pmatrix}, C_1 = \begin{pmatrix} 1 & 0 \\ 0 & 2 \end{pmatrix}$$

$$\mu_1 = \begin{pmatrix} 1 \\ 0 \end{pmatrix}, \mu_2 = \begin{pmatrix} 0 \\ -1 \end{pmatrix}, \mu_3 = \begin{pmatrix} 0 \\ 0 \end{pmatrix}$$

$$p(C_1) = p(C_2) = p(C_3) = \frac{1}{3}$$

3. Find the error probability of the Bayes classifier applied for Problem 1.

4. In Problem 1 choose $p(C_1) = \alpha$, $p(C_2) = 1 - \alpha$ and draw the error probability as a function of α.

5. Consider a 2-D 2-class classification problem with normally distributed patterns. Assume that the vector patterns $(0,0)^T$, $(1,0)^T$, $(0,1)^T$, $(1,1)^T$ belong to C_1 and $(-1,0)^T$, $(0,-1)^T$, $(-1,-1)^T$, $(-2,-2)^T$ to C_2. Approximate μ_i, C_i, $i = 1,2$ using *only* these classified patterns and use the results to obtain the decision boundary between the classes.

4.4 ESTIMATION   OF   PROBABILITY   DENSITY

FUNCTIONS

The most important task in implementing a statistical approach for solving pattern classification problems is estimating the density functions $p(x|C_i)$, $1 \leq i \leq m$. We will first show how to use the *maximum entropy principle* to obtain the *form* of probability density functions.

4.4.1   Form of the Density Function

The principle of maximum entropy states that in the case where a probability density function of a random variable is not known, the function which maximizes the entropy of this variable subject to known specified constraints is an appropriate choice. Any other choice would show a bias to some information obtained from the given data. The maximum entropy solution is easily derived when the constraints are given in the form of averages associated with the probability density function. Given a probability density function $p(x)$, the associated entropy is

$$E = -\int_x p(x)\ln[p(x)]dx \qquad (4.4.1)$$

and we assume the constraints

$$\int_x f_i(x)p(x)dx = \alpha_i, \quad 0 \leq i \leq M \qquad (4.4.2)$$

where $f_0(x) = 1$ and $\alpha_0 = 1$. We wish to obtain $p(x)$ which satisfies Eq. (4.4.2) while minimizing the entropy E of Eq. (4.4.1). This is done using Lagrange multipliers. Define

$$E_1 = E + \sum_{i=0}^{M} \lambda_i [\int_x f_i(x)p(x)dx - \alpha_i] \qquad (4.4.3)$$

where the constants λ_i, $0 \le i \le M$ are yet to be determined. By virtue of Eq. (4.4.1) we get

$$E_1 = -\int_x p(x)[\ln[p(x)] - \sum_{i=0}^{M} \lambda_i f_i(x)]dx - \sum_{i=0}^{M} \lambda_i \alpha_i \qquad (4.4.4)$$

The partial derivative of E_1 with respect to $p(x)$ is

$$\frac{\partial E_1}{\partial [p(x)]} = -\int_x \left[\ln[p(x)] - \sum_{i=0}^{M} \lambda_i f_i(x) + 1\right]dx \qquad (4.4.5)$$

and to obtain the maximum entropy solution the integrand must vanish, i.e.

$$p(x) = \exp\left[\sum_{i=0}^{M} \lambda_i f_i(x) - 1\right] \qquad (4.4.6)$$

We still have freedom of choosing λ_i, $a \le i \le m$ and these coefficients are chosen so that Eq. (4.4.2) holds. Once the form of the probability density function is known, we may turn and perform the next step: estimating the parameters of this density.

■   **Example 4.4.1**   Consider a random variable x which is characterized by

$$a < x < b, \quad \int_0^\infty p(x)dx = 1$$

By virtue of Eq. (4.4.6) we obtain

$$p(x) = \exp(\lambda_0 - 1), \quad \int_a^b \exp(\lambda_0 - 1)dx = 1$$

and therefore

$$p(x) = \begin{cases} \dfrac{1}{b-a} & , \quad a < x < b \\ \\ 0 & , \quad \text{otherwise} \end{cases}$$

♠

■ **Example 4.4.2** Assume that the *a priori* information about x is

$$x \geq 0 \ , \ \int_0^\infty p(x)dx = 1 \ , \ \int_0^\infty xp(x)dx = \mu$$

Using Eq. (4.4.6) we obtain

$$p(x) = \exp(\lambda_0 - 1 + \lambda_1 x)$$

and in order to satisfy the two constraints the density function must be

$$p(x) = \begin{cases} (1/\mu)\exp(-x/\mu) & , \quad x \geq 0 \\ 0 & , \quad \text{otherwise} \end{cases}$$

♠

4.4.2 Estimating the Mean Vector and Covariance Matrix

Consider a pattern population with probability density function $p(x)$. The mean vector of this population is given by

$$\mu = E(x) = \int_x xp(x)dx \qquad (4.4.7)$$

If the patterns are in R^n, then μ is a vector with n components $(\mu_1, \ldots, \mu_n)$. Let $\{x_i\}_{i=1}^N$ denote the given patterns. An approximate to μ is simply

$$\mu \approx \frac{1}{N}\sum_{i=1}^N x_i \qquad (4.4.8)$$

The covariance matrix $C = (c_{jk})$, $1 \le j,k \le n$ satisfies

$$c_{jk} = \int_{-\infty}^{\infty} \int_{-\infty}^{\infty} (x_j - \mu_j)(x_k - \mu_k) p(x_j, x_k) dx_j dx_k \qquad (4.4.9)$$

We can also rewrite C as

$$\begin{aligned} C &= E[(x - \mu)(x - \mu)^T] \\ &= E[xx^T - 2x\mu^T + \mu\mu^T] \\ &= E[xx^T] - \mu\mu^T \end{aligned} \qquad (4.4.10)$$

and use the new expression to approximate C as

$$C \approx \frac{1}{N} \sum_{i=1}^{N} x_i x_i^T - \mu\mu^T \qquad (4.4.11)$$

Both estimates for μ and for C can be conveniently used in a recursive manner. Let N be the current number of sample patterns and assume on additional incoming pattern. Denote by $\mu(N), C(N)$ the current mean vector and covariance matrix. Then

$$\mu(N+1) = \frac{1}{N+1} \sum_{i=1}^{N+1} x_i$$

$$= \frac{1}{N+1} \left(\sum_{i=1}^{N+1} x_i + x_{N+1} \right)$$

$$= \frac{1}{N+1} (N\mu(N) + x_{N+1}) \qquad (4.4.12)$$

where $\mu(1) = x_1$. This recursive expression updates the mean vector.

In the case of the covariance matrix we obtain

$$C(N+1) = \frac{1}{N+1} \sum_{i=1}^{N+1} x_i x_i^T - \mu(N+1)\mu^T(N+1)$$

$$= \frac{1}{N+1} \left(\sum_{i=1}^{N} x_i x_i^T + x_{N+1} x_{N+1}^T \right) - \mu(N+1)\mu^T(N+1)$$

$$= \frac{1}{N+1} (NC(N) + N\mu(N)\mu^T(N) + x_{N+1} x_{N+1}^T)$$

$$- \frac{1}{(N+1)^2} (N\mu(N) + x_{N+1})(N\mu^T(N) + x_{N+1}^T) \qquad (4.4.13)$$

To start the calculation of $C(N)$ we use the relation

$$C(1) = x_1 x_1^T - \mu(1)\mu^T(1)$$

to obtain $C(1)=0$.

■ **Example 4.4.3** Consider the sample patterns

$$x_1 = \begin{pmatrix} 0 \\ 0 \end{pmatrix}, \quad x_2 = \begin{pmatrix} 1 \\ 0 \end{pmatrix}, \quad x_3 = \begin{pmatrix} 1 \\ 1 \end{pmatrix}, \quad x_4 = \begin{pmatrix} 1 \\ 2 \end{pmatrix}$$

To start the recursive procedure we set

$$\mu(1) = x_1 = \begin{pmatrix} 0 \\ 0 \end{pmatrix}, \quad C_1 = \begin{pmatrix} 0 & 0 \\ 0 & 0 \end{pmatrix}$$

and then, using Eqs. (4.4.12-13), obtain

$$\mu(2) = \begin{pmatrix} 1/2 \\ 0 \end{pmatrix}, \quad \mu(3) = \begin{pmatrix} 2/3 \\ 1/3 \end{pmatrix}, \quad \mu(4) = \begin{pmatrix} 3/4 \\ 3/4 \end{pmatrix},$$

$$C(2) = \begin{pmatrix} 1/4 & 0 \\ 0 & 0 \end{pmatrix}, \quad C(3) = \begin{pmatrix} 2/9 & 1/9 \\ 1/9 & 2/9 \end{pmatrix}, \quad C(4) = \begin{pmatrix} 3/16 & 3/16 \\ 3/16 & 11/16 \end{pmatrix}$$

♠

4.4.3   Estimation by Functional Approximation

If the form of the density function is not known we may estimate it directly using functional approximation.

Let $p(x)$ denote the probability density function $p(x \mid C)$ and consider an approximate $\tilde{p}(x)$ given by

$$\tilde{p}(x) = \sum_{i=1}^{m} a_i \phi_i(x) \tag{4.4.14}$$

where $\{\phi_i(x)\}_{i=1}^{m}$ are specified basis functions. We wish to minimize

$$E = \int_x w(x)[p(x) - \tilde{p}(x)]^2 dx \tag{4.4.15}$$

or

$$E = \int_x w(x)\left[p(x) - \sum_{i=1}^{m} a_i \phi_i(x) \right]^2 dx \tag{4.4.16}$$

where $w(x)$ is a specified weight function. Solving the system

$$\frac{\partial E}{\partial a_i} = 0, \quad i = 1, \ldots, m \tag{4.4.17}$$

provides a set of linear equations

$$\sum_{j=1}^{m} a_i \int_x w(x)\phi_j(x)\phi_i(x)dx = \int_x w(x)\phi_i(x)p(x)dx, \quad 1 \le i \le m \tag{4.4.18}$$

The right-hand sides of these equations are simply the expected values of $w(x)\phi_i(x)$, $1 \le i \le m$. If $\{x_k\}_{k=1}^{N}$ are given samples which belong to C, these expected values can be estimated as

$$\int_x w(x)\phi_i(x)p(x)dx \approx \frac{1}{N} \sum_{k=1}^{N} w(x_k)\phi_i(x_k) \tag{4.4.19}$$

We thus replace the system given by Eq. (4.4.18) by

$$\sum_{j=1}^{m} a_i \int_x w(x)\phi_j(x)\phi_i(x)dx = \frac{1}{N}\sum_{k=1}^{N} w(x_k)\phi_i(x_k), \quad 1 \le i \le m \qquad (4.4.20)$$

In the particular case where $\phi_i(x)$, $1 \le i \le k$ are orthogonal with respect to $w(x)$, we have

$$\int_x w(x)\phi_j(x)\phi_i(x)dx = \begin{cases} A_i, & j=i \\ 0, & j \ne i \end{cases} \qquad (4.4.21)$$

and consequently

$$a_i = \frac{1}{NA_i}\sum_{k=1}^{N} w(x_k)\phi_i(x_k) \qquad (4.4.22)$$

The expression given by Eq. (4.4.22) provides an easy way to obtain $a_i(N+1)$ from $a_i(N)$. Indeed

$$a_i(N+1) = \frac{1}{(N+1)A_i}\sum_{k=1}^{N+1} w(x_k)\phi_i(x_k)$$

$$= \frac{1}{(N+1)A_i}\left[NA_i a_i(N) + w(x_{N+1})\phi_i(x_{N+1})\right] \qquad (4.4.23)$$

In decision making problems, since the terms $w(x_k)$ in Eq. (4.4.22) are independent of i and are therefore common to all the coefficients, they can usually be eliminated from the process, without violating the discriminatory characteristics of the coefficients. We may usually therefore, for such problems, apply a simpler relation

$$a_i = \frac{1}{N}\sum_{k=1}^{N} \phi_i(x_k) \qquad (4.4.24)$$

i.e. relate to the orthogonal basis functions, as if they were orthonormal and simplifying the computations.

Since $p(x)$ is not known, one may not be able to decide how large m should be. Usually we start with a prefixed m and experiment with the training set to determine whether $\tilde{p}(x)$ is an acceptable approximate to $p(x)$. If the classification performance of $\tilde{p}(x)$ is poor, we increase m until we reach a 'saturation' state, i.e. until adding new terms has no effect on the classification quality of $\tilde{p}(x)$. It can be shown that in general $\tilde{p}(x)$ approaches $p(x)$ as $m \to \infty$ and $N \to \infty$.

■ **Example 4.4.4** Consider the two-class classification problem given in Fig. 4.4.1

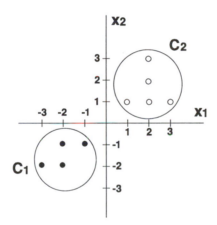

■ **Figure 4.4.1**   Bayes classification using functional approximation.

Assuming that the entire domain of the patterns is the whole plane, one is tempted to use the Hermite polynomials which are orthogonal over the interval $(-\infty, \infty)$. The first two polynomials are $H_0(x) = 1, H_1(x) = 2x$. If four basis functions are considered we may choose

$$\phi_1(x) = H_0(x_1)H_0(x_2) = 1$$

$$\phi_2(x) = H_1(x_1)H_0(x_2) = 2x_1$$

$$\phi_3(x) = H_0(x_1)H_1(x_2) = 2x_2$$

$$\phi_4(x) = H_1(x_1)H_1(x_2) = 4x_1x_2$$

We may treat the functions as if they were orthonormal and obtain

$$a_i^{(l)} = \frac{1}{N_l}\sum_{k=1}^{N_l}\phi_i\left(x_k^{(l)}\right), \quad 1 \le l \le 2$$

where $a_i^{(l)}$ are the coefficients associated with class l, N_l – the number of patterns in class l, and $x_k^{(l)}$ are the patterns in class l. Thus

$$a_1^{(1)} = \frac{1}{4}(1+1+1+1) = 1 , \qquad a_2^{(1)} = \frac{1}{4}(-2-4-4-6) = -4$$

$$a_3^{(1)} = \frac{1}{4}(-2-2-4-4) = -3 , \qquad a_4^{(1)} = \frac{1}{4}(4+8+16+24) = 13$$

$$a_1^{(2)} = \frac{1}{5}(1+1+1+1+1) = 1 , \qquad a_2^{(2)} = \frac{1}{5}(2+4+4+4+6) = 4$$

$$a_3^{(2)} = \frac{1}{5}(2+2+2+4+6) = 3.2 , \qquad a_4^{(2)} = \frac{1}{5}(4+8+12+16+24) = 12.8$$

and consequently

$$\tilde{p}(x \mid C_1) = 1 - 8x_1 - 6x_2 + 52x_1x_2$$

$$\tilde{p}(x \mid C_1) = 1 + 8x_1 + 6.4x_2 + 51.2x_1x_2$$

The decision functions are

$$d_1(x) = \tilde{p}(x \mid C_1) p(C_1)$$

$$d_2(x) = \tilde{p}(x \mid C_2) p(C_2)$$

and by assuming $p(C_1) = p(C_2) = 1/2$ we get

$$d_1(x) = \frac{1}{2} - 4x_1 - 3x_2 + 26x_1 x_2$$

$$d_2(x) = \frac{1}{2} + 4x_1 + 3.2x_2 + 25.6x_1 x_2$$

The decision boundary is therefore

$$d_{12}(x) = d_1(x) - d_2(x) = -8x_1 - 6.2x_2 + 0.4x_1 x_2 = 0$$

♠

PROBLEMS

1. Use the maximum entropy principle to obtain the probability density function if the information

$$-\infty < x < \infty, \quad \int_{-\infty}^{\infty} p(x)dx = 1, \quad \int_{-\infty}^{\infty} xp(x)dx = \mu, \quad \int_{-\infty}^{\infty} x^2 p(x)dx = \sigma^2$$

is *a priori* known.

2. Given the sample patterns

$$x_1 = \begin{pmatrix} 1 \\ 0 \\ 1 \end{pmatrix}, \quad x_2 = \begin{pmatrix} 2 \\ 0 \\ 0 \end{pmatrix}, \quad x_3 = \begin{pmatrix} 1 \\ -1 \\ 1 \end{pmatrix}, \quad x_4 = \begin{pmatrix} 1 \\ 1 \\ 1 \end{pmatrix}$$

Use Eqs. (4.4.12-13) to estimate $\mu(i)$, $C(i)$, $1 \leq i \leq 4$.

3. Apply the method of functional approximation to get estimates of $p(x|C_1)$ and $p(x|C_2)$ where

$$C_1 = \{(1,0)^T, \ (1, 1)^T, (2,1)^T, (3,0)^T, (4,1)^T\}$$

$$C_2 = \{(-1,0)^T, \ (-2, 0)^T, (-2,-1)^T, (-3,1)^T, (-3,2)^T\}$$

Use the first three 2-D Hermite polynomials and Eq. (4.4.24) to obtain the coefficients.

4. Repeat problem 3 but use the first four Hermite polynomials.

5. Repeat problems 3 and 4 using Hermite orthonormal functions. Replace $H_k(x)$ by

$$H_k^*(x) = \frac{\exp(-x^2/2)}{\sqrt{2^k k! \sqrt{\pi}}} H_k(x)$$

but still use Eq. (4.4.24).

5 FEATURE SELECTION

5.1 INTRODUCTION

Any pattern which can be classified in some category must possess a number of *features*. The first step in the process of classification is to consider the problem, what features to select and how to *extract* (measure) them. This problem could be complicated since sometimes the important features are not easily measured, while sometimes economic considerations forbid their measurement.

As an example, consider the problem of oil prospecting. This is clearly a two-class classification problem since any given location is either positive or negative for oil. In order to classify an arbitrary location there is a foolproof procedure: one should start drilling oil wells until either oil is found in significant quantities, or there are already enough dry wells in this location to declare it oil-free. Although by doing so we are *measuring* the most significant features of the location, it is quite clear that this procedure is economically impractical, unless time and money do not count — which usually is not the case.

Instead, we must consider other features which provide less information but are economically reasonable and practical. For example, we detonate dynamite at several points on the surface at the specific location. The features that we measure are some seismic events obtained from the low frequency reflection waves caused by the explosions. Using these features, a map of the earth's inner crust is obtained and each location is classified as having or lacking a *potential* of having oil. Obviously, a more conclusive map would be desired but as one finds, a trade-off between feature selection and classification performance is a constraint which exists here and in many other pattern recognition problems where economical considerations must be considered.

Three types of features may be considered:

1. Physical features

2. Structural features

3. Mathematical features

Physical and structural features are easily detected by sensory organs and are therefore commonly used by humans (and animals) for pattern recognition.   Color and weight for example are considered physical features while geometrical properties are structural features.   In this chapter we only discuss mathematical features which are for example correlation coefficients, eigenvalues of covariance matrices and other mathematical invariants.   In automatic pattern recognition, physical and structural features are used mainly for image processing and they are problem oriented.   For example, to identify crops by aerial photographs one should definitely use color as a prime feature.   On the other hand, in order to identify a setup of missiles or airplanes, the use of structural features is needed.   However, it is impossible to develop general guidelines how to select physical or structural features.

Mathematical pattern preprocessing consists of two tasks: clustering transformation and feature selection.   A central problem is the development of decision functions from given sets of patterns so that these functions will partition the measurement space into regions, each of which contains the sample patterns of a single pattern class.   This brings the concept of clustering transformation which operates on the measurement space and clusters the points representing the patterns of that class.   A clustering transformation is expected to maximize the *interset distance* which is the mean square distance between patterns that belong to different classes, and at the same time to minimize the *intraset distance* which is the mean square distance between patterns that belong to the same class.   In the process of selecting the most effective features, the dimensionality of the vectors representing the patterns may be reduced.

The maximization or the minimization of some criterion function dictates the optimum feature selection. Another approach is to attach the feature selection to the performance of the classification procedure, for example to the probability of correct classification. If the feature distribution is known for each class we may perform feature selection by entropy minimization or by maximizing a divergence function which measures the dissimilarity between classes. If the feature distribution for each class is unknown we use nonparametric feature selection based on direct estimate of the error probability.

5.2   DISTANCE MEASURES

In processing pattern samples, distance measures play a significant role and are applied in designing a feature extraction procedure. We open this section with the definitions of point-to-point, point-to-set and set-to-set distances in an n-dimensional Euclidean space.

■ **Definition 5.2.1**   For   arbitrary   patterns $x = (x_1, x_2, \ldots, x_n)^T$ and $y = (y_1, y_2, \ldots, y_n)^T$ in R^n, the quantity

$$d(x, y) = \left[\sum_{i=1}^{n} (x_i - y_i)^2 \right]^{1/2}$$

(5.2.1)

is called the distance (*point-to-point distance*) between x and y. It is also denoted by $\|x - y\|$ (*norm*).

Let $C = \{x^{(1)}, x^{(2)}, \ldots, x^{(m)}\}$ denote a class of patterns in R^n.

■ **Definition 5.2.2**   Given an arbitrary pattern $x = (x_1, x_2, \ldots, x_n)^T$ in R^n, the distance of x from C (*point-to-set distance*) is the mean square distance between x and $x^{(i)}$, $1 \le i \le m$, and is denoted by

$$d^2(x, C) = \frac{1}{m} \sum_{i=1}^{m} d^2(x, x^{(i)})$$

$$= \frac{1}{m}\sum_{i=1}^{m}\sum_{j=1}^{n}(x_{j} - x_{j}^{(i)})^{2}$$

(5.2.2)

For arbitrary $x^{(j)} \in C$ we thus have

$$d^{2}(x^{(j)}, C - \{x^{(j)}\}) = \frac{1}{m-1}\sum_{i\neq j}\sum_{k=1}^{n}(x_{k}^{(j)} - x_{k}^{(i)})^{2}$$

(5.2.3)

and since $d(x^{(j)}, x^{(j)}) = 0$ we obtain also

$$d^{2}(x^{(j)}, C - \{x^{(j)}\}) = \frac{1}{m-1}\sum_{i=1}^{m}\sum_{k=1}^{n}(x_{k}^{(j)} - x_{k}^{(i)})^{2}$$

(5.2.4)

The intraset distance associated with C is defined next.

■ **Definition 5.2.3** The mean of $d(x^{(j)}, C - \{x^{(j)}\})$ over C is called the *intraset distance* of C and is denoted by

$$D^{2}(C) = \frac{1}{m}\sum_{j=1}^{m} d^{2}(x^{(j)}, C - \{x^{(j)}\})$$

$$= \frac{1}{m(m-1)}\sum_{j=1}^{m}\sum_{i=1}^{m}\sum_{k=1}^{n}(x_{k}^{(j)} - x_{k}^{(i)})^{2}$$

(5.2.5)

■ **Example 5.2.1** Consider the class $C = \{(0,0)^{T}, (1,0)^{T}, (-1,0)^{T}, (1,1)^{T}\}$ in R^{2}. Here

$$d^{2}(x^{(1)}, C - \{x^{(1)}\}) = \frac{1^{2} + 1^{2} + (1^{2} + 1^{2})}{3} = 1.333$$

$$d^{2}(x^{(2)}, C - \{x^{(2)}\}) = \frac{1^{2} + 2^{2} + 1^{2}}{3} = 2$$

$$d^2\left(x^{(3)}, C - \left\{x^{(3)}\right\}\right) = \frac{1^2 + 2^2 + (2^2 + 1^2)}{3} = 3.333$$

$$d^2\left(x^{(4)}, C - \left\{x^{(4)}\right\}\right) = \frac{(1^2 + 1^2) + 1^2 + (2^2 + 1^2)}{3} = 2.667$$

i.e.,

$$D^2(C) = \frac{1.333 + 2 + 3.333 + 2.667}{4} = 2.333$$

♠

By conveniently rearranging the elements in the triple summation of Eq. (5.2.5) we will now express the intraset distance $D^2(C)$ in terms of the variances of the components of the given patterns. Indeed,

$$D^2(C) = \frac{m}{m-1} \sum_{k=1}^{n} \left[\frac{1}{m^2} \sum_{j=1}^{m} \sum_{i=1}^{m} \left(x_k^{(j)} - x_k^{(i)}\right)^2 \right]$$

$$= \frac{m}{m-1} \sum_{k=1}^{n} \left[\frac{1}{m^2} \sum_{j=1}^{m} \sum_{i=1}^{m} \left(x_k^{(j)}\right)^2 - \frac{2}{m^2} \sum_{j=1}^{m} \sum_{i=1}^{m} x_k^{(j)} x_k^{(i)} + \frac{1}{m^2} \sum_{j=1}^{m} \sum_{i=1}^{m} \left(x_k^{(i)}\right)^2 \right]$$

We now denote

$$\overline{x_k^{(j)}} = \frac{1}{m} \sum_{j=1}^{m} x_k^{(j)} \quad , \quad \overline{\left(x_k^{(j)}\right)^2} = \frac{1}{m} \sum_{j=1}^{m} (x_k^{(j)})^2$$

and obtain

$$D^2(C) = \frac{m}{m-1} \sum_{k=1}^{n} \left[\frac{1}{m} \sum_{i=1}^{m} \overline{\left(x_k^{(j)}\right)^2} - 2 \overline{x_k^{(j)}} \; \overline{x_k^{(i)}} + \frac{1}{m} \sum_{j=1}^{m} \overline{\left(x_k^{(i)}\right)^2} \right]$$

$$= \frac{2m}{m-1} \sum_{k=1}^{n} \left[\overline{\left(x_k^{(i)}\right)^2} - \overline{\left(x_k^{(i)}\right)}^2 \right] \tag{5.2.6}$$

since obviously $\overline{x_k^{(i)}} = \overline{x_k^{(j)}}$ and $\overline{(x_k^{(i)})^2} = \overline{(x_k^{(j)})^2}$ for arbitrary i and j.   The unbiased variance of $x_k^{(i)}$, $1 \le i \le m$ is given by

$$
\begin{aligned}
\sigma_k^2 &= \frac{1}{m-1} \sum_{i=1}^{m} (x_k^{(i)} - \overline{x_k^{(i)}})^2 \\
&= \frac{1}{m-1} \left[\overline{m(x_k^{(i)})^2} - 2m \overline{(x_k^{(i)})^2} + m \overline{(x_k^{(i)})^2} \right] \\
&= \frac{m}{m-1} \left[\overline{(x_k^{(i)})^2} - \overline{(x_k^{(i)})^2} \right]
\end{aligned}
$$

Therefore,

$$
D^2(C) = 2 \sum_{k=1}^{n} \sigma_k^2 \tag{5.2.7}
$$

i.e., the intraset distance of a pattern class C is twice the sum of the variances of the single components of the patterns.

■ **Example 5.2.2** In the previous example the means of the components are $\mu_1 = \mu_2 = 0.25$ providing the unbiased variances $\sigma_1^2 = (44/48)$, $\sigma_2^2 = (12/48)$ and

$$
D^2(C) = 2 \left(\frac{44}{48} + \frac{12}{48} \right) = 2.333
$$

as expected.

♠

We finally define the interset distance.

■ **Definition 5.2.4**   For   arbitrary   pattern   classes
$C_1 = \{x^{(1)}, x^{(2)},..., x^{(m_1)}\}$ and $C_2 = \{y^{(1)}, y^{(2)},..., y^{(m_2)}\}$,   the   *interset*
distance (*set-to-set distance*) between C_1 and C_2 is the mean square
distance between a pattern in C_1, and a pattern in C_2. It is denoted by

$$D^2(C_1, C_2) = \frac{1}{m_1 m_2} \sum_{i=1}^{m_1} \sum_{j=1}^{m_2} d^2(x^{(i)}, y^{(j)}) \qquad (5.2.8)$$

5.3 CLUSTERING TRANSFORMATIONS

Consider a pattern $x = (x_1, x_2,..., x_n)^T$ in R^n.   The measurements
x_i , $1 \le i \le n$ which represent the sample and by which one is supposed
to classify the pattern are usually not equally important.   Clearly,
measurements of less importance should be assigned *smaller* weights. The
process of *feature weighting* can be carried through a linear transformation
which will operate on initially scattered patterns in such a way that the
transformed pattern points will be highly clustered in the new space.
    Consider arbitrary patterns x, y in R^n and a *weight matrix*

$$W = \begin{pmatrix} w_{11} & w_{12} \cdots w_{1n} \\ w_{21} & w_{22} \cdots w_{2n} \\ \vdots & \quad \vdots \\ w_{n1} & w_{n2} \cdots w_{nn} \end{pmatrix} \qquad (5.3.1)$$

Using W to transform the given patterns we get

$$x' = Wx \quad , \quad y' = Wy$$

and the distance between the patterns in the new space is

$$d(x', y') = \left[\sum_{i=1}^{n} (x'_i - y'_i)^2 \right]^{1/2}.$$

$$= \left[\sum_{i=1}^{n} \left(\sum_{j=1}^{n} w_{ij}(x_j - y_j) \right)^2 \right]^{1/2} \qquad (5.3.2)$$

We now assume only scale-factor transformation where each coordinate is simply multiplied by an associated factor. In this case $w_{ij} = 0$ if $i \neq j$ and the matrix W is diagonal. Instead of Eq. (5.3.2) we obtain

$$d(x', y') = \left[\sum_{i=1}^{n} w_{ii}^2 (x_i - y_i)^2 \right]^{1/2} \qquad (5.3.3)$$

where w_{ii} is the $i-$th feature weight.

Consider the following problem: Given a pattern class $C = \{x^{(1)}, x^{(2)}, \ldots x^{(m)}\}$ in R^n, find a scale-factor transformation that will minimize the intraset distance of the new pattern class in the new space.

It is easily seen that the class C' of the transformed pattern satisfies

$$D^2(C') = 2\sum_{i=1}^{n} (w_{ii}\sigma_i)^2 \qquad (5.3.4)$$

where σ_i^2 is the unbiased variance associated with the $i-$th component in the original space (throughout the calculations in the previous section we simply replace each $x_i^{(j)}$ by $w_{ii}x_i^{(j)}$). To minimize the right-hand side of Eq. (5.3.4) we must add a single constraint on the numbers w_{ii}, $1 \leq i \leq n$.

Case 1.   Assume the constraint

$$\sum_{i=1}^{n} w_{ii} = 1 \qquad (5.3.5)$$

Minimizing $D^2(C')$ is equivalent to minimizing the expression (Lagrange multipliers procedure)

$$A = 2\sum_{i=1}^{n}(w_{ii}\sigma_{ii})^2 - \alpha\left(\sum_{i=1}^{n}w_{ii} - 1\right)$$ (5.3.6)

since Eq. (5.3.5) holds. Thus

$$\frac{\partial A}{\partial w_{ii}} = 4w_{ii}\sigma_i^2 - \alpha = 0 \ , \quad 1 \le i \le n$$ (5.3.7)

which yields

$$w_{ii} = \frac{\alpha}{4\sigma_i^2} \ , \quad 1 \le i \le n$$ (5.3.8)

In addition Eq. (5.3.5) holds. Consequently

$$\alpha = \frac{4}{\displaystyle\sum_{i=1}^{n}\sigma_i^{-2}}$$ (5.3.9)

and

$$w_{ii} = \frac{1}{\sigma_i^2\displaystyle\sum_{i=1}^{n}\sigma_i^{-2}}$$ (5.3.10)

■ **Example 5.3.1** Consider the pattern class in Example 5.2.1. By Example 5.2.2 $\sigma_1^2 = (44/48)$ and $\sigma_2^2 = (12/48)$. To minimize $D^2(C')$ we apply Eq. (5.3.10) and choose

$$w_{11} = \frac{1}{(44/48)[(48/44)+(48/12)]} = 0.214$$

$$w_{22} = 1 - w_{11} = 0.786$$

The intraset distance in the new space is

$$2[(w_{11}\sigma_1)^2 + (w_{22}\sigma_2)^2] = 0.393$$

The intraset distance in the original space is

$$2(\sigma_1^2 + \sigma_2^2) = 2.333$$

♠

This example demonstrates how a clustering transformation is designed. We use a feature weighting process, where the feature with a larger variance is assigned a smaller weight, since the associated measurement is clearly less reliable or less important.

Case 2. Again we assume that W is a scale-factor transformation subject to the constraint

$$\prod_{i=1}^{n} w_{ii} = 1 \qquad\qquad (5.3.11)$$

Here, minimizing $D^2(C')$ is equivalent to minimizing

$$B = 2\sum_{i=1}^{n}(w_{ii}\sigma_i)^2 - \beta\left(\prod_{i=1}^{n}w_{ii} - 1\right) \qquad\qquad (5.3.12)$$

under the constraint of Eq. (5.3.11). Therefore,

$$\frac{\partial B}{\partial w_{ii}} = 4w_{ii}\sigma_i^2 - \beta\prod_{j\neq i}w_{jj}, \quad 1\leq i\leq n \qquad\qquad (5.3.13)$$

and consequently

$$w_{ii} = \frac{\sqrt{\beta}}{2\sigma_i}, \quad 1\leq i\leq n \qquad\qquad (5.3.14)$$

Since Eq. (5.3.11) holds we obtain

$$\beta = 4\left(\prod_{i=1}^{n}\sigma_i\right)^{(2/n)} \tag{5.3.15}$$

and the feature-weighing process is given by

$$w_{ii} = \frac{1}{\sigma_i}\left(\prod_{i=1}^{n}\sigma_i\right)^{(1/n)} \tag{5.3.16}$$

i.e., w_{ii} is inversely proportional to the standard deviation of the $i-$ th measurement.

■ **Example 5.3.2** Using the pattern class of Example 5.2.1 we obtain

$$\sigma_1 = \sqrt{\frac{44}{48}} = 0.957 \;,\; \sigma_2 = \sqrt{\frac{12}{48}} = 0.5$$

$$w_{11} = 0.723 \;,\;\; w_{22} = 1.384$$

and

$$2[(w_{11}\sigma_1)^2 + (w_{22}\sigma_2)^2] = 1.915$$

Clearly the clustering transformation of Example 5.3.1 yields better clustering

♠

So far we obtained a clustering transformation W under given constraints, that minimized the intraset distance in the new space. We will now define a second transformation in the new space that will clarify which components have smaller variances and will thus enable us to proceed with the feature selection. This transformation is given by

$$x'' = Ax' \tag{5.3.17}$$

and A will be chosen so that the covariance matrix of the pattern class in the space $X'' = \{x''\}$ will be diagonal. In order to keep the distances in $X' = \{x'\}$ unchanged A will be chosen as an orthonormal matrix. Denote by C, C', C'' the covariance matrices associated with the pattern class in the spaces $X = \{x\}$, X', X'' respectively. Let the corresponding means of the pattern class be μ, μ' and μ'' respectively. Then

$$\mu' = W\mu \quad , \quad x' - \mu' = W(x - \mu) \tag{5.3.18}$$

and

$$
\begin{aligned}
C' &= E\{(x' - \mu')(x' - \mu')^T\} \\
&= E\{W(x - \mu)(x - \mu)^T W^T \\
&= WCW^T
\end{aligned}
\tag{5.3.19}
$$

where E denotes the expectation operator. Similarly

$$C'' = AC'A^T \tag{5.3.20}$$

and since A is chosen orthonormal

$$C'' = AC'A^{-1} \tag{5.3.21}$$

i.e., C'' and C' are similar. To obtain a diagonal C'' we choose

$$A^{-1} = \{e'_1, e'_2, \ldots, e'_n\} \tag{5.3.22}$$

where e'_i, $1 \le i \le n$ are the normalized eigenvectors of C' which define an orthonormal set. Consequently

$$C'' = \begin{pmatrix} \lambda_1 & & & \\ & \lambda_2 & & 0 \\ & & \ddots & \\ 0 & & & \\ & & & \lambda_n \end{pmatrix} \tag{5.3.23}$$

where $\{\lambda_k\}_1^n$ are the eigenvalves of C' and can be shown to satisfy

$$\lambda_k = \sigma_k^2, \ 1 \le k \le n \tag{5.3.24}$$

Thus, the transformation A converts the covariance matrix C' into a diagonal matrix whose entries are the unbiased sample variances. The measurements corresponding to small variances are more reliable and should be considered as more important features.

However, to obtain the eigenvectors of C' from those of C is not simple. Instead we reverse the order of steps. We choose an orthonormal matrix A whose rows are the eigenvectors of the covariance matrix C. It converts C into a diagonal matrix C'. We then construct a diagonal matrix W which minimizes the intraset distance in space X'' under some given constraint.

5.4   FEATURE SELECTION BY ENTROPY MINIMIZATION

The concept of entropy introduces a statistical measure of uncertainty. For a given set of patterns, a good measure of intraset dispersion is the population entropy

$$T = -E_p[\ln(p)] \tag{5.4.1}$$

where p is the probability density associated with the given patterns. In this section we will use the entropy as a criterion in designing an optimal feature selection process. Features which decrease the uncertainty of a situation are more meaningful than others. Since entropy measures uncertainty, an appropriate feature selection tool should choose those features which minimize the entropy of the given pattern classes. Clearly, this is equivalent to minimizing the dispersion of the given pattern populations and the process should therefore have clustering properties.

Consider M pattern classes $C_1, \ldots, C_M$ whose populations are determined by the probabilities $\{p(x \mid C_i)\}_{i=1}^M$. The entropies of these populations are given by

$$T_i = -\int_x p(x \mid C_i) \ln[p(x \mid C_i)] \, dx \qquad (5.4.2)$$

where integration is performed over the whole pattern space.

We will now assume that the given densities are normal probability density functions, i.e.

$$p(x \mid C_i) = N(\mu_i, C_i) \qquad (5.4.3)$$

where μ_i and C_i are the mean and covariance matrix of the i-th population. We also assume $C_i = C$.

The basic idea now is to determine a linear transformation matrix A which transforms the given pattern vectors to new vectors with lower dimension. The transformation is

$$y = Ax \qquad (5.4.4)$$

where A is determined by minimizing the entropies of the given pattern classes. The vectors x are n-dimensional, the image vectors y are m-dimensional where $m < n$ and $A = A(m \times n)$. The rows of A are m feature vectors $\{a_i\}_1^m$, which are chosen so that the entropy of the image pattern vectors will be minimized.

■ **Theorem 5.4.1**

Given M pattern classes which are characterized by normal distribution density functions with identical covariance matrices, the entropies T_i, $1 \le i \le M$ are minimized by

$$A = \begin{pmatrix} a_1^T \\ \vdots \\ a_m^T \end{pmatrix} \tag{5.4.5}$$

where $\{a_i\}_1^m$ are the normalized eigenvectors associated with the m smallest eigenvalues of the matrix C.

The proof of this theorem is beyond the scope of this book.

■ **Example 5.4.1** Consider two classes C_1, C_2 given as (Fig. 5.4.1):

$$C_1 = \left\{ (-1,0)^T, (1,0)^T, (1,1)^T, (2,0)^T \right\}$$

$$C_2 = \left\{ (-2,0)^T, (-1,1)^T, (-3,0)^T, (-2,-1)^T \right\}$$

The estimates for the mean vectors μ_1, μ_2 are given by

$$\mu_i = \frac{1}{N_i} \sum_{j=1}^{N_i} x_{ij}, \quad i = 1, 2$$

where N_i are the numbers of patterns in C_i, i.e.

$$\mu_1 = \begin{pmatrix} 1 \\ 0 \end{pmatrix}, \quad \mu_2 = \begin{pmatrix} -2 \\ 0 \end{pmatrix}$$

The estimates for the covariance matrices are

$$C_i = \frac{1}{N_i} \sum_{j=1}^{N_i} x_{ij} x_{ij}^T - \mu_i \mu_i^T , \quad i = 1, 2$$

which yield

$$C_i = C_2 = C = \begin{pmatrix} 0.5 & 0.25 \\ 0.25 & 0.5 \end{pmatrix}$$

The eigenvalues of C are $\lambda_1 = \frac{1}{4}$, $\lambda_2 = \frac{3}{4}$. The normalized corresponding eigenvectors are (for example)

$$e_1 = \frac{1}{\sqrt{2}} (1, -1)^T$$

$$e_2 = \frac{1}{\sqrt{2}} (1, 1)^T$$

respectively. Let us decide to decrease the dimensionality by 1 and choose for example e_1 to define A:

$$A = \begin{pmatrix} 1/\sqrt{2} & -1/\sqrt{2} \end{pmatrix}$$

The image patterns obtained by Eq. (5.4.4) are

C_1	C_2
$1/\sqrt{2}$	$-\sqrt{2}$
$1/\sqrt{2}$	$-\sqrt{2}$
0	$-3/\sqrt{2}$
$\sqrt{2}$	$-3/\sqrt{2}$

and the clustering effect is obvious.

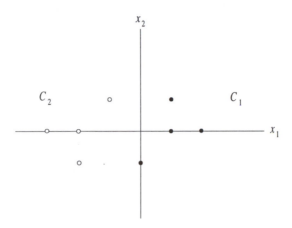

■ **Figure 5.4.1** Original patterns in R^2.

5.5 FEATURE SELECTION USING FUNCTIONAL APPROXIMATION

Assume that the features of a given pattern class can be characterized by a function $f(x)$ whose values are determined for the observed data. Then, the feature selection problem becomes a problem of functional approximation. Given the training patterns x_1, x_2, ..., x_N and the associated values of the feature function: $f(x_i)$, $1 \leq i \leq n$, we search for an approximate $\bar{f}(x)$ to $f(x)$ such that a given performance criterion is optimized. In this section we consider a method of functional expansion and a method of stochastic approximation to approximate feature functions.

Function expansion

Let C_1, ..., C_M be M pattern classes where

$$C_i = \{x_{ik}\}, \quad 1 \leq k \leq N_i \tag{5.5.1}$$

and let $f_i(x)$ be associated feature functions. In the process of determining approximates $\bar{f}_i(x)$ to the unknown feature functions, an agreeable performance criterion is that for each i: $1 \le i \le M$, the error sum

$$E_i = \sum_{k=1}^{N_i} w_i(x_{ik})[f_i(x_{ik}) - \bar{f}_i(x_{ik})]^2 \qquad (5.5.2)$$

where w_i is a given associated weight function, is minimized. Each approximate $\bar{f}_i(x)$ is expressed as a linear combination of basis functions, i.e.

$$\bar{f}_i(x) = \sum_{j=1}^{n_i} c_{ij}\phi_{ij}(x) = c_i^T \phi_i(x) \qquad (5.5.3)$$

where

$$c_i^T = (c_{i1}, c_{i2}, \ldots, c_{in_i}) \qquad (5.5.4)$$

and

$$\phi_i(x) = (\phi_{i1}(x), \phi_{i2}(x), \ldots, \phi_{in_i}(x))^T \qquad (5.5.5)$$

and $n_i (\le N_i)$ is the number of basis functions which are chosen to approximate the feature function of the i-th pattern class. The choice $n_i = N_i$ means that the number of basis functions equals the number of training patterns in the i-th class and in this case the error some E_i is reduced to zero.

To minimize E_i one must solve the system

$$\frac{\partial E_i}{\partial c_{ij}}, \quad j = 1, 2, \ldots, n_i \qquad (5.5.6)$$

for $i=1$, 2, ..., M.   Once $\phi_{ij}(x)$ are chosen and c_{ij} computed the approximate feature functions are obtained by Eq. (5.5.3). Simple algebra replaces Eq. (5.5.6) by

$$A_i c_i = b_i \ , \quad 1 \le i \le m \tag{5.5.7}$$

where A_i is an $n_i \times n_i$ positive definite symmetric matrix (consequently A_i^{-1} exists) with entries

$$\left(A_i \right)_{jk} = \sum_{l=1}^{N_i} w_i(x_{il}) \phi_{ij}(x_{il}) \phi_{ik}(x_{il}) \tag{5.5.8}$$

and b_i is a vector of size n_i, whose components are

$$b_{ij} = \sum_{l=1}^{N_i} w_i(x_{il}) \phi_{ij}(x_{il}) f_i(x_{il}) \tag{5.5.9}$$

By virtue of Eq. (5.5.7) we obtain

$$c_i = A_i^{-1} b_i \ , \quad 1 \le i \le m \tag{5.5.10}$$

The process may be simplified if ϕ_{ij} are chosen to be orthogonal with respect to the factors $w_i(x_{il})$. Then A_i is a diagonal matrix and we simply get

$$c_{ij} = \frac{\sum_{l=1}^{N_i} w_i(x_{il}) \phi_{ij}(x_{il}) f_i(x_{il})}{\sum_{l=1}^{N_i} w_i(x_{il}) \phi_{il}^2(x_{il})} \tag{5.5.11}$$

If furthermore ϕ_{ij} are orthonormal with respect to w_i, then

$$c_{ij} = \sum_{l=1}^{N_i} w_i(x_{il}) \phi_{ij}(x_{il}) f_i(x_{il}) \tag{5.5.12}$$

The advantage of this approach is that if for a given n_i, the error sum E_i is not small enough, we may obtain a higher order approximation by taking an additional term $c_{i,n_i+1}\phi_{i,n_i+1}(x)$ where $\phi_{i,n_i+1}(x)$ is another orthonormal function. The previously determined $c_{i1}, c_{i2}, \ldots, c_{in_i}$ remain the same, and we just calculate the additional c_{i,n_i+1}.

■ **Example 5.5.1** Consider the pattern classes

$$C_1 \qquad\qquad\qquad\qquad C_2$$

$$
\begin{aligned}
x_{11} &= (0,0)^T & x_{21} &= (2,2)^T \\
x_{12} &= (-2,0)^T & x_{22} &= (-2,2)^T \\
x_{13} &= (-2,-4)^T & x_{23} &= (3,0)^T \\
x_{14} &= (1,-1)^T &
\end{aligned}
$$

whose features are characterized by some unknown feature functions $f_1(x)$, $f_2(x)$ respectively. The values of these functions at the training patterns are known and given by

$$
\begin{aligned}
f_1(x_{11}) &= -3 & f_2(x_{21}) &= 2 \\
f_1(x_{12}) &= -4 & f_2(x_{22}) &= 1 \\
f_1(x_{13}) &= -2 & f_2(x_{23}) &= 3 \\
f_1(x_{14}) &= -1 &
\end{aligned}
$$

and based upon this information it is desired to approximate $f_i(x)$ by $\bar{f}_i(x)$ for $i = 1,2$. To simplify the computation we choose $w_i = 1$, $i=1,2$. The choice $n_i = 2$, $\phi_{i1}(x) = x_1$, $\phi_{i2}(x) = x_2$ for $i=1,2$ yields

$$A_1 = \begin{pmatrix} 9 & 7 \\ 7 & 17 \end{pmatrix}, \quad A_2 = \begin{pmatrix} 17 & 0 \\ 0 & 8 \end{pmatrix}$$

$$b_1 = \begin{pmatrix} 11 \\ 9 \end{pmatrix}, \quad b_2 = \begin{pmatrix} 11 \\ 6 \end{pmatrix}$$

and consequently

$$c_{11} = \frac{31}{26}, \quad c_{12} = \frac{1}{26}, \quad c_{21} = \frac{21}{17}, \quad c_{22} = \frac{3}{4}$$

Thus, the approximate feature functions are

$$\bar{f}_1(x) = \frac{31}{26}x_1 + \frac{1}{26}x_2, \quad \bar{f}_2(x) = \frac{21}{17}x_1 + \frac{3}{4}x_2$$

The error sums are

$$E_1 \sim 19.6, \quad E_2 \sim 8.3$$

and are not particularly small. This suggests introducing an additional basis function, for example

$$\phi_{i3} = 1, \quad 1 \le i \le 2; \quad w_3 = 1$$

Adding a constant basis function is essential since $f_1(x_{11}) = -3$ while $x_{11} = (0,0)$. We now obtain

$$A_1 = \begin{pmatrix} 9 & 7 & -3 \\ 7 & 17 & -5 \\ 3 & -5 & 4 \end{pmatrix}, \quad A_2 = \begin{pmatrix} 17 & 0 & 3 \\ 0 & 8 & 4 \\ 3 & 4 & 3 \end{pmatrix}$$

$$b_1 = \begin{pmatrix} 11 \\ 9 \\ -10 \end{pmatrix}, \qquad b_2 = \begin{pmatrix} 11 \\ 6 \\ 6 \end{pmatrix}$$

and finally get

$$c_{11} = 0.790 , \quad c_{12} = -0.565 , \quad c_{13} = -2.613$$
$$c_{21} = 0.250 , \quad c_{22} = -0.375 , \quad c_{23} = 2.250$$

The approximate feature functions are now

$$\bar{f}_1(x) = -2.613 + 0.790x_1 - 0.565x_2$$
$$\bar{f}_2(x) = 2.250 + 0.250x_1 - 0.375x_2$$

and the reduced error sums are

$$E_1 \sim 0.26 , \quad E_2 = 0 \quad (\text{since } n_2 = N_2 = 3)$$

♠

Stochastic approximation

Sometimes the observed values of the feature functions $f_i(x)$ at the given training patterns are random variables which are characterized by unknown probability density functions. In this case the error criterion that should be used is: minimize the quantities

$$E_i = \int_{x \in C_i} w_i(x)[f_i(x) - \bar{f}_i(x)]^2 \, p(x \mid C_i)dx , \quad 1 \le i \le M \qquad (5.5.13)$$

We express each $\bar{f}_i(x)$ as a linear combination of basis functions, i.e.

$$\bar{f}_i(x) = \sum_{j=1}^{n_i} c_{ij}\phi_{ij}(x), \quad 1 \le i \le M \tag{5.5.14}$$

where $n_i \le N_i$ for all $1 \le i \le M$. The minimization procedure implies

$$\frac{\partial E_i}{\partial c_{ij}} = 2 \int_{x \in C_i} \left[f_i(x) - \sum_{k=1}^{n_i} c_{ik}\phi_{ik}(x) \right] \phi_{ij}(x) p(x \mid C_i) \, dx = 0 \tag{5.5.15}$$

for all $1 \le i \le M$ and $1 \le j \le n_i$. Since Eq. (5.5.15) includes the unknown probability density function $p(x \mid C_i)$ a method of stochastic approximation should be applied. The Robbins-Mouro algorithm provides the recursive procedure

$$c_{ij}(k+1) = c_{ij}(k) + \alpha_k \left[f_i(x_{ik}) - \sum_{l=1}^{n_i} c_{il}(k)\phi_{il}(x_{ik}) \right] \phi_{ij}(x_{ik}) \tag{5.5.16}$$

Where k denotes the k-th iteration and α_k, $k = 1, 2\ldots$ are positive numbers which satisfy

$$\sum_{k=1}^{\infty} \alpha_k = \infty, \quad \sum_{k=1}^{\infty} \alpha_k^2 < \infty \tag{5.5.17}$$

The quality of the coefficients $c_{ij}(k)$ improve as k increases and if $c_{ij}^{(0)}$ denote the exact solution, then

$$prob\left[\lim_{k \to \infty} c_{ij}(k) = c_{ij}^{(0)} \right] = 1 \tag{5.5.18}$$

PROBLEMS

1. Given the pattern class $C_1 = \{x_i\}_{i=1}^4$ with

$$x_1 = \begin{pmatrix} 1 \\ 0 \\ 1 \end{pmatrix}, \quad x_2 = \begin{pmatrix} 1 \\ 1 \\ 1 \end{pmatrix}, \quad x_3 = \begin{pmatrix} 2 \\ 1 \\ 0 \end{pmatrix}, \quad x_4 = \begin{pmatrix} 0 \\ 1 \\ 1 \end{pmatrix}$$

   obtain the intraset distance of C_1.

2. Let $C_2 = \{y_j\}_{j=1}^3$ where

$$y_1 = \begin{pmatrix} 3 \\ 2 \\ 0 \end{pmatrix}, \quad y_2 = \begin{pmatrix} 2 \\ 2 \\ 1 \end{pmatrix}, \quad y_3 = \begin{pmatrix} 4 \\ 5 \\ -1 \end{pmatrix}$$

   Calculate the interset distance between C_2 and C_1 of problem 1.

3. Let C denote a class of patterns in R^4. The variances of the single components satisfy $\sigma_i^2 \le 1/8$, $1 \le i \le 3$ and $\sigma_4^2 \le \dfrac{1}{16}$. What can be said about the intraset distance of C.

4. Given class C_1 of problem 1 obtain a scale-factor transformation $x' = Wx$ that would minimize the intraset distance in the new space under the constraint

   (a) $\sum w_{ii} = 1$
   (b) $\prod w_{ii} = 1$

5. Let C be a class of four patterns given by

$$x_1 = \begin{pmatrix} 2 \\ 6 \end{pmatrix}, \quad x_2 = \begin{pmatrix} 1 \\ 5 \end{pmatrix}, \quad x_3 = \begin{pmatrix} 1 \\ 6 \end{pmatrix}, \quad x_4 = \begin{pmatrix} 2 \\ 5 \end{pmatrix}$$

Reduce the dimensionality of x_i, $1 \le i \le 4$ to one by using the minimum entropy transformation given by Eq. (5.4.5)

6. Repeat problem 5 in the case of

$$C = \left\{ (0,0)^T, (1,5)^T, (5,1)^T, (6,6)^T \right\}$$

and observe the formation of a cluster.

7. Consider the two pattern classes $C_i = \left\{ x_{ij} \right\}_{j=1}^{n_i}$, $1 \le i \le 2$:

$$C_1 = \left\{ (0,1)^T, (1,0)^T, (1,1)^T \right\}$$
$$C_2 = \left\{ (0,2)^T, (1,-3)^T, (-1,-3)^T, (-2,-2)^T \right\}$$

whose features are characterized by unknown feature functions $f_1(x)$ and $f_2(x)$ respectively. The values of the feature functions at the given training patterns are

$$
\begin{array}{ll}
f_1(x_{11}) = -5 & f_2(x_{21}) = 1 \\
f_1(x_{12}) = -8 & f_2(x_{22}) = 2 \\
f_1(x_{13}) = -6 & f_2(x_{23}) = 0 \\
& f_2(x_{24}) = -1
\end{array}
$$

Approximate $f_i(x)$, $1 \le i \le 2$ by $\bar{f}_i(x)$, $1 \le i \le 2$ using three basis functions: $1, x_1, x_2$. In the minimization procedure assume weight functions $w_i(x) = 1$, $1 \le i \le 2$.

6 FUZZY CLASSIFICATION AND PATTERN RECOGNITION

6.1 FUZZY SETS THEORY

In this section we present the basic principles of Fuzzy Sets Theory (FST). Advanced techniques in pattern recognition using this theory are treated in Sections 2-5.

Uncertainty

Several mathematical disciplines deal with the principles of uncertainty. For example, stochastic uncertainty deals with issues related to the future occurrence of a *certain event*. The event itself is defined precisely but the uncertainty involved is qualified by a degree of probability that this particular certain event will occur.

Another kind of uncertainty is related to lexical uncertainty which deals with the imprecision and ambiguity that is inherent in human languages. Researchers in the field of psycholinguistics investigate the way humans evaluate concepts and derive decisions in these complex structures, usually related to subjective categories. Analysis of this kind of uncertainty usually results in a perceived probability rather than the mathematically defined mobility. The third kind of uncertainty, which is the main topic of this section, is the theory of fuzzy sets. This theory assists us in updating linguistic uncertainty in an adequate fashion. The main feature of any fuzzy system in the *linguistic variable* which is closely related to the concept of a *fuzzy event*; mainly, an event which is not certain but has a grade of membership associated with it. Thus, now we can have a transformation from a linguistic variable to a Linguistic Mathematical Description (LMD).

Since 1965, when Lotfi A. Zadeh published his controversial paper on fuzziness and also coined its name, a large number of methods using fuzzy sets have been developed. It should be emphasized that these methods are not based on "sloppy" mathematics or "fuzzy" mathematics, but are descriptions of precise mathematical handling of fuzzy and uncertain events, data, and concepts. Fuzzy techniques mimic human decision-making and evaluation processes. Therefore, a good defuzzification technique is required in transforming the results of Approximated Reasoning (AR) to deterministic action.

6.1.1   Fuzzy Sets

Fuzzy set theory, introduced by Lotfi A. Zadeh in 1965, is a generalization of crisp set theory.

A *fuzzy set* consists of objects and their respective grades of membership in the set. The *grade of membership* of an object in the fuzzy set is given by a subjectively defined *membership function*. The value of the grade of membership of an object can range from 0 to 1 where the value of 1 denotes full membership, and the closer the value is to 0, the weaker is the object's membership in the fuzzy set.

The single most important feature of fuzzy set theory is the ability to express in numerical format the amount of imprecision and ambiguity in human thinking and decision-making. The encoding and processing of fuzzy data, improve knowledge, and ambiguous procedures are relatively easy and intuitive, since in fuzzy set theory, the truth of any statement is a matter of degree.

Essentially, fuzziness is a type of imprecision that stems from a grouping of elements into classes that do not have sharply defined boundaries. Such classes - called fuzzy sets - arise, for example, whenever we describe ambiguity, vagueness, and ambivalence in mathematical models of empirical phenomena. Since certain aspects of reality always escape such models, the strictly binary (and even the ternary) approach to the treatment of physical phenomena is not always adequate to describe systems in the real world; and the attributes of the system variables often emerge from an elusive fuzziness, a readjustment to context, or an effect of human imprecision. In many cases, however, even if the model is precise, fuzziness may be a concomitant of complexity. Systems of high carnality are rampant in real life and their computer simulations require some kind of mathematical formulation to deal with the imprecise descriptions.

The theory of fuzzy sets has as one of its aims the development of a methodology for the formulation and solution of problems that are too complex or too ill-defined to be susceptible of analysis by conventional techniques.

Intuitively, a fuzzy set is a class that admits the possibility of *partial membership* in it.

■ **Definition 6.1.1** Let $X = \{x\}$ denote a space of objects. Then a fuzzy set A is a set of ordered pairs

$$A = \{x, \chi_A(x)\}, \; x \in X \tag{6.1.1}$$

where $\chi_A(x)$, a number in the interval $[0,1]$ is the grade of membership of x in A. The grades 1 and 0 represent respectively, full *membership* and *nonmembership* in a fuzzy set. We assume that an exact comparison is possible for the truths of any two inexact statements "$x \in A$" and "$y \in A$," and that the exact relation so obtained satisfies the minimal consistency requirements of *transitivity* and *reflexivity*; the ordering $x \geq y$ means "x is at least as true as y" with $x \leq y$ denoting "x is not truer than y."

The grades of membership reflect an "ordering" of the objects in the universe; it is interesting to note that the grade-of-membership value $\chi_A(x)$ of an object x in A can be interpreted as the degree of compatibility of the predicate associated with A and the object x. It is also possible to interpret $\chi_A(x)$ as the degree of possibility that x is the value of a parameter fuzzily restricted by A.

If $X = \{x_1, x_2, \ldots, x_n\}$ is finite we often express it as

$$X = \sum_{i=1}^{n} x_i = x_1 + x_2 + \ldots + x_n$$

where the plus sign (+) plays the role of "union" rather than the arithmetic sign. We extend this notation to a fuzzy set A and express it as

$$A = \sum_{i=1}^{n} \chi_A(x_i)/x_i = \chi_A(x_1)/x_1 + \chi_A(x_2)/x_2 + \ldots + \chi_A(x_n)/x_n \qquad (6.1.2)$$

If A is infinite we use the notation

$$A = \int_X \chi_A(x)/x \qquad (6.1.3)$$

■   **Example 6.1.1**   Let the universe X be the interval $[0, 120]$, with x interpreted as age. A fuzzy set A of X labeled *old* may be defined by a grade of membership function such as

$$\chi_A(x) = \begin{cases} 0 & , \quad 0 \le x \le 40 \\ \left[1 + \left(\dfrac{x-40}{5} \right)^{-2} \right]^{-1} & , \quad 40 < x < 120 \end{cases} \qquad (6.1.4)$$

The *support* of A which is the set of points in X at which $\chi_A(x) > 0$ is the interval $(40, 120]$. The *height* of A which is supremum of $\chi_A(x)$ over X is effectively 1. The *crossover* point where the grade of membership gets the value 0.5 is 45. The membership function of *old* is illustrated in Fig. 6.1.1.

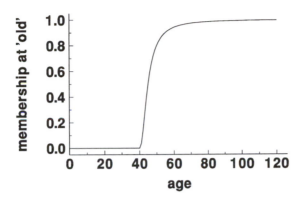

■ **Figure 6.1.1** Membership function of *old* (Eq. 6.1.4).

Basic Set-Theoretic Operations for Fuzzy Sets

Among the basic operations that can be performed on fuzzy sets are the following:

■ **Definition 6.1.2** The *complement* of a fuzzy set A denoted by $\overline{A}$, is defined by

$$\overline{A} = \int_X [1 - \chi_A (x)]/x$$

The operation of complementation is equivalent to negation.

■ **Definition 6.1.3** The *union* of fuzzy sets A and B denoted by $A \cup B$, is defined by

$$A \cup B = \int_X [\chi_A (x) \vee \chi_B (x)]/ x$$

where $\vee$ is the symbol for max.

The union corresponds to the connective OR. Thus, if A and B are labels of fuzzy sets, then A OR B is expressed as $A \cup B$.

■ **Definition 6.1.4** The *intersection* of fuzzy sets A and B denoted by $A \cap B$, is defined by

$$A \cap B = \int_X \left[\chi_A (x) \wedge \chi_B (x) \right] / x$$

where $\wedge$ is the symbol for min.

The intersection corresponds to the connective AND. Hence A AND B is interpreted as $A \cap B$.

Comment: It should be pointed out that $\vee$ and $\wedge$ are not the only operators used as interpretations of the union and intersection, respectively. In particular, when AND is identified with $\wedge$ (i.e., min), it represents a "hard" AND in the sense that no trade-off is allowed between its operands. By contrast, an AND that is interpreted in terms of the arithmetic product of the operands, acts as a "soft" AND. Which of these or other possible interpretations is more appropriate depends on the applications in which OR and AND are used.

■ **Definition 6.1.5** The *product* of fuzzy sets A and B denoted by AB, is defined by

$$AB = \int_X \chi_A (x) \cdot \chi_B (x) / x$$

Also, A^α, where α is any positive number, is defined by

$$A^\alpha = \int_X [\chi_A (x)]^\alpha / x$$

Two operations that are defined as special cases of A are useful in the representation of linguistic hedges. The operation of *concentration* denoted by CON (A), is defined by

$$\text{CON}(A) = A^2$$

The concentration is an interpretation of VERY. Thus, if A is a label of a fuzzy set, then VERY A corresponds to $\text{CON}(A)$. The operation of *dilation* denoted by $\text{DIL}(A)$, is expressed by

$$\text{DIL}(A) = A^{0.5}$$

If A is a label of a fuzzy set, the APPROXIMATELY A is interpreted as $\text{DIL}(A)$.

If w is any nonnegative real number such that $w \cdot \text{height}(A) \leq 1$, we define

$$wA = \int_X w \cdot \chi_A(x)/x$$

■ **Example 6.1.2** Consider the universe of discourse $X = 1 + 2 + \ldots + 8$

and the fuzzy sets

$$A = 0.8/3 + 1/5 + 0.6/6$$
$$B = 0.7/3 + 1/4 + 0.5/6$$

Then

$$A \cup B = 0.8/3 + 1/4 + 1/5 + 0.6/6$$
$$A \cap B = 0.7/3 + 0.5/6$$
$$\bar{A} = 1/1 + 1/2 + 0.2/3 + 1/4 + 0.4/6 + 1/7 + 1/8$$
$$AB = 0.56/3 + 0.3/6$$
$$A^2 = 0.64/3 + 1/5 + 0.36/6$$
$$0.5A = 0.4/3 + 0.5/5 + 0.3/6$$
$$\text{CON}(B) = 0.49/3 + 1/4 + 0.25/6$$
$$\text{DIL}(A) = 0.89/3 + 1/5 + 0.77/6$$

♠

α -Cuts

When we want to exhibit an element $x \in X$ that typically belongs to a fuzzy set A, we may demand that its membership value be greater than some threshold $\alpha \in [0,1]$. The ordinary set of such elements is the α-cut A_α of A, i.e.

$$A_\alpha = \{x \mid x \in X \text{ and } \chi_A(x) \geq \alpha\} \tag{6.1.5}$$

The *strong* α-cut is defined as

$$A_{\bar{\alpha}} = \{x \mid x \in X \text{ and } \chi_A(x) > \alpha\} \tag{6.1.6}$$

Consequently

$$\chi_A(x) = \sup_{0 < \alpha \leq 1} \min[\alpha, \chi_{A_\alpha}(x)] \tag{6.1.7}$$

where

$$\chi_{A_\alpha}(x) = \begin{cases} 1 & \text{iff } x \in A_\alpha \\ 0 & \text{otherwise} \end{cases} \tag{6.1.8}$$

It is easily seen that the relations

$$(A \cup B)_\alpha = A_\alpha \cup B_\alpha, (A \cap B)_\alpha = A_\alpha \cap B_\alpha$$

hold. However, for $\alpha \neq 0.5$ we obtain

$$(\bar{A})_{\bar{\alpha}} = \overline{(A_{1-\alpha})} \neq \overline{(A_\alpha)}$$

This result stems from the fact that usually, there are elements that belong neither to A_α nor to $(\bar{A})_\alpha$, i.e.

$$A_\alpha \cup (\bar{A})_\alpha \neq X$$

The *level fuzzy sets* of a fuzzy set A are defined as the fuzzy sets $\tilde{A}_\alpha, 0 < \alpha < 1$ such that

$$\tilde{A}_\alpha = \{(x, \chi_A(x)), x \in A_\alpha\} \tag{6.1.9}$$

The *strong level fuzzy sets* are defined as

$$\tilde{A}_{\bar{\alpha}} = \{(x, \chi_A(x)), x \in A_{\bar{\alpha}}\} \tag{6.1.10}$$

By virtue of Eq. (6.1.9) we easily obtain

$$A = \int_0^1 \alpha A_\alpha = \sum_\alpha \alpha A_\alpha \tag{6.1.11}$$

where the integral (or sum) is the union of αA_α with α ranging from 0 to 1.

■ **Example 6.1.3** Consider the fuzzy set

$$A = 0.1/2 + 0.3/4 + 0.5/7 + 0.9/8 + 1/9$$

Then, A can be rewritten as

$$\begin{aligned}
A = {} & 0.1/2 + 0.1/4 + 0.1/7 + 0.1/8 + 0.1/9 \\
& + 0.3/4 + 0.3/7 + 0.3/8 + 0.3/9 \\
& + 0.5/7 + 0.5/8 + 0.5/9 \\
& + 0.9/8 + 0.9/9 \\
& + 1.0/9
\end{aligned}$$

or

$$A = 0.1 \ (1/2 + 1/4 + 1/7 + 1/8 + 1/9)$$
$$+ \ 0.3 \ (1/4 + 1/7 + 1/8 + 1/9)$$
$$+ \ 0.5 \ (1/7 + 1/8 + 1/9)$$
$$+ \ 0.9 \ (1/8 + 1/9)$$
$$+ \ 1.0 \ (1/9)$$

i.e.

$$A = 0.1A_{0.1} + 0.3A_{0.3} + 0.5A_{0.5} + 0.9A_{0.9} + 1.0A_{1.0}$$

♠

6.1.2 The Extension Principle

One of the basic ideas of fuzzy set theory, which provides a general extension of nonfuzzy mathematical concepts to fuzzy environments, is the *extension principle*. This is a basic identity that allows the domain of the definition of a mapping or a relation to be extended from points in X to fuzzy subsets of X.

More specifically, suppose that f is a mapping from X to Y and A is a fuzzy subset of X expressed as

$$A = \chi_1/x_1 + \ldots + \chi_n/x_n.$$

The extension principle asserts that

$$f(A) = f(\chi_1/x_1 + \ldots + \chi_n/x_n) \equiv \chi_1/f(x_1) + \ldots + \chi_n/f(x_n)$$

Thus the image of A under f can be deduced from the knowledge of the images of $x_1, \ldots, x_n$ under f.

If we have an n-ary function f, which is a mapping from the Cartesian product $X_1 \times X_2 \times \ldots \times X_n$ to a universe Y such that $y = f(x_1, \ldots, x_n)$, and $A_1, \ldots, A_n$, are n fuzzy sets in $X_1, X_2, \ldots, X_n$, respectively, characterized by a set of membership functions $\{\chi_{A_i}(x_i)\}_{i=1}^{n}$, then the extension principle allows us to induce from the fuzzy sets $\{A_i\}_{i=1}^{n}$ a fuzzy set F on Y such that

$$\chi_F(y) = \sup_{\substack{x_1,\ldots,x_n \\ y = f(x_1,\ldots,x_n)}} \min[\chi_{A_i}(x_1),\ldots,\chi_{A_n}(x_n)]$$

$$\chi_F(y) = 0 \quad \text{if } f^{-1}(y) = \varnothing$$

■ **Example 6.1.4** Let $X = 1 + 2 \ldots + 7$ and let *small* be a fuzzy subset on X defined as

$$small = 1/1 + 1/2 + 0.8/3 + 0.5/4$$

Let f be the operation of squaring. Then

$$f(small) = 1/1 + 1/4 + 0.8/9 + 0.5/16$$

♠

■ **Example 6.1.5** Let $X_1 = X_2 = 1 + 2 + \ldots + 7$ and let

$$A_1 = approximately\, 2 = 0.6/1 + 1/2 + 0.8/3$$

$$A_2 = approximtely\, 4 = 0.8/3 + 1/4 + 0.7/5$$

Then

$$A_1 \times A_2 = 0.6/3 + 0.6/4 + 0.6/5 + 0.8/6 + 1/8 + 0.8/9 + 0.7/10 + 0.8/12 + 0.7/15$$

♠

6.1.3 Fuzzy Relations

■ **Definition 6.1.6** Let X denote a cartesian product of n universes of discourse $X_1,\ldots,X_n$. An arbitrary fuzzy subset R of X given by

$$R = \int\limits_{X_1 \times \ldots \times X_n} \chi_R(x_1,\ldots,x_n)/(x_1,\ldots,x_n) \qquad (6.1.12)$$

is called a *fuzzy relation*.

Common examples of (binary) fuzzy relations are: *much greater than, resembles, is relevant to* and *is close to*.   For example, if $X_1 = X_2 = (-\infty, \infty)$ the relation *is close to* may be defined by

$$is\, close\, to \equiv \int\limits_{X_1+X_2} e^{-\alpha|x_1-x_2|}/(x_1, x_2)$$

where α is same scale factor. Similarly, if

$$X_1 = X_2 = 1+2+3+4$$

the relation *much greater than* may be defined by the relation matrix

R	1	2	3	4
1	0	0.4	0.8	1
2	0	0	0.4	0.8
3	0	0	0	0.4
4	0	0	0	0

in which the (i, j) entry is $\chi_R(x_1,x_2)$ for the i-th value of x_1 and the j-th value of x_2.

The fuzzy relation "x is much greater than y" in N (the natural numbers) may be defined subjectively by a membership function such as

$$\chi(x,y) = \begin{cases} 0 & , & x-y \le 0 \\ \left[1+10(x-y)^{-1}\right]^{-1} & , & x-y > 0 \end{cases}$$

■   **Definition 6.1.7**   Let A and B denote binary fuzzy relations in a cartesian product of a universe X by itself. The composition of A and B, denoted by $B \circ A$, is a fuzzy relation in X^2, whose membership function is

$$\chi_{B \circ A}(x, y) = \sup_v \left[\min[\chi_A(x,v), \chi_B(v,y)]\right], \quad v, x, y \in X \qquad (6.1.13)$$

■   **Example 6.1.6**   Let $X = 1 + 2 + 3 + 4$ and let R denote the fuzzy relation *much greater than*, previously defined. Then

$$\chi_{R \circ R}(1, 1) = \chi_{R \circ R}(2, 2) = \chi_{R \circ R}(3,3) = \chi_{R \circ R}(4,4) = 0$$

$$\chi_{R \circ R}(1, 2) = \chi_{R \circ R}(2, 3) = \chi_{R \circ R}(3, 4) = 0$$

$$\chi_{R \circ R}(1, 3) = \chi_{R \circ R}(2, 4) = \chi_{R \circ R}(1, 4) = 0.4$$

♠

A particular important type of fuzzy relation is a *similarity relation* which is essentially a generalization of the concept of an equivalence relation.

Similarity Relations

■   **Definition 6.1.8**   A fuzzy similarity relation S, is a fuzzy relation in XxX that is reflexive, symmetric and transitive, i.e.

(a) $\chi_S(x, x) = 1$ for all $x \in X$ (reflexivity).

(b) $\chi_S(x, y) = \chi_S(y, x)$ for all $x, y \in X$ (symmetry).

(c) $\chi_S(x, z) \geq \max_{y \in X}[\min(\chi_S(x, y), \chi_S(y, z))]$ for all $x, z \in X$

A fuzzy relation that satisfies requirements (a) and (b) of definition 6.1.8, is called a *fuzzy tolerance relation*. If R is fuzzy tolerance relation in X^2, where X is a finite universe of size n, R can be represented by a symmetric matrix.

$$R = (r_{ij}), \ 1 \le i, j \le n$$

where $r_{ij} = 1, \ 1 \le i \le n$ and $r_{ij} = r_{ji}, \ 1 \le i, j \le n.$

■   **Theorem 6.1.1** [Kandel 1982]

Let a fuzzy tolerance relation be represented by a matrix R of size n and define

$$R^{(2)} \equiv R \circ R \ ; \ R^{(k)} \equiv R^{k-1} \circ R, \ k \ge 3$$

Then, by performing at the most $(n-1)$ compositions, we obtain a matrix $R' = R^k, \ k \le n$ with elements $r'_{ij}, \ 1 \le i, j \le n$ such that

$$r'_{ij} \ge r_{ij}, \ \ 1 \le i, j \le n$$

$$r'_{ij} \ge \max_{1 \le k \le n}[\min(r'_{jk}, r'_{kj})], \ 1 \le i, j \le n$$

i.e. R' represents a fuzzy similarity relation.

■   **Example 6.1.7** Consider a fuzzy tolerance relation given by the matrix

$$R = \begin{pmatrix} 1 & 0.6 & 0.3 & 0.8 \\ 0.6 & 1 & 0.1 & 0.4 \\ 0.3 & 0.1 & 1 & 0.5 \\ 0.8 & 0.4 & 0.5 & 1 \end{pmatrix}$$

Since $r_{23} = 0.1$ and $\min(r_{24}, r_{43}) = 0.4 > 0.1$ R is not a similarity relation. The composition of R by itself provides

$$R^{(2)} = R \circ R = \begin{pmatrix} 1 & 0.6 & 0.5 & 0.8 \\ 0.6 & 1 & 0.4 & 0.6 \\ 0.5 & 0.4 & 1 & 0.5 \\ 0.8 & 0.6 & 0.5 & 1 \end{pmatrix}$$

for which $r_{23}^{(2)} = 0.4$ and $\min\left(r_{24}^{(2)}, r_{43}^{(2)}\right) = 0.5 > 0.4$. Thus, $R^{(2)}$ is also not a similarity relation. An additional composition yields

$$R^{(3)} = \begin{pmatrix} 1 & 0.6 & 0.5 & 0.8 \\ 0.6 & 1 & 0.5 & 0.6 \\ 0.5 & 0.5 & 1 & 0.5 \\ 0.8 & 0.6 & 0.5 & 0.8 \end{pmatrix}$$

which already represents a fuzzy similarity relation.

♠

6.2   FUZZY AND CRISP CLASSIFICATIONS

The classification methods discussed in Chapter 3 have one thing in common: an arbitrary pattern is classified in a *unique* cluster or not classified at all. For example, consider a two class classification problem where the classes are 'apples' and 'pears.' If each incoming pattern is either an apple or a pear it will be classified accordingly. If the pattern is a watermelon it will not be classified. If the pattern is a pear which also resembles an apple it could be mistaken for an apple and classified as such. However, once classified, the incoming pattern is seen as *either* an apple *or* a pear. This is the main feature of a *crisp* classification, where each pattern belongs to a single class. The union of the disjoint classes produces the whole universe of patterns.

■   **Example 6.2.1** In R^2 we classifiy a set of patterns using the following rule for arbitrary incoming sample $x = (x_1, x_2)^T$:

$$x \in C_1 \quad iff \quad x_1^2 + x_2^2 < 1$$
$$x \in C_2 \quad iff \quad (x_1 - 3)^2 + (x_2 - 3)^2 < 1 \qquad (6.2.1)$$
$$x \text{ is not classified, } otherwise$$

Since x cannot belong to C_1 and C_2 simultaneously, this is clearly a crisp classification. For example, consider the patterns

$$\left\{ (0,0)^T, \ (2.5, 3.5)^T, (3,5)^T, (0.5, 0.5)^T, (3, 3.5)^T \right\}$$

By applying Eq. (6.2.1) we obtain

$$(0, \ 0)^T, \ (0.5, \ 0.5)^T \in C_1$$
$$(2.5, \ 3.5)^T, \ (3, \ 3.5)^T \in C_2$$

while the pattern $(3, \ 5)^T$ is not classified.

♠

The next example is a classification problem where the different categories are defined by linguistic descriptors.

■ **Example 6.2.2** Consider a classification problem where we classify people according to height. We define three classes - 'tall', 'medium' and 'short.' If these classes are observed as fuzzy sets, then each person is classified in *each* class with some grade of membership. If a person x is for example is 5' 9" tall, he may be classified simultaneously as

x is 0.3 ' tall'
x is 0.6 ' medium'
x is 0.1 ' short'

Consequently x belongs to *every* class. If x is 6'7" he may be classified as

x is 0.9 ' tall'
x is 0.1 ' medium'

i.e. x belongs to 'tall' and to 'medium' but not to 'short'.

♠

Example 6.2.2 is a simple case of 'fuzzy classification' where each pattern *may* belong at the same time to *each* of the existing classes with various grades of membership. Usually it is reasonable to require that the sum of the membership values is 1. A general fuzzy classification problem can be represented by a pattern space X and a fuzzy $m-$ partition of X by fuzzy sets $C_1, C_2, \ldots, C_m$. Each pattern $x_j \in X$ is a member of C_i with grade of membership μ_{ij} such that

$$\sum_{i=1}^{m} \mu_{ij} = 1 \qquad (6.2.2)$$

If for arbitrary $x_j \in X$ we have a unique $i_0(j)$ for which

$$\mu_{i_0(j)j} = 1; \mu_{ij} = 0, i \neq i_0(j) \qquad (6.2.3)$$

we obtain the particular case of crisp classification and crisp $m-$ partition of X.

■ **Example 6.2.3** Consider the sets of heights

$$X = \{x_1, x_2, x_3, x_4, x_5\} = \{6'1", 5'5", 4'2", 5'10", 6'8"\}$$

and let C_1, C_2, C_3 denote the fuzzy sets 'tall', 'medium' and 'short' respectively. A possible fuzzy 3-partition of X by C_i $1 \leq i \leq 3$ is given in Table 6.2.1.

■ **Table 6.2.1** Membership values in fuzzy classification.

	x_1	x_2	x_3	x_4	x_5
C_1	0.60	0.20	0.00	0.35	0.95
C_2	0.35	0.45	0.10	0.45	0.05
C_3	0.05	0.35	0.90	0.20	0.00

If only crisp classification is considered, a reasonable 3-partition of X is

■ **Table 6.2.2**   A crisp classification of X.

	x_1	x_2	x_3	x_4	x_5
C_1	1	0	0	0	1
C_2	0	1	0	1	0
C_3	0	0	1	0	0

    A fuzzy classification clearly provides more *information* about the given data than a crisp classification.   We will now discuss two popular approaches for representing fuzzy classification.

6.3   CLASSIFICATION BY EQUIVALENT RELATIONS

Let R denote an equivalent relation defined over a pattern space X, i.e. for arbitrary $x, y, z \in X$

1. $(x, x) \in R$ (reflexivity).
2. If $(x, y) \in R$ then $(y, x) \in R$ (symmetry).
3. If $(x, y) \in R$ and $(y, z) \in R$ then $(x, z) \in R$ (transitivity).

Let X be a union of a finite number of equivalent classes, i.e.

$$X = \bigcup_{i=1}^{m} C_i ; \quad C_i \bigcap C_j = \varnothing ; \quad i \neq j \qquad (6.3.1)$$

Then for arbitrary $x, y \in X$

$$(x, y) \in R \text{ if } x, y \in C_i \text{ for some } i$$

$$(x, y) \notin R \text{ if } x \in C_i, \ y \in C_j, \ i \neq j \qquad (6.3.2)$$

If the rule for classification is "x and y are in the same class if and only if $(x,y) \in R$" then the classes obtained $C_1,...,C_m$ form an $m-$partition of X, i.e. present X as a union of disjoint non-empty subsets.

■ **Example 6.3.1**   Let $X = \{x_i\}_{i=1}^{7} = \{2,4,6,9,11,12,17\}$ and consider the relation

$$(x,y) \in R \ iff \ x \equiv y \ \mod(5) \tag{6.3.3}$$

We define the *relation matrix* $A_R = (a_{ij})$, $1 \le i, j \le 7$ by

$$a_{ij} = \begin{cases} 1, & (x_i, x_j) \in R \\ 0, & (x_i, x_j) \notin R \end{cases} \tag{6.3.4}$$

and obtain

$$A_R = \begin{array}{c} \\ 2 \\ 4 \\ 6 \\ 9 \\ 11 \\ 12 \\ 17 \end{array} \begin{array}{c} \begin{array}{ccccccc} 2 & 4 & 6 & 9 & 11 & 12 & 17 \end{array} \\ \left[\begin{array}{ccccccc} 1 & 0 & 0 & 0 & 0 & 1 & 1 \\ 0 & 1 & 0 & 1 & 0 & 0 & 0 \\ 0 & 0 & 1 & 0 & 1 & 0 & 0 \\ 0 & 1 & 0 & 1 & 0 & 0 & 0 \\ 0 & 0 & 1 & 0 & 1 & 0 & 0 \\ 1 & 0 & 0 & 0 & 0 & 1 & 1 \\ 1 & 0 & 0 & 0 & 0 & 1 & 1 \end{array} \right] \end{array}$$

Since arbitrary patterns x_i and x_j are classified in the same class if and only if $x_i \equiv x_j \ \mod(5)$ we obtain

$$C_1 = \{2, 12, 17\}, \ C_2 = \{4, 9\}, \ C_3 = \{6, 11\}$$

♠

If the relation R is not an equivalent relation, the classification rule

$$x \text{ and } y \text{ are in the same class } iff \ (x,y) \in R \qquad (6.3.5)$$

would usually produce inconsistencies.   For example, if $(x, y) \in R$, $(y, z) \in R$ then x, y, z belong to the same class, but if $(x, z) \notin R$ (i.e. R is not transitive) then x and z must belong to different classes!

If R is at least reflexive and symmetric, i.e. a *tolerance relation*, we apply the following result previously stated (Section 6.1) to obtain an equivalent relation from R:

Let R denote a tolerance relation over a pattern space of size n. Then by performing at most $n-1$ max-min compositions of R with itself, we obtain an equivalent relation R' with relation matrix $A_{R'} = (a'_{ij})$ such that

$$a_{ij} \leq a'_{ij} \text{ for all } i, j \qquad (6.3.6)$$

If R is only a tolerance relation, we first perform the appropriate number of compositions of R with itself to obtain R' (which is a modified R) and then apply Eq. (6.3.5) for R' to classify the patterns of X.

■ **Example 6.3.2** Let $X = \{3,\ 5,\ 8,\ 14,\ 18\}$, i.e. $n = 5$ and consider the relation

$$(x, y) \in R \quad iff \ |x - y| \leq 4$$

with the relation matrix

$$A_R = \begin{bmatrix} 1 & 1 & 0 & 0 & 0 \\ 1 & 1 & 1 & 0 & 0 \\ 0 & 1 & 1 & 0 & 0 \\ 0 & 0 & 0 & 1 & 1 \\ 0 & 0 & 0 & 1 & 1 \end{bmatrix}$$

Clearly, R is a tolerance relation but not transitive. For example

$$(3, 5) \in R, \quad (5, 8) \in R, \quad (3, 8) \notin R$$

The composition relation $R \circ R$ has the relation matrix

$$A_{R \circ R} = (b_{ij}), \quad 1 \le i, j \le n$$

where

$$b_{ij} = \max_{1 \le k \le n} \{\min(a_{ik}, a_{kj})\}, \quad 1 \le i, j \le n \tag{6.3.7}$$

i.e.

$$A_{R \circ R} = \begin{bmatrix} 1 & 1 & 1 & 0 & 0 \\ 1 & 1 & 1 & 0 & 0 \\ 1 & 1 & 1 & 0 & 0 \\ 0 & 0 & 0 & 1 & 1 \\ 0 & 0 & 0 & 1 & 1 \end{bmatrix}$$

The new matrix defines an equivalent relation and the equivalent classes are

$$C_1 = \{3, 5, 8\}, \quad C_2 = \{14, 18\}$$

Replacing R with $R' = R \circ R$ enables us to classify 3, 5 and 8 in the same class although the distance between 3 and 8 exceeds (slightly) 4.

♠

Classification Using Fuzzy Relations

Theorem 6.3.1 can be applied in the case of a *fuzzy* tolerance relation as well. Let R_f and R'_f denote a fuzzy tolerance relation and its associated fuzzy equivalent relation respectively. Then, by using $\alpha-$cuts we obtain crisp equivalent relations, i.e. crisp classifications of the pattern space. Usually, the number of classes increases with α.

■ **Example 6.3.3** Consider six patterns and a fuzzy tolerance relation R_f given by the matrix

$$A_{R_f} = (a_{ij}) = \begin{bmatrix} 1 & 0.2 & 0.8 & 0.9 & 0.3 & 0.5 \\ 0.2 & 1 & 0.7 & 0.5 & 0.1 & 0.6 \\ 0.8 & 0.7 & 1 & 0.8 & 0.2 & 0.5 \\ 0.9 & 0.5 & 0.8 & 1 & 0.6 & 0.2 \\ 0.3 & 0.1 & 0.2 & 0.6 & 1 & 0.9 \\ 0.5 & 0.6 & 0.5 & 0.2 & 0.9 & 1 \end{bmatrix}$$

Since $a_{12} = 0.2 < \min(a_{14}, a_{42}) = 0.5$, R_f is not transitive. Two compositions are needed to obtain a fuzzy equivalent relation with matrix

$$A_{R'_f} = \begin{bmatrix} 1 & 0.7 & 0.8 & 0.9 & 0.6 & 0.6 \\ 0.7 & 1 & 0.7 & 0.7 & 0.6 & 0.6 \\ 0.8 & 0.7 & 1 & 0.8 & 0.6 & 0.6 \\ 0.9 & 0.7 & 0.8 & 1 & 0.6 & 0.6 \\ 0.6 & 0.6 & 0.6 & 0.6 & 1 & 0.9 \\ 0.6 & 0.6 & 0.6 & 0.6 & 0.9 & 1 \end{bmatrix}$$

The various $\alpha-$cuts of R'_f are obtained for $\alpha = 1, 0.9, 0.8, 0.7, 0.6$. Each matrix denoted by $A_{R'_f}(\alpha)$ presents a different classification. In this particular example we obtain five possible classifications. Let x_i, $1 \le i \le 6$ denote the given patterns. An arbitrary classification is represented by $\{C_{1,\alpha}, C_{2,\alpha}, \ldots, C_{m(\alpha),\alpha}\}$ where $C_{i,\alpha}$, $1 \leq i \leq m(\alpha)$ are disjoint classes and

$$\bigcup_{i=1}^{m(\alpha)} C_{i,\alpha} = \{x_1, x_2, \ldots, x_6\}$$

The matrices $A_{R'_f}(\alpha)$ and their associated classifications are

$$A_{R'_f}(1) = \begin{bmatrix} 1 & 0 & 0 & 0 & 0 & 0 \\ 0 & 1 & 0 & 0 & 0 & 0 \\ 0 & 0 & 1 & 0 & 0 & 0 \\ 0 & 0 & 0 & 1 & 0 & 0 \\ 0 & 0 & 0 & 0 & 1 & 0 \\ 0 & 0 & 0 & 0 & 0 & 1 \end{bmatrix}$$

$$C_{1,1} = \{x_1\}, \ C_{2,1} = \{x_2\}, \ C_{3,1} = \{x_3\}, \ C_{4,1} = \{x_4\}, \ C_{5,1} = \{x_5\}, \ C_{6,1} = \{x_6\}$$

$$A_{R'_f}(0.9) = \begin{bmatrix} 1 & 0 & 0 & 1 & 0 & 0 \\ 0 & 1 & 0 & 0 & 0 & 0 \\ 0 & 0 & 1 & 0 & 0 & 0 \\ 1 & 0 & 0 & 1 & 0 & 0 \\ 0 & 0 & 0 & 0 & 1 & 1 \\ 0 & 0 & 0 & 0 & 1 & 1 \end{bmatrix}$$

$$C_{1,0.9} = \{x_1, x_4\}, \ C_{2,0.9} = \{x_2\}, \ C_{3,0.9} = \{x_3\}, \ C_{4,0.9} = \{x_5, x_6\}$$

$$A_{R'_f}(0.8) = \begin{bmatrix} 1 & 0 & 1 & 1 & 0 & 0 \\ 0 & 1 & 0 & 0 & 0 & 0 \\ 1 & 0 & 1 & 1 & 0 & 0 \\ 1 & 0 & 1 & 1 & 0 & 0 \\ 0 & 0 & 0 & 0 & 1 & 1 \\ 0 & 0 & 0 & 0 & 1 & 1 \end{bmatrix}$$

$$C_{1,0.8} = \{x_1, x_3, x_4\}, \ C_{2,0.8} = \{x_2\}, \ C_{3,0.8} = \{x_5, x_6\}$$

$$A_{R'_f}(0.7) = \begin{bmatrix} 1 & 1 & 1 & 1 & 0 & 0 \\ 1 & 1 & 1 & 1 & 0 & 0 \\ 1 & 1 & 1 & 1 & 0 & 0 \\ 1 & 1 & 1 & 1 & 0 & 0 \\ 0 & 0 & 0 & 0 & 1 & 1 \\ 0 & 0 & 0 & 0 & 1 & 1 \end{bmatrix}$$

$$C_{1,0.7} = \{x_1, x_2, x_3, x_4\}, \ C_{2,0.7} = \{x_5, x_6\}$$

$$A_{R'_f}(0.6) = \begin{bmatrix} 1 & 1 & 1 & 1 & 1 & 1 \\ 1 & 1 & 1 & 1 & 1 & 1 \\ 1 & 1 & 1 & 1 & 1 & 1 \\ 1 & 1 & 1 & 1 & 1 & 1 \\ 1 & 1 & 1 & 1 & 1 & 1 \\ 1 & 1 & 1 & 1 & 1 & 1 \end{bmatrix}$$

$$C_{1,0.6} = \{x_1, x_2, x_3, x_4, x_5, x_6\}$$

♠

Thus, classification based on a fuzzy relation is not unique but depends on the choice of α. Still, if α is prefixed the classification is completely deterministic and can be regarded as a crisp one. The equivalent relation defined by $A_{R'_f}(\alpha)$ is the $\alpha-$ *defuzzified relation*. The two extreme cases are obtained for $\alpha = 0$ and $\alpha = 1$. If $\alpha = 0$, all the patterns are classified in the same class. The finest classification occurs when $\alpha = 1$: each pattern has its own class. In general the optimal choice of α is problem dependent.

■ **Example 6.3.4** An interesting problem that was treated via fuzzy relations is the following [Kandel 1975, 1979]: Ten different hurricanes were photographed ten times each. An expert not familiar with the dates of the pictures got a well mixed package of a hundred pictures and determined their resemblance to one another. The result was a similarity relation matrix (r_{ij}) $1 \le i, j \le 100$. After carrying several compositions between the matrix and itself a modified equivalent similarity relation was obtained. The $\alpha-$ cut of $\alpha = 0.65$ provided the original partition of photographs (i.e. the original ten sets of the ten hurricanes) with 95% success.

♠

It should again be noted that although classification via a fuzzy relation generally provides several solutions, i.e. all the α-cuts of the similarity matrix, we obtain a crisp classification for any prefixed α. Thus, the terminology 'fuzzy classification' refers in this case to the *uncertainty* associated with arbitrary choices of α.

The next approach to fuzzy classification does not provide *several* crisp classifications. Instead, the pattern space is represented as a union of *fuzzy clusters*.

PROBLEMS

1. Consider the pattern space $X = \{1.0, 1.8, 1.2, 2.1, 1.4, 2.3, 0.9\}$ and the relation R defined over X by $(x,y) \in R$ iff $|x - y| < 0.3, x, y \in X$

    (a) Calculate the relation matrix A_R.
    (b) Is R an equivalent relation over X ?
    (c) If R is not an equivalent relation, use max-min compositions of R with itself to obtain an equivalent relation R'.
    (d) Calculate $A_{R'}$ and classify the patterns of X with respect to R'.

2. A fuzzy tolerance relation R_f over a pattern space of five patterns is given by the matrix

$$
A_{R_f} = \begin{bmatrix}
1 & 0.1 & 0.6 & 0.3 & 0.9 \\
0.1 & 1 & 0.8 & 0.7 & 0.5 \\
0.6 & 0.8 & 1 & 0.3 & 0.2 \\
0.3 & 0.7 & 0.3 & 1 & 0.8 \\
0.9 & 0.5 & 0.2 & 0.8 & 1
\end{bmatrix}
$$

    (a) Show that R_f is not a fuzzy equivalent relation.
    (b) Use max-min compositions to obtain such a relation R'_f.
    (c) Find the various α-cuts of R'_f.

3. (a) Find the matrix of the general fuzzy tolerance relation over a pattern space with three patterns.
   (b) Obtain necessary and sufficient conditions for this matrix to represent a fuzzy equivalent relation.
   (c) What are the $\alpha-$cuts associated with this matrix?

6.4   FUZZY CLUSTERING

Consider a pattern space $X = \{x_1, x_2, ..., x_m\}$ where x_i, $1 \le i \le m$ are vectors in R^n, i.e. each pattern is characterized by n features. Clustering the patterns means partitioning X into c clusters $C_1, C_2, ..., C_c$ such that

$$\bigcup_{i=1}^{c} C_i = X \qquad (6.4.1)$$

$$C_i \cap C_j = \varnothing, \; i \ne j, \; 1 \le i, j \le c \qquad (6.4.2)$$

$$\varnothing \subset C_i \subset X \qquad (6.4.3)$$

The requirement given by Eq. (6.4.3) excludes empty clusters and the trivial case $c = 1$ where the whole pattern space is regarded as a single cluster. Another trivial case is obtained if $c = m$ i.e. each single pattern is a cluster by itself. Since it is reasonable to exclude this possibility as well, we request $1 < c < m$. A partitioning of X which satisfies the requirements given by Eqs. (6.4.1) through (6.4.3) defines a crisp classification of the pattern space X where each pattern x_i, $1 \le i \le m$ belongs *fully* to a unique cluster (class).

Prior to defining 'fuzzy clustering' we will represent the crisp model of clustering using characteristic functions χ_{C_i}, $1 \le i \le c$ defined by

$$\chi_{C_i}(x_j) = \begin{cases} 1, & x_j \in C_i \\ 0, & x_j \notin C_i \end{cases} \qquad (6.4.4)$$

These functions which obtain the values 0 or 1 according to whether a given pattern is a member of a particular cluster, satisfy

$$\max_{1 \le i \le c}[\chi_{C_i}(x_j)] = 1,\ 1 \le j \le m \tag{6.4.5}$$

$$\sum_{i=1}^{c} \chi_{C_i}(x_j) = 1,\ 1 \le j \le m \tag{6.4.6}$$

$$\min[\chi_{C_i}(x_j),\ \chi_{C_k}(x_j)] = 0,\ 1 \le j \le m \tag{6.4.7}$$

$$0 < \sum_{j=1}^{m} \chi_{C_i}(x_j) < m,\ 1 \le i \le c \tag{6.4.8}$$

The first three equations (Eq. (6.4.5) through Eq. (6.4.7)) follows from the crisp classification request that an arbitrary pattern of X must fully belong to a unique cluster. The fourth equation (Eq. (6.4.8)) excludes the possibility of empty clusters and the case in which the whole universe is a single cluster.

An arbitrary crisp classification of X is completely determined by the numbers $\chi_{ij} = \chi_{C_i}(x_j)$, $1 \le i \le c$, $1 \le j \le m$, i.e. by the $c \times m$ matrix $A_c = (\chi_{ij})$. The set of all matrices of the *crisp* partitions with c clusters is

$$P_c = \left\{ A_c \,|\, \chi_{ij} \in \{0,1\},\ \sum_{i=1}^{c} \chi_{ij} = 1,\ 0 < \sum_{j=1}^{m} \chi_{ij} < m \right\} \tag{6.4.9}$$

Using mathematical induction one can show that the total number of partitions in P_c, if the clusters are not labeled, is

$$N(m,\ c) = \frac{1}{c!} \left[\sum_{i=1}^{c} (-1)^{c-i} \binom{c}{i} i^m \right] \tag{6.4.10}$$

If we seek to cluster X using c clusters, the immediate question is which of the $N(m,c)$ partitions should be chosen. In Chapter 3 we suggested minimizing an appropriate performance index. However, carrying the minimization process over the complete set P_c is impractical, since $N(m,c)$ increases rapidly with m and c. Even for a moderate classification problem, for example $m = 30$, $c = 3$ we already obtain

$$N(30,3) = \frac{1}{3!}\left[3^{30} - \binom{3}{2}2^{30} + \binom{3}{1}\right] \sim 3.4 \cdot 10^{13}$$

The $c-$means algorithm introduced in Chapter 3, is an iterative procedure which instead of minimizing a single global performance index, minimizes c *local* performance indices. Each performance index is the total variance of a cluster's members with respect to its new unknown center. The minimization process defines a new cluster center - arithmetic mean of all the patterns which were classified in this particular cluster. The number of iterations needed for convergence is usually relatively low.

The 'crisp' $c-$means algorithm for clustering can be generalized to include fuzzy clustering where each pattern may belong to *several* clusters.

- **Definition 6.4.1** Given   a   pattern   space $X = \{x_1, x_2, \ldots, x_m\}$ let $\tilde{C}_1, \tilde{C}_2, \ldots, \tilde{C}_c$ denote c fuzzy sets over X, and let χ_{ij} denote the grade of membership of x_j in $\tilde{C}_i$. If

$$\sum_{i=1}^{c} \chi_{ij} = 1, \ 1 \le j \le m \tag{6.4.11}$$

$$0 < \sum_{j=1}^{m} \chi_{ij} < m, \ 1 \le i \le c \tag{6.4.12}$$

the set $\tilde{C}_1, \tilde{C}_2, \ldots, \tilde{C}_c$ is called a $c-fuzzy\ partition$ of X.

A typical fuzzy partition is given in Example 6.2.3.

The set of all fuzzy partitions having c sets is given by

$$P_f = \left\{ A_c \mid \chi_{ij} \in [0,1], \ \sum_{i=1}^{c} \chi_{ij} = 1, \ 0 < \sum_{j=1}^{m} \chi_{ij} < m \right\} \tag{6.4.13}$$

where $A_c = (\chi_{ij})$, $1 \le i \le c$, $1 \le j \le m$. As in the case of a crisp partition, it is required that no $\tilde{C}_i$ is empty and that $c > 1$.

In order to introduce fuzzy clustering (classification) we must first define a grade of membership of an arbitrary pattern x_j in a given cluster C_i centered at y_i. Let d_{ij} denote the Euclidean distance $\|x_j - y_i\|$ between x_j and y_i i.e.

$$d_{ij} = \|x_j - y_i\|, \ 1 \leq i \leq c, \ 1 \leq j \leq m \qquad (6.4.14)$$

The membership value x_j in C_i is defined by

$$\chi_{ij} = \left[\sum_{k=1}^{c} \left(\frac{d_{ij}}{d_{kj}} \right)^{2/(\beta-1)} \right]^{-1}, \ 1 \leq i \leq c, \ 1 \leq j \leq m \qquad (6.4.15)$$

where $\beta > 1$ is a tuning parameter which controls the *degree of fuzziness* in the clustering process, provided that $d_{kj} \neq 0$ for all $1 \leq k \leq c$. If $d_{ij} = 0$ for some i and j we define

$$\chi_{ij} = 1; \ \chi_{kj} = 0, \ k \neq i \qquad (6.4.16)$$

Thus, the membership values *always* satisfy Eq. (6.4.11) and unless a pattern coincides with one of cluster centers, it maintains a positive membership value in every cluster.

A *fuzzy clustering process* is defined as the process of finding cluster centers $y_1, y_2, \ldots, y_c$ which minimize the fuzzy performance index

$$I_f = \sum_{j=1}^{m} \sum_{i=1}^{c} \chi_{ij} \|z_i - x_j\|^2 ; \ z_i \in R^n, \ 1 \leq i \leq c \qquad (6.4.17)$$

Clearly, χ_{ij} include the unknowns z_i, $1 \leq i \leq c$ and the problem is generally a complex nonlinear problem. We bypass this difficulty by using an iterative scheme, the fuzzy c-means algorithm which updates

z_i, $1 \le i \le c$ using the already known last iteration's membership values. Updating z_i is done by minimizing c local performance indices, namely

$$I_f(i) = \sum_{j=1}^{m} \chi_{ij} \|z_i - x_j\|^2 \ , \ 1 \le i \le c \tag{6.4.18}$$

This algorithm is similar to the 'crisp' c−means algorithm (CMI) given in Chapter 3. The updating of the center of an arbitrary *fuzzy cluster* $\tilde{C}_i$ is therefore given by

$$y_i^{(k+1)} = \frac{\sum_{j=1}^{m} \chi_{ij}^{(k)} x_j}{\sum_{j=1}^{m} \chi_{ij}^{(k)}} \tag{6.4.19}$$

where $\chi_{ij}^{(k)}$ denotes the membership value of x_j in $\tilde{C}_i$ after the k−th iteration. As in the crisp case there is no guarantee that the final cluster centers are indeed the *optimal* solution, i.e. the solution which minimizes I_f of Eq. (6.4.17).

6.4.1   Fuzzy c−Means Iterative Algorithm (FCMI)
        [Similar to Bezdek 1981]

Given a pattern space $X = \{x_1, x_2, \ldots, x_m\}$ we assume the existence of c fuzzy clusters, whose centers are unknown and are given the initial values $y_{10}, y_{20}, \ldots, y_{c0}$. At each iteration, the patterns' membership values in the various clusters are obtained. The cluster centers are then updated by minimizing the performance indices $I_f(i)$ of Eq. (6.4.18). The process terminates when the difference between two consecutive iterations does not exceed a given tolerance.

Algorithm 6.4.1.

(A fuzzy c−Means iterative clustering procedure: FCMI).

Input: $n-$ the patterns' dimension.

                   $m-$ the number of patterns.

$c-$ the number of clusters.

$X = \{x_i\}$, $1 \le i \le m -$ the given patterns in R^n

$Y_0 = \{y_{i0}\}$, $1 \le i \le c -$ the initial c cluster centers.

$N -$ maximum number of iterations allowed.

$\varepsilon -$ a given tolerance.

$\beta -$ a tuning parameter which controls the degree of fuzziness in the process.

Output: $Y = \{y_i\}$, $1 \le i \le c -$ the final cluster centers.

(χ_{ij}), $1 \le i \le c$, $1 \le j \le m$ – the final matrix of membership values.

$it -$ the number of iterations performed.

Step 1. Initialization: set $k = 0$ and $y_i^{(0)} = y_{i0}$, $1 \le i \le c$.

Step 2. For $1 \le i \le c$ and $1 \le j \le m$ calculate

$$d_{ij}^{(k)} = \left\| x_j - y_i^{(k)} \right\|$$

Step 3. For $1 \le i \le c$ and $1 \le j \le m$ calculate

$$\chi_{ij}^{(k)} = \left[\sum_{l=1}^{c} \left(\frac{d_{ij}^{(k)}}{d_{lj}^{(k)}} \right)^{2/(\beta-1)} \right]^{-1}$$

Step 4. If $d_{ij}^{(k)} = 0$ for some $l = l_0$, set $\chi_{l_0 j}^{(k)} = 1$ and $\chi_{ij}^{(k)} = 0$ for all $i \ne l_0$. For $1 \le i \le c$ update the cluster centers, using Eq. (6.4.19).

Step 5.   If

$$\left[\sum_{i=1}^{c} \left\| y_i^{(k+1)} - y_i^{(k)} \right\|^2 \right]^{1/2} < \varepsilon \tag{6.4.20}$$

set $y_i = y_i^{(k+1)}\ 1 \le i \le c$; $\chi_{ij} = \chi_{ij}^{(k)}$, $1 \le i \le c$, $1 \le j \le m$;
$it = k+1$; output y_i, χ_{ij} for $1 \le i \le c$, $1 \le j \le m$ it and stop.
Otherwise continue.

Step 6.   If $k = N$ output 'no convergence' and stop.   Otherwise, set
$k \leftarrow k+1$ and go to Step 2.

A subroutine FCMI based on Algorithm 6.4.1, is given in the appendix.

■ **Example 6.4.1** Consider a 2-D fuzzy classification problem with five
patterns, distributed as shown in Fig. 6.4.1. The patterns are $x_1 = (0,0)^T$,
$x_2 = (0,1)^T$, $x_3 = (1,1)^T$, $x_4 = (3,3)^T$, $x_5 = (4,2)^T$.

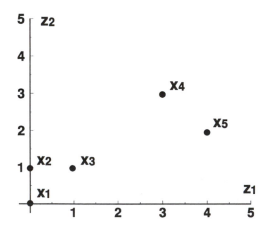

■ **Figure 6.4.1**   A 2-D   5-pattern fuzzy classification problem.

It is assumed that the patterns cluster around two centers, initially approximated by $y_{10} = (0,0)^T$ and $y_{20} = (3,2)^T$. To apply the FCMI algorithm we prefix $N = 10$, $\varepsilon = 5 \cdot 10^{-3}$ and $\beta = 2$. The first iteration consists of calculating $d_{ij}^{(0)}$ and $\chi_{ij}^{(0)}$. The pairs $(d_{ij}^{(0)}, \chi_{ij}^{(0)})$ are given in Table 6.4.1.

- **Table 6.4.1**   Calculating $(d_{ij}^{(0)}, \chi_{ij}^{(0)})$.

	x_1	x_2	x_3	x_4	x_5
$y_1^{(0)}$	$(0.000,1.000)^T$	$(1.000,0.909)^T$	$(1.414,0.714)^T$	$(4.243,0.053)^T$	$(4.472,0.048)^T$
$y_2^{(0)}$	$(3.606,0.000)^T$	$(3.162,0.091)^T$	$(2.236,0.286)^T$	$(1.000,0.947)^T$	$(1.000,0.952)^T$

The next step is updating the cluster centers. Using Eq. (6.4.19) we obtain $y_1^{(1)} = (0.390,0.689)^T$ and $y_2^{(1)} = (3.048,2.251)^T$. The error, i.e. the left hand-side of Eq. (6.4.20), is $e_1 = 0.832 > \varepsilon = 0.005$ and the iterative process continues. The next four iterations are given in detail in Table 6.4.2.

Since $e_5 < \varepsilon$ the fuzzy clustering terminates and $y_1^{(5)}$, $y_2^{(5)}$ are considered the final cluster centers - obtained after five iterations. The membership values of x_i in the clusters C_1 and C_2 (centered at $y_1^{(5)}$, $y_2^{(5)}$ respectively) are given in Table 6.4.3.

If *defuzzification*, i.e. *unique* classification for arbitrary x_i is requested, then Table 6.4.3 would be replaced by Table 6.4.4 which consists of values which are either 1 or 0.

- **Table 6.4.2**   Calculating $\left(d_{ij}^{(k)}, \chi_{ij}^{(k)}\right)$ and $y_i^{(k+1)}$, $1 \le k \le 4$.

	x_1	x_2	x_3	x_4	x_5
$y_1^{(1)}$	$(0.792,0.958)^T$	$(0.499,0.978)^T$	$(0.685,0.925)^T$	$(3.486,0.044)^T$	$(3.841,0.062)^T$
$y_2^{(1)}$	$(3.789,0.042)^T$	$(3.294,0.022)^T$	$(2.399,0.075)^T$	$(0.751,0.956)^T$	$(0.985,0.938)^T$

$$y_1^{(2)} = (0.440,0.728)^T, \qquad y_2^{(2)} = (3.293,2.381)^T, \qquad e_2 = 0.284$$

$y_1^{(2)}$	$(0.850,0.958)^T$	$(0.517,0.979)^T$	$(0.623,0.949)^T$	$(3.423,0.038)^T$	$(3.781,0.043)^T$
$y_2^{(2)}$	$(4.063,0.042)^T$	$(3.570,0.021)^T$	$(2.676,0.051)^T$	$(0.685,0.962)^T$	$(0.803,0.957)^T$

$$y_1^{(3)} = (0.417,0.718)^T, \qquad y_2^{(3)} = (3.328,2.396)^T, \qquad e_3 = 0.046$$

$y_1^{(3)}$	$(0.830,0.961)^T$	$(0.503,0.981)^T$	$(0.648,0.946)^T$	$(3.447,0.038)^T$	$(3.806,0.040)^T$
$y_2^{(3)}$	$(4.101,0.039)^T$	$(3.609,0.019)^T$	$(2.715,0.054)^T$	$(0.687,0.962)^T$	$(0.780,0.960)^T$

$$y_1^{(4)} = (0.412,0.715)^T, \qquad y_2^{(4)} = (3.333,2.398)^T, \qquad e_4 = 0.008$$

$y_1^{(4)}$	$(0.826,0.961)^T$	$(0.501,0.981)^T$	$(0.653,0.945)^T$	$(3.452,0.038)^T$	$(3.811,0.040)^T$
$y_2^{(4)}$	$(4.106,0.039)^T$	$(3.614,0.019)^T$	$(2.720,0.055)^T$	$(0.688,0.962)^T$	$(0.777,0.960)^T$

$$y_1^{(5)} = (0.411,0.715)^T, \qquad y_2^{(5)} = (3.333,2.399)^T, \qquad e_5 = 0.001$$

- **Table 6.4.3**   Membership values of x_i, $1 \le i \le 5$.

	x_1	x_2	x_3	x_4	x_5
C_1	0.961	0.981	0.946	0.038	0.040
C_2	0.039	0.019	0.054	0.962	0.960

- **Table 6.4.4**   *Hardening* the results of Table 6.4.3.

	x_1	x_2	x_3	x_4	x_5
C_1	1	1	1	0	0
C_2	0	0	0	1	1

♠

6.4.2 Defuzzifying the Fuzzy Partition

In many applications the fuzzy partition of the given patterns must be further processed to obtain a crisp partition. If the nature of the problem is such that a crisp classification should be the final output, a defuzzification procedure must follow the fuzzy classification. Two equivalent approaches for defuzzification are usually considered.

(a) Maximum membership classifier

For an arbitrary sample x_j let $i_0(j)$ satisfy

$$\chi_{i_0(j)j} = \max_{1 \le i \le c}(\chi_{ij}) \tag{6.4.21}$$

The modified membership values of x_j are defined by

$$\chi'_{i_0(j)j} = 1; \chi'_{ij} = 0, \ 1 \le i \le c, \ i \ne i_0(j) \tag{6.4.22}$$

(b) Nearest center classifier

For an arbitrary sample x_j let $i_1(j)$ satisfy

$$d_{i_1(j)j} = \min_{1 \le i \le c} d_{ij} \tag{6.4.23}$$

Define

$$\chi'_{i_1(j)j} = 1; \ \chi'_{ij} = 0, \ 1 \le i \le c, \ i \ne i_1(j) \tag{6.4.24}$$

As mentioned above, the two approaches are equivalent, i.e. $i_0(j) = i_1(j)$ for all j. This follows directly from the next result.

Lemma 6.4.1.

For arbitrary $i, k: 1 \leq i, k \leq c$, $i \neq k$ and $j: 1 \leq j \leq m$

$$\chi_{ij} \leq \chi_{kj} \text{ iff } d_{ij} \leq d_{kj} \tag{6.4.25}$$

Proof.

By virtue of Eq. (6.4.15) we have

$$\frac{\chi_{ij}}{\chi_{kj}} = \left(\frac{d_{kj}}{d_{ij}}\right)^{\alpha} \tag{6.4.26}$$

where $\alpha = 2/(\beta - 1) > 0$. Consequently, Eq. (6.4.25) must hold.

□

6.4.3 Fuzzy Clustering and Fuzzy Similarity

Consider a general classification problem whose solution is represented by a $c-$partition of a pattern space X, given by

$$C = \{C_1, C_2, \ldots, C_c\} \tag{6.4.27}$$

If arbitrary patterns x and y belong to the same class C_i, one may correctly state that the *features* by which the patterns of X are classified, are similar for x and y. In other words, if $x, y \in C_i$ then x and y are *similar*. They may not be similar in *every* respect, but they are expected to show similarity with regard to *each* feature which *participates* in the classification process.

In the case of fuzzy classification this is not true, i.e. x and y may belong to the same fuzzy cluster C_i without being *similar* to each other. For example if x and y belong to $\tilde{C}_i$ with membership values 0.9 and 0.2 respectively, then there is no similarity between the two patterns. If on the other hand, the membership values are 0.9 and 0.75 respectively, the statement 'x and y are similar' is certainly true. One could be tempted to observe x and y as similar patterns if and only if a fuzzy cluster $\tilde{C}_i$ can be found such that the membership values of x and y in $\tilde{C}_i$ are *high*. The following example, however, suggests that this approach is sometimes wrong.

■ **Example 6.4.2** Consider a fuzzy partition of humans where the only classes are 'tall' and 'short'. Let X consist of four persons: $x_1 = 3'9''$, $x_2 = 6'10''$, $x_3 = 5'8''$ and $x_4 = 5'4''$. Reasonable membership values are given in Table 6.4.5.

■ **Table 6.4.5**   Membership values in 'tall' and 'short'.

	x_1	x_2	x_3	x_4
'tall'	0.10	0.85	0.48	0.37
'short'	0.90	0.15	0.52	0.63

By applying the previous concept for determining similarity, since no two persons obtain high membership values in the *same* cluster, no two persons are similar. However, x_3 and x_4 *are* similar (both have medium height) and this is reflected by the fact that both have 'close' membership values in *both* 'tall' and 'short'. Thus any definition of *fuzzy similarity* must be in agreement with the *fact* that the persons x_3 and x_4 are similar.

Let a fuzzy classification problem yield the $c-$fuzzy partition

$$\tilde{C} = \left\{\tilde{C}_1, \tilde{C}_2, \ldots, \tilde{C}_c\right\} \tag{6.4.28}$$

of a given pattern space $X = \{x_1, x_2, \ldots, x_m\}$.

■ **Definition 6.4.2** For arbitrary x_i, $x_j \in X$, the quantity

$$s_{ij} = \sum_{k=1}^{c} \min\left(\chi_{ki}, \chi_{kj}\right) \equiv \sum_{k=1}^{c} \left(\chi_{ki} \wedge \chi_{kj}\right) \tag{6.4.29}$$

is called the *fuzzy similarity* between x_i and x_j. The matrix

$$\tilde{S} = (s_{ij}), \ 1 \le i, j \le m \tag{6.4.30}$$

is the *fuzzy similarity relation* of the fuzzy classification.

■   **Example 6.4.3** Consider the fuzzy classification in Example 6.4.2. Based on Table 6.4.5 and Eqs. (6.4.11) and (6.4.29) we obtain $s_{ii} = 1$, $1 \le i \le 4$ and

$$\tilde{S} = \begin{pmatrix} 1 & 0.25 & 0.62 & 0.73 \\ 0.25 & 1 & 0.63 & 0.52 \\ 0.62 & 0.63 & 1 & 0.89 \\ 0.73 & 0.52 & 0.89 & 1 \end{pmatrix}$$

and the two persons mostly similar to one another are x_3 and x_4.

♠

It should be also noted that by using Eq. (6.4.29) to define fuzzy similarity, we guarantee that the similarity between an arbitrary pattern and itself is always 1. The alternative approach for defining similarity would be

$$s'_{ij} = \max_{1 \le k \le c} \{ \min(\chi_{ki}, \chi_{kj}) \} \tag{6.4.31}$$

and would lead to absurdity. For example, the similarity between x_3 and itself using Eq. (6.4.31) is 0.52!

6.4.4 Measuring the Fuzziness in a c – Fuzzy Partition

Consider an arbitrary pattern x_j in a c – fuzzy partition of a given pattern space. Let χ_{ij} and χ_{kj} denote the membership values of x_j in the fuzzy clusters $\tilde{C}_i$ and $\tilde{C}_k$ respectively. The quantity

$$m_{ik}^{(j)} = \min\{\chi_{ij}, \chi_{kj}\} \tag{6.4.32}$$

is called the *unshared* membership which x_j possesses in both $\tilde{C}_i$ and $\tilde{C}_k$. A single number which is commonly used to measure the *hardness* of a given $c-$fuzzy partition is

$$H_c(\tilde{C}) = \frac{tr(MM^T)}{m} \tag{6.4.33}$$

where $\tilde{C}$ is the given $c-$fuzzy partition and M is the cxm matrix of membership values, i.e.

$$M = (\chi_{ij}), \; 1 \le i \le c, \; 1 \le j \le m \tag{6.4.34}$$

Alternatively, the number $F_c(\tilde{C}) = 1 - H_c(\tilde{C})$ measures the *fuzziness* of the partition. The matrix MM^T is clearly a cxc matrix and in the particular case of a crisp partition, it is a diagonal matrix with trace m, i.e. $H_c = 1$. Another extreme case is when each pattern has the same membership value in each cluster, i.e. $\chi_{ij} = \frac{1}{c}$, $1 \le i \le c$, $1 \le j \le m$. This is a case of total ambiguity. We have

$$MM^T = \frac{m}{c^2} \begin{pmatrix} 1 & 1 & \cdots & 1 \\ 1 & 1 & \cdots & 1 \\ \vdots & \vdots & & \vdots \\ 1 & 1 & \cdots & 1 \end{pmatrix} \tag{6.4.35}$$

and consequently $H_c = \left(\frac{m}{c^2} \cdot c\right) / m = \frac{1}{c}$. The case of a general $c-$fuzzy partition is considered next.

■ **Theorem 6.4.1** For an arbitrary pattern space and a $c-$fuzzy partition, the hardness defined by Eq. (6.4.33) satisfies

$$\frac{1}{c} \le H_c(\tilde{C}) \le 1 \tag{6.4.36}$$

Proof.

Let $MM^T = (a_{ij})$, $1 \le i, j \le c$. Then

$$a_{ii} = \sum_{k=1}^{m} \chi_{ik}^2 \tag{6.4.37}$$

and

$$tr(MM^T) = \sum_{i=1}^{c} \sum_{k=1}^{m} \chi_{ik}^2 = \sum_{k=1}^{m} \sum_{i=1}^{c} \chi_{ik}^2 \tag{6.4.38}$$

Since $0 \le \chi_{ik} \le 1$ we have $\chi_{ik}^2 \le \chi_{ik}$ and therefore

$$\sum_{i=1}^{c} \chi_{ik}^2 \le \sum_{i=1}^{c} \chi_{ik} = 1 \tag{6.4.39}$$

Consequently, by virtue of Eqs. (6.4.38-39), $tr(MM^T) \le m$ which implies $H_c(\tilde{C}) \le 1$.

To show the second part of the theorem we apply the Cauchy-Schartz inequality to obtain

$$1 = \left(\sum_{i=1}^{c} \chi_{ik} \right)^2 = \left(\sum_{i=1}^{c} \chi_{ik} \cdot 1 \right)^2 \le \sum_{i=1}^{c} \chi_{ik}^2 \sum_{i=1}^{c} 1^2 = c \sum_{i=1}^{c} \chi_{ik}^2$$

or

$$\frac{1}{c} \le \sum_{i=1}^{c} \chi_{ik}^2 \tag{6.4.40}$$

By substituting in Eq. (6.4.38) we get

$$tr(MM^T) \ge \frac{m}{c} \tag{6.4.41}$$

and the proof of Eq. (6.4.36) is concluded.

□

A direct consequence of Theorem 6.4.1 is

$$0 \le F_c(\tilde{C}) \le 1 - \frac{1}{c} \tag{6.4.42}$$

i.e. the maximum fuzziness in an arbitrary $c-$fuzzy partition is $1-1/c$. If $c=1$ there is *no* fuzziness since each pattern *fully* belongs to the only existing cluster.

PROBLEMS

1. Show the validity of Eq. (6.4.10) in the case $c=2$.

2. Show the validity of Eq. (6.4.19).

3. Obtain the physical meaning of β in Eq. (6.4.15).

4. Consider a 3-class fuzzy classification problem where the final cluster centers are

$$y_1 = (2,1)^T, \; y_2 = (4,4)^T, \; y_3 = (-1,0)^T$$

(a) Calculate the membership values of the following patterns in the fuzzy clusters: $x_1 = (1,1)^T$, $x_2 = (1,-1)^T$, $x_3 = (1,3)^T$. Use the expression given in Eq. (6.4.15) with (i) $\beta = 1.5$ (ii) $\beta = 2.5$ (iii) $\beta = 10$

(b) Discuss the results of (a).

5. Use FCMI to obtain fuzzy classification of the samples in Fig. 6.4.2, using $N = 20$, $\beta = 2$, $\varepsilon = 10^{-3}$. Assume $c = 3$ and start with the initial cluster centers

$$y_{10} = (3,2)^T, \ y_{20} = (0,4)^T, \ y_3 = (-1,0)^T$$

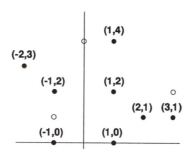

■ **Figure 6.4.2**   Fuzzy classification, $c = 3$.

6. Repeat and solve problem 5 using (a) $\beta = 1.5$ (b) $\beta = 4$.

7. Four patients are associated with two diseases (categories). From each patient we obtain test results which are in some way connected with these diseases: blood sugar rate (S) and cholesterol level (C).

$$\begin{array}{ccccc} & x_1 & x_2 & x_3 & x_4 \\ S & 160 & 180 & 155 & 230 \\ C & 300 & 130 & 270 & 180 \end{array}$$

Classify the patients in the two fuzzy clusters whose initial centers are chosen as $y_{10} = (150,250)^T$, $y_{20} = (200,150)^T$. Use a fuzzy tuning parameter $\beta = 1.5$, tolerance $\varepsilon = 0.0001$ and allow 50 iterations.

8. Solve problem 7 with $\beta = 2$ while keeping the remaining input data unchanged.

9. Solve problem 7 using the initial cluster centers

(a) $y_{10} = (10,1)^T$, $y_{20} = (8,2)^T$

(b) $y_{10} = (10,2)^T$, $y_{20} = (7,1)^T$

without changing the remaining input data.

10. Six person - denoted by $\{x_i\}_{i=1}^6$ are classified into two categories according to their blood pressure (B.P.) and pulse. The given measurements are

$$\begin{array}{ccccccc} & x_1 & x_2 & x_3 & x_4 & x_5 & x_6 \\ \text{low B.P.} & 65 & 70 & 100 & 95 & 83 & 85 \\ \text{high B.P.} & 110 & 130 & 138 & 140 & 113 & 127 \\ \text{pulse} & 63 & 75 & 77 & 88 & 70 & 90 \end{array}$$

The initial cluster centers are $y_{10} = (80,120,70)^T$, $y_{20} = (100,150,90)^T$. Use $\varepsilon = 0.1$ and find the cluster centers for (a) $\beta = 1.5$ (b) $\beta = 2$ (c) $\beta = 2.5$. In each case allow 20 iterations. Explain the results of case (c).

11. We seek fuzzy classification for the data given in Fig. 6.4.3, assuming two or three categories. Use $\beta = 2$, $\varepsilon = 0.001$, allow 50 iterations and classify in the following cases:

   (a) $c=2$, $\mathbf{y}_{10} = (1,0)^T$, $\mathbf{y}_{20}=(2,2)^T$.

   (b) $c = 3$, $\mathbf{y}_{10} = (1,0)^T$, $\mathbf{y}_{20} = (3,0)^T$, $\mathbf{y}_{30} = (2,2)^T$.

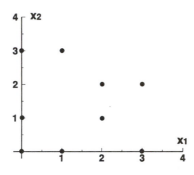

■ **Figure 6.4.3**   Fuzzy classification using $c = 2,3$.

12. Use the performance index criteria to determine which of the classifications performed in the previous problem is better.

13. (a) In problem 11 harden the classifications and obtain crisp c-partitions of the data.

   (b) Perform the hardening using a threshold value $t = 0.6$, i.e. a pattern $\mathbf{x}_j$ is classified if and only if $\max(\chi_{ij})$, $1 \le i \le c$ exceeds t. Otherwise it is considered 'noise' and deleted.

14. Calculate the fuzzy similarity relation matrix for both classifications of problem 11.

6.5 FUZZY PATTERN RECOGNITION

A crisp pattern recognition system consists of c well defined categories into which incoming unknown patterns are classified. It is expected that two *similar* patterns i.e. two patterns with similar features, will belong to the same class. In this section we will extend these principles to obtain *fuzzy pattern recognition systems*.

We first introduce the concept of *fuzzy typical pattern* which is presented as a fuzzy set $\tilde{A}$ over the pattern space X.

■ **Example 6.5.1** Let X denote all the simple four-sided polygons in R^2 and let $\tilde{A}$ be the fuzzy set 'rectangle' defined as follows: each $x \in X$ with angles α_i, $1 \le i \le 4$ (which must satisfy $\sum_{i=1}^{4} \alpha = 2\pi$) belongs to $\tilde{A}$ with grade of membership

$$\chi(x) = \left[1 + \sum_{i=1}^{4} \left(\alpha_i - \frac{\pi}{2} \right)^2 \right]^{-1} \tag{6.5.1}$$

The fuzzy typical pattern 'rectangle' is thus represented by $\tilde{A}$.

♠

6.5.1 Single Sample Identification

Consider c fuzzy typical patterns represented by fuzzy sets $\tilde{C}_1$, $\tilde{C}_2 ...$, $\tilde{C}_c$ over a pattern space X. Let x denote an incoming pattern in X. The *maximum membership principle* states that x will be assigned to $\tilde{C}_i$ which satisfies

$$\chi_{\tilde{C}_i}(x) = \max_{1 \le j \le c} \{ \chi_{\tilde{C}_j}(x) \} \tag{6.5.2}$$

If this is fulfilled by several i's, we may decide that x belongs to $\tilde{C}_{i_0}$ where i_0 is the smallest i which satisfies Eq. (6.5.2). Another option is to carry further tests on x, which may lead to a reasonable unique choice.

■   **Example 6.5.2** Let X be the set of all real numbers and consider the fuzzy sets $\tilde{C}_i$, $1 \le i \le 3$ in Fig. 6.5.1.

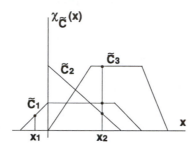

■   **Figure 6.5.1**   The maximum membership principle.

Using Eq. (6.5.2) we obtain $x_1 \in \tilde{C}_1$ and $x_2 \in \tilde{C}_3$

♠

It should be noted that assigning $x \in X$ to an arbitrary $\tilde{C}_i$ simply expresses the fact that x resembles $\tilde{C}_i$ more than any other fuzzy typical pattern.

In the next example we classify an arbitrary triangle.

■   **Example 6.5.3**   Let X denote the set of all the triangles in a plane. Five fuzzy typical patterns are considered: *right, right and isosceles, equilateral, isosceles* and '*all other*' triangles. The corresponding fuzzy sets are denoted by $\tilde{R}$, $\tilde{RI}$, $\tilde{E}$, $\tilde{I}$ $\tilde{O}$ respectively. The grades of membership of an arbitrary triangle x with angles α, β, γ given in an increasing order, in $\tilde{R}$, $\tilde{RI}$, $\tilde{E}$, $\tilde{I}$, $\tilde{O}$ are defined by

$$\chi_{\tilde{R}}(x) = 1 - \frac{|\gamma - 90|}{90}$$

$$\chi_{\tilde{RI}}(x) = 1 - \left(\frac{|\gamma - 90|}{90} + \frac{|\beta - 45|}{45} + \frac{|\alpha - 45|}{45} \right) / 3$$

$$\chi_{\tilde{E}}(x) = 1 - \max \left\{ \frac{|\gamma - 60|}{60}, \frac{|\beta - 60|}{60}, \frac{|\alpha - 60|}{60} \right\} \tag{6.5.3}$$

$$\chi_{\tilde{I}}(x) = 1 - \min \left\{ \frac{\beta - \alpha}{\alpha + \beta}, \frac{\gamma - \beta}{\gamma + \beta} \right\}$$

$$\chi_{\tilde{O}}(x) = 1 - \max \left\{ X_{\tilde{R}}(x), X_{\tilde{RI}}(x), X_{\tilde{E}}(x), X_{\tilde{I}}(x) \right\}$$

and if any of the right-hand sides of Eq. (6.5.3) is negative, the corresponding membership is defined as 0. Consider an incoming pattern which is the triangle $x = (27^0, 58^0, 95^0)$. The membership values of x in the five fuzzy sets are

$$\chi_{\tilde{R}}(x) = 1 - \frac{5}{90} = 0.944$$

$$\chi_{\tilde{RI}}(x) = 1 - \left(\frac{5}{90} + \frac{13}{45} + \frac{18}{45} \right) / 3 = 0.752$$

$$\chi_{\tilde{E}}(x) = 1 - \max \left\{ \frac{35}{60}, \frac{2}{60}, \frac{33}{60} \right\} = 0.417$$

$$\chi_{\tilde{I}}(x) = 1 - \min \left\{ \frac{31}{85}, \frac{37}{153} \right\} = 0.758$$

$$\chi_{\tilde{O}}(x) = 1 - \max \left\{ 0.944, 0.752, 0.417, 0.758 \right\} = 0.056$$

Using Eq. (6.5.2), the triangle mostly resembles a right triangle. If $x = (5^0, 35^0, 140^0)$ we obtain $\chi_{\tilde{R}}(x) = 0.444$, $\chi_{\tilde{RI}}(x) = 0.444$, $\chi_{\tilde{E}}(x) = 0$,

$\chi_{\tilde{I}}(x) = 0.4$, $\chi_{\tilde{o}}(x) = 0.556$ and the triangle has a maximum membership value in the fuzzy set of 'all other' triangles.

♠

Let us now assume that the incoming pattern instead of being a crisp vector in X, is given as fuzzy set $\tilde{A}$ over X. This could occur for example if the new pattern is determined by *several* observations whose distribution can be represented by a fuzzy set. We are interested in obtaining a fuzzy set $\tilde{C}_i$ which is most resembled by $\tilde{A}$. The degree of similarity between two fuzzy sets $\tilde{A}$ and $\tilde{B}$ over a pattern space X is most frequently defined by one of the expressions:

$$s_1(\tilde{A},\tilde{B}) = \min[(\tilde{A} \bullet \tilde{B}), (\overline{\tilde{A} \oplus \tilde{B}})] \qquad (6.5.4)$$

$$s_2(\tilde{A},\tilde{B}) = (1/2)[(\tilde{A} \bullet \tilde{B}) + (\overline{\tilde{A} \oplus \tilde{B}})] \qquad (6.5.5)$$

where $\tilde{A} \bullet \tilde{B}$ and $\overline{\tilde{A} \oplus \tilde{B}}$ are the inner and outer products of $\tilde{A}$ and $\tilde{B}$, i.e.

$$\tilde{A} \bullet \tilde{B} = \max\{\min[\chi_{\tilde{A}}(x), \chi_{\tilde{B}}(x)], x \in X\} \qquad (6.5.6)$$

$$\tilde{A} \oplus \tilde{B} = \min\{\max[\chi_{\tilde{A}}(x), \chi_{\tilde{B}}(x)], x \in X\} \qquad (6.5.7)$$

and

$$\overline{\tilde{A} \oplus \tilde{B}} = 1 - \tilde{A} \oplus \tilde{B} \qquad (6.5.8)$$

■ **Example 6.5.4** Consider the pattern space $X = \{x_i\}_{i=1}^6$ and the fuzzy sets

$$\tilde{A} = \{1/x_1 \; ; \; 1/x_2 \; ; \; 0/x_3 \; ; \; 0/x_4 \; ; \; 0/x_5 \; ; \; 0/x_6\}$$
$$\tilde{B} = \{0/x_1 \; ; \; 0/x_2 \; ; \; 1/x_3 \; ; \; 1/x_4 \; ; \; 1/x_5 \; ; \; 1/x_6\}$$

The inner and outer products of $\tilde{A}$ and $\tilde{B}$ are $\tilde{A} \bullet \tilde{B} = 0$ and $\tilde{A} \oplus \tilde{B} = 1$ respectively. Consequently $\overline{\tilde{A} \oplus \tilde{B}} = 0$ and

$$s_1\left(\tilde{A}, \tilde{B}\right) = s_2\left(\tilde{A}, \tilde{B}\right) = 0$$

i.e. $\tilde{A}$ and $\tilde{B}$ are *completely* dissimilar by either approach

♠

In the particular case $\tilde{A} = \tilde{B}$ one should expect full similarity between the two fuzzy sets. To obtain that we require

$$\max \chi_{\tilde{A}}(x) = 1, \ \min \chi_{\tilde{A}}(x) = 0$$

for arbitrary fuzzy set $\tilde{A}$. Then, $\tilde{A} = \tilde{B}$ leads to

$$\tilde{A} \bullet \tilde{B} = \max \chi_{\tilde{A}}(x) = 1, \ \tilde{A} \oplus \tilde{B} = \min \chi_{\tilde{A}}(x) = 0$$

i.e. $s_1\left(\tilde{A}, \tilde{B}\right) = s_2\left(\tilde{A}, \tilde{B}\right) = 1$.

We will now denote either $s_1\left(\tilde{A}, \tilde{B}\right)$ or $s_2\left(\tilde{A}, \tilde{B}\right)$ by $s\left(\tilde{A}, \tilde{B}\right)$.

■ **Definition 6.5.1** Let c sample patterns be represented by the fuzzy sets $\tilde{C}_1, \tilde{C}_2, ..., \tilde{C}_c$ and let an arbitrary new pattern be represented by a fuzzy set $\tilde{A}$. Then the pattern $\tilde{A}$ is said to most resemble $\tilde{C}_i$, if

$$s\left(\tilde{A}, \tilde{C}_i\right) = \max_{1 \le j \le c} [s(\tilde{A}, \tilde{C}_j)] \tag{6.5.9}$$

■ **Example 6.5.5** Let $\tilde{C}_1$ and $\tilde{C}_2$ be the fuzzy sets $\tilde{A}, \tilde{B}$ of the previous example respectively and consider an incoming pattern which is represented by the fuzzy set

$$\tilde{E} = \left\{0.9/x_1; \ 0.2/x_2; \ 0.8/x_3; \ 0.9/x_4; \ 0.9/x_5; \ 0.8/x_6\right\}$$

Then $s_1\big(\tilde{E},\tilde{C}_1\big)=0.2$, $s_1\big(\tilde{E},\tilde{C}_2\big)=0.8$ and therefore $\tilde{E}$ most resembles $\tilde{C}_2$ if s_1 is used. If s_2 is applied, we obtain $s_2\big(\tilde{E},\tilde{C}_1\big)=0.55$, $s_2\big(\tilde{E},\tilde{C}_2\big)=0.85$ and again $\tilde{E}$ most resembles $\tilde{C}_2$.

♠

An incoming pattern represented by a fuzzy set is called a *fuzzy pattern*.

■ **Example 6.5.6** Let $\tilde{C}_1$ and $\tilde{C}_2$ over $X:\ -\infty<x<\infty$ represent fuzzy typical patterns with Gaussian membership functions given by (Fig. 6.5.2)

$$\chi_{\tilde{C}_i}(x)=\exp[-(x-\mu_i)^2/\sigma_i^2],\ 1\le i\le 2 \qquad (6.5.10)$$

Clearly $\tilde{C}_1\bullet\tilde{C}_2=\chi_{\tilde{C}_1}(x_0)=\chi_{\tilde{C}_2}(x_0)$ and the unique x_0 must satisfy

$$\left(\frac{x_0-\mu_1}{\sigma_1}\right)^2=\left(\frac{x_0-\mu_2}{\sigma_2}\right)^2$$

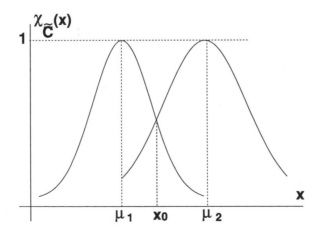

■ **Figure 6.5.2**   Patterns with Gaussian membership functions.

If $\mu_1 \le \mu_2$ then $(x_0 - \mu_1)/\sigma_1 = (\mu_2 - x_0)/\sigma_2$ and consequently

$$x_0 = \frac{\mu_2 \sigma_1 + \mu_1 \sigma_2}{\sigma_1 + \sigma_2} , \quad \chi_{\tilde{C}_i}(x_0) = \exp\left[-\left(\frac{\mu_1 - \mu_2}{\sigma_1 + \sigma_2}\right)^2\right] \qquad (6.5.11)$$

The outer product of $\tilde{C}_1$ and $\tilde{C}_2$ is zero and thus $\overline{\tilde{C}_1 \oplus \tilde{C}_2} = 1$ leading to

$$s_1\left(\tilde{C}_1, \tilde{C}_2\right) = \min\{1, \chi_{\tilde{C}_i}(x_0)\} = \exp\left[-\left(\frac{\mu_1 - \mu_2}{\sigma_1 + \sigma_2}\right)^2\right]$$

$$s_2\left(\tilde{C}_1, \tilde{C}_2\right) = [1 + \chi_{\tilde{C}_i}(x_0)] / 2$$

♠

Given c known fuzzy patterns $\{\tilde{C}_i\}_{i=1}^c$ and an *unknown* incoming fuzzy pattern $\tilde{A}$, the criteria given by Eq. (6.5.9) for obtaining the known pattern which $\tilde{A}$ most closely resembles is called the *maximum approaching degree* principle [Dong, 1987].

Previously we discussed mainly fuzzy pattern recognition problems where only a single feature was considered. A multi-feature problem is more realistic. For example, we may want to identify a hurricane not only by its intensity, but to consider also additional features as the number of casualties. The general multi-feature fuzzy pattern recognition problem is discussed next.

6.5.2   A Multi-Feature Pattern Recognition Problem

Let X denote a universe of m sample patterns $x_1, x_2, \ldots, x_m$ each characterized by n features, i.e.

$$x_i = (x_{i1}, x_{i2}, \ldots, x_{in})^T , \quad 1 \le i \le m \qquad (6.5.12)$$

By implementing a fuzzy classification approach (given the number of desired classes $-c$) we obtain a $c-$fuzzy partition, which using a hardening procedure can be then replaced by a crisp classification. The final clusters are $C_1, C_2, \ldots, C_c$ and they satisfies

$$X = \bigcup_{i=1}^{c} C_i \ ; \ C_i \cap C_j = \varnothing, \ i \neq j \tag{6.5.13}$$

A pattern recognition scheme will classify an arbitrary incoming pattern $x_0 = (x_{01}, x_{02}, \ldots, x_{0n})^T$ in one of the classes C_i, $1 \leq i \leq c$ according to a prechosen approach. Three of the popular approaches are the following:

1. Nearest neighbor classifier

If x_i satisfies

$$\|x_0 - x_i\| = \min_{1 \leq j \leq m} \|x_0 - x_j\| \ , \ x_i \in C_k \tag{6.5.14}$$

then x_0 is classified in C_k .

2. Nearest cluster classifier

Let $y_1, y_2, \ldots, y_c$ denote the centers of the c fuzzy clusters generated during the fuzzy classification process. If

$$\|x_0 - y_i\| = \min_{1 \leq j \leq c} \|x_0 - y_j\| \tag{6.5.15}$$

then x_0 is classified in C_i .

3. Weighted maximum approaching degree

Let each known sample pattern be characterized by n features and represented by an $n-$dimensional fuzzy vector set. If c known patterns are considered, they are given by

$$\tilde{C}_i = \left(\tilde{C}_{i1}, \tilde{C}_{i2}, \ldots, \tilde{C}_{in}\right)^T, \ 1 \le i \le c \tag{6.5.16}$$

where $\{\tilde{C}_{ij}\}_{j=1}^n$ are non-interactive fuzzy sets which represent the n features of the $i-$th pattern respectively. Let

$$\tilde{A} = (\tilde{A}_1, \tilde{A}_2, \ldots, \tilde{A}_n)^T \tag{6.5.17}$$

represent a new incoming pattern. Since in general some features are more significant in determining similarity (consider for example medical diagnosis where some symptoms are more significant than others in determining the patient's prognosis), we define the approaching degree between $\tilde{A}$ and $\tilde{C}_i$ by

$$s(\tilde{A}, \tilde{C}_i) \triangleq \sum_{j=1}^n w_j [s(\tilde{A}_j, \tilde{C}_{ij})], \ 1 \le i \le c \tag{6.5.18}$$

where $w_j, \ 1 \le j \le n$ are appropriate weights which indicate the relative significance of the various features and satisfy

$$\sum_{j=1}^n w_j = 1$$

As in the case of a single feature, $\tilde{A}$ most closely resembles $\tilde{C}_i$ if

$$s(\tilde{A}, \tilde{C}_i) = \max_{1 \le j \le c}[s(\tilde{A}, \tilde{C}_j)] \tag{6.5.19}$$

If instead of a fuzzy incoming pattern we have a crisp feature vector $x = (x_1, x_2, \ldots, x_n)^T$, Eq. (6.5.18) is replaced by

$$\chi_{\tilde{C}_i}(x) \triangleq \sum_{j=1}^n w_j \chi_{\tilde{C}_{ij}}(x_j), \ 1 \le i \le c \tag{6.5.20}$$

and x most closely resembles $\tilde{C}_i$ for which

$$\chi_{\tilde{C}_i}(x) = \max_{1 \le j \le c}[\chi_{\tilde{C}_j}(x)] \tag{6.5.21}$$

■ **Example 6.5.7** Consider a two-feature problem with two known patterns $\tilde{C}_1$ and $\tilde{C}_2$, where each feature is represented by a fuzzy set with Gaussian membership function. Thus

$$\tilde{C}_i = (\tilde{C}_{i1}, \tilde{C}_{i2})^T , \; \chi_{\tilde{C}_{ij}}(t) = \exp\left[-(t-\mu_{ij})^2/\sigma_{ij}^2\right] \tag{6.5.22}$$

for $1 \le i \le 2$ and $-\infty < t < \infty$. Let $\tilde{A} = (\tilde{A}_1, \tilde{A}_2)$ denote a new pattern for which

$$\chi_{\tilde{A}_i}(t) = \exp\left[-(t-\mu_i)^2/\sigma_i^2\right], \; 1 \le i \le 2 \tag{6.5.23}$$

and we seek a known pattern which most closely resembles $\tilde{A}$. The known patterns as well as the new pattern are derived from table 6.5.1.

■ **Table 6.5.1**   Input to Example 6.5.7.

	$\tilde{C}_{11}$	$\tilde{C}_{12}$	$\tilde{C}_{21}$	$\tilde{C}_{22}$	$\tilde{A}_1$	$\tilde{A}_2$
μ	10	15	7	20	9	18
σ	3	5	2	8	4	6

The inner products $\tilde{A}_i \bullet \tilde{C}_{ji}$ are

$$\tilde{A}_1 \bullet \tilde{C}_{11} = 0.980 , \; \tilde{A}_1 \bullet \tilde{C}_{21} = 0.895 , \; \tilde{A}_2 \bullet \tilde{C}_{12} = 0.928 , \; \tilde{A}_2 \bullet \tilde{C}_{22} = 0.980$$

and $\overline{\tilde{A}_i \oplus \tilde{C}_{ji}} = 1$ for all i and j. Assume that the two features are not equally important and that $w_1 = 0.7$, $w_2 = 0.3$. If the measure of similarity is given by s_1 then

$$s_1(\tilde{A}, \tilde{C}_1) = 0.7(\tilde{A}_1 \bullet \tilde{C}_{11}) + 0.3(\tilde{A}_2 \bullet \tilde{C}_{12}) = 0.964$$

$$s_1(\tilde{A}, \tilde{C}_2) = 0.7(\tilde{A}_1 \bullet \tilde{C}_{21}) + 0.3(\tilde{A}_2 \bullet \tilde{C}_{22}) = 0.921$$

Therefore, $\tilde{A}$ most closely resembles the first known pattern $\tilde{C}_1$

♠

The next example is medical in nature. An arbitrary patient is characterized by 'medical features' and accordingly classified in one of several risk groups.

■ **Example 6.5.8** Three features which have a significant effect on a patient's state of health are the rates of blood sugar, cholesterol and smoking of the patient. We assume that the rates of blood sugar and cholesterol are each represented by three fuzzy sets - 'high' (H), 'normal' (N) and 'low' (L). The rate of smoking may be 'low' (L) or 'high' (H). The geometrical representations of these fuzzy sets are given in Fig. 6.5.3 (blood sugar), Fig. 6.5.4 (cholesterol) and Fig. 6.5.5 (smoking).

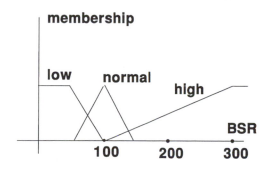

■ **Figure 6.5.3** Fuzzy set representation of blood sugar rate (BSR).

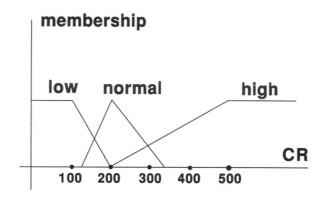

■ **Figure 6.5.4**   Fuzzy set representation of cholesterol (CR).

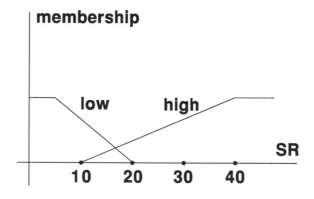

■ **Figure 6.5.5**   Fuzzy set representation of smoking (SR).

The number of known patterns is $3 \cdot 3 \cdot 2 = 18$ and they are classified by Table 6.5.2 in six risk groups: very risky (VR), risky (R), relatively risky(RR), relatively safe (RS), safe (S) and very safe (VS).

■ **Table 6.5.2**   Assigning new patients to risk groups.

risk group	blood sugar	cholesterol	smoking
R	L	L	L
VS	N	L	L
R	H	L	L
RS	L	N	L
VS	N	N	L
RR	H	N	L
RR	L	H	L
S	N	H	L
VR	H	H	L
R	L	L	H
RS	N	L	H
VR	H	L	H
RR	L	N	H
RS	N	N	H
R	H	N	H
R	L	H	H
RR	N	H	H
VR	H	H	H

The classification of new patterns is based on medical experience and indicates for example that high blood sugar is considered *in general* more risky than high cholesterol. The weights that we assign to the features are also based on medical experience. They are:

$$w(\text{blood sugar}) = 0.45, \quad w(\text{cholesterol}) = 0.30, \quad w(\text{smoking}) = 0.25$$

Consider now a patient with $BSR = 130$, $CR = 150$, $SR = 25$ (see Figs. 6.5.4-6). The patient is denoted in short by $x \, (=(130,150,25)^T)$. Using Eq. (6.5.21) we obtain $\chi_{\tilde{C}_i}(x)$, $1 \le i \le 18$ where (Table 6.5.2)

$$\tilde{C}_1 = (L,L,L)^T, \quad \tilde{C}_2 = (N,L,L)^T, \ldots, \quad \tilde{C}_{18} = (H,H,H)^T$$

These numbers are given in Table 6.5.3.

■ **Table 6.5.3**   Membership values of the pattern x in $\tilde{C}_i$.

i	blood sugar	cholesterol	smoking	$\chi_{\tilde{C}_i}(x)$
1	L	L	L	0.15
2	N	L	L	0.33
3	H	L	L	0.22
4	L	N	L	0.11
5	N	N	L	0.29
6	H	N	L	0.18
7	L	H	L	0
8	N	H	L	0.18
9	H	H	L	0.07
10	L	L	H	0.28
11	N	L	H	0.46
12	H	L	H	0.34
13	L	N	H	0.24
14	N	N	H	0.42
15	H	N	H	0.31
16	L	H	H	0.13
17	N	H	H	0.31
18	H	H	H	0.19

For example:

$$\chi_{\tilde{C}_{12}}(x) = 0.45 \cdot \chi_{\tilde{C}_{12,1}}(130) + 0.30 \cdot \chi_{\tilde{C}_{12,2}}(150) + 0.25 \cdot \chi_{\tilde{C}_{12,3}}(25)$$

where $\chi_{\tilde{C}_{12,i}}$ (130), $1 \le i \le 3$ are the membership values of the new patient at 'high blood sugar rate', 'low cholesterol rate' and 'high smoking rate' respectively. From Table 6.5.3 we obtain that the new patient most closely resembles $\tilde{C}_{11}$, i.e. the patient is assigned to the group 'relatively safe' (RS). The second best choice is $\tilde{C}_{14}$ but the patient is still assigned to RS, a result which indicates the consistency of the previous knowledge used to provide the input parameters.

♠

PROBLEMS

1. Obtain the smallest grade of membership in 'rectangle' for arbitrary four-sided polygon. Use Eq. (6.5.1).

2. Use Eq. (6.5.3) to classify the following triangles: (i) $(20^0, 109^0, 51^0)^T$ (ii) $(38^0, 58^0, 84^0)^T$ (iii) $(40^0, 60^0, 80^0)^T$

3. Use Eq. (6.5.3) to classify the triangle $(30^0, 30^0 + \alpha, 120^0 - \alpha)^T$ as a function of α (given in degrees), where $0 \le \alpha \le 45$.

4. (a) For the following fuzzy sets $\tilde{A}$ and $\tilde{B}$ obtain $\tilde{A} \bullet \tilde{B}$ and $\tilde{A} \oplus \tilde{B}$:

$$\tilde{A} = \{0.2/x_1; \ 0.5/x_2; \ 0.1/x_3; \ 0.6/x_4; \ 0.3/x_5; 0.4/x_6\}$$
$$\tilde{B} = \{0.4/x_1; \ 0.7/x_2; \ 0.05/x_3; \ 0.7/x_4; \ 0.15/x_5; 0.3/x_6\}$$

(b) Calculate $s_1(\tilde{A}, \tilde{B})$ and $s_2(\tilde{A}, \tilde{B})$.

5. (a) For fuzzy typical patterns $\tilde{C}_1$ and $\tilde{C}_2$ represented by Gaussian membership functions, show the validity of Eq. (6.5.11).

(b) Show $\tilde{C}_1 \oplus \tilde{C}_2 = 0$ for arbitrary Gaussian patterns $\tilde{C}_1$ and $\tilde{C}_2$.

6. Assume four known fuzzy patterns which are A, B, C, D. Each pattern is characterized by two features: color, and weight. The fuzzy sets which represent the features are shown in Figs. 6.5.6-7 respectively. They are triangulars for A, B, C, and Gaussian for D. The unit for color is normalized to a non-dimensional unit while the unit for weight is 1 lb. The assumed weights are $w(\text{color}) = 0.55$, $w(\text{weight}) = 0.45$. Classify a new crisp pattern $x = (0.65, 8.5)^T$.

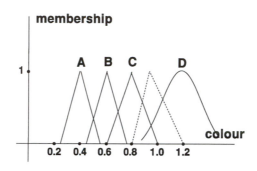

■ **Figure 6.5.6**   Representation of the patterns in terms of color.

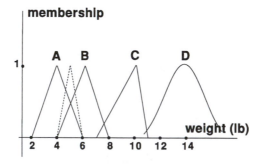

■ **Figure 6.5.7**   Representation of the patterns in terms of weight.

7. Solve Problem 6 if the new pattern's features are fuzzy sets given by the dashed triangles in Figs. 6.5.6-7.

7 SYNTACTIC PATTERN

RECOGNITION

7.1 INTRODUCTION

Ideally we would have liked a solution to a pattern recognition problem to consist of the following stages:

1. Find a feature vector x.
2. Train a system using a set of training patterns whose classification is *a priori* known.
3. Classify unknown incoming patterns.

Unfortunately, for most practical problems this approach is not feasible. The reason is that usually, a pattern contains some *relational information* from which it is difficult and sometime impossible to derive an appropriate feature vector. Therefore, the analytical approaches which process the patterns only on a quantitative basis but ignore the interrelationships between the components of the patterns quite often fail.

The premise of syntactic pattern recognition is that the *structure* of the pattern, so far ignored, is now the most important element in the recognition process. This structure is used for two purposes:
(a) Describing the pattern (b) Classifying the pattern. A general scheme of a syntactic pattern recognition system is shown in Fig. 7.1.1.

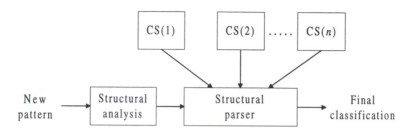

■ **Figure 7.1.1** Classification using syntactic pattern recognition.

We consider n different classes and each of them is associated with a specific 'structure': Class Structure (CS), which is typical only to patterns in this class. Each unknown pattern is processed to obtain its structural analysis. Then starts the process of 'structural parsing' in which the pattern structure is compared with the existing CS(1),...,CS(n). If a match occurs with CS(i), the pattern is classified in class i. Otherwise it is rejected.

Most techniques in syntactic pattern recognition are based on transforming complex patterns using hierarchical decomposition into simpler subpatterns, just as a sentence in a natural language may be decomposed into words (and then into letters). This process of decomposing may continue several times until we obtain the *pattern primitives* which are not being decomposed. For example, the picture A consists of a triangle B and a rectangle C, while each of them may be decomposed to its edges.

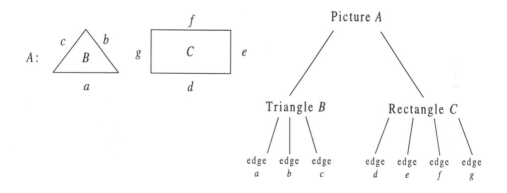

The tree decomposition indicates the similarity between the structure of a sentence and the structural description of a pattern. Thus, patterns are designed by using primitives and later subpatterns, just as sentences are constructed using letters and words.

A pattern's structural description is obtained by a specific *language*. The collection of the rules which determine the process of composing primitives into patterns is the language *grammar*.

For an unknown pattern we first find and identify all its primitives and then start syntax analysis called *parsing* which will finally determine whether the pattern is a legitimate member (sentence) of the class (language). The similarity between structural description of a pattern and the structure of a paragraph, sentence and words-obeying a set of rules (grammar) suggests the introducing of the basic concepts of a formal language, based on a formal grammar.

7.2   PRELIMINARIES

The following definitions present basic concepts which play a major role in the study of formal language theory.

- **Definition 7.2.1** An *alphabet* is a finite set of symbols

$$V = \{x_1, x_2, \ldots, x_n\} \tag{7.2.1}$$

and a *sentence* over V is a finite string of ordered symbols (from left to right) from V.

- **Example 7.2.1** If the alphabet is $V = \{a,b,c\}$, valid sentences are: 'abb', 'abba', 'aaa' and also the *empty* sentence which has no symbols.

♠

The *length* of a sentence s is the number of its symbols and is denoted by $|s|$. The null sentence is denoted by ε and satisfies $|\varepsilon| = 0$.

■ **Definition 7.2.2** For arbitrary strings $s_1 = x_1 x_2 \ldots x_m$ and $s_2 = y_1 y_2 \ldots y_n$ the *concatenation* of s_1 and s_2 denoted by $s_1 \circ s_2$ is the sentence

$$s_3 = s_1 \circ s_2 = x_1 x_2 \ldots x_m y_1 \ldots y_n \qquad (7.2.2)$$

with length $|s_3| = m + n$. A particular case is the concatenation of two symbols x, y which provides the sentence xy.

Given an alphabet V, we denote by

$$\underbrace{V \circ V \circ \ldots \circ V}_{(n-1)\,\text{times}} = V^n \qquad (7.2.3)$$

the set of all sentences with n symbols over V. The set

$$V^+ = V \cup V^2 \cup V^3 \cup \ldots = \overset{\infty}{\underset{k=1}{\cup}} V^k \qquad (7.2.4)$$

denotes all the nonempty sentences over V. The set

$$V^* = \epsilon \cup V^+ \qquad (7.2.5)$$

is called the *closure* of V.

■ **Example 7.2.2** If $V = \{a\}$ then

$$V^+ = \{a, a^2, a^3, \ldots, a^n, \ldots\}$$

where

$$a^1 = a; \, a^n = a^{n-1} \circ a \,, n \geq 2 \qquad (7.2.6)$$

and

$$V^* = \{\varepsilon, a, a^2, a^3, \ldots, a^n, \ldots\}$$

♠

- **Definition 7.2.3** An arbitrary subset L of V^* is called a *language*

- **Example 7.2.3** Let $V = \{0,1\}$. Then

$$L_1 = \{001,110,111,0,\varepsilon\}$$

is a *finite language* while

$$L_2 = \{s \mid s = 1^n 0^2 1^m, n \geq 1, \ 1 \leq m \leq 10\}$$

is an *infinite language*.

♠

- **Definition 7.2.4** For arbitrary languages L_1 and L_2, the set

$$L_1 \circ L_2 = \{s \mid s = s_1 s_2, s_1 \in L_1 \text{ and } s_2 \in L_2\} \tag{7.2.7}$$

is called the *concatenation* of L_1 and L_2. The set

$$L_1^{it} = \{s \mid s = s_1 s_2 \ldots s_n, \ n \geq 0 \text{ and } s_i \in L_1\} \tag{7.2.8}$$

is called the *iterate* of L_1.

Clearly, $L_1 \circ L_2$ and L_1^{it} are also languages.

- **Example 7.2.4** Consider the alphabet $V = \{a,b\}$ and the languages

$$L_1 = \{aa,ab,bb\}, \ L_2 = \{a,b\}$$

Then

$$L_1 \circ L_2 = \{a_1^3 aba, b^2 a, a^2 b, ab_1^2 b^3\}$$

The language L_1^{it} is obviously infinite. Its elements for $n \leq 2$ are

$$\left\{ \varepsilon, a^2, ab, b^2, a^4, a^3b, a^2b^2, aba^2, abab, ab^3, b^2a^2, b^2ab, b^4 \right\}$$

♠

■ **Definition 7.2.5** For arbitrary strings $s, t \in V^*$, s is called a *substring* of t if

$$t = usv \qquad\qquad (7.2.9)$$

for some strings $u, v \in V^*$.

Since u and/or v may be the null string, each string s is also a substring of itself.

■ **Example 7.2.5** For $V = \{a, b\}$ the string $s = abab$ is a substring of $t = aaabab$. In this particular case $v = \varepsilon$ (Eq. (7.2.9)).

♠

As in natural languages, a thorough study of a formal language theory must concentrate on grammars and their properties.

Grammars

A grammar is defined as a four-entity substance

$$G = \{V_T, V_N, P, S\} \qquad\qquad (7.2.10)$$

The entities are:

1. A set of *terminal symbols*, often called *primitives* which is denoted by V_T and is a subset of the alphabet V.

2. A set of *nonterminal symbols*, often called *variables* which are used as intermediate quantities in the process of generating an arbitrary outcome. The outcome is *always* composed of terminal symbols, i.e.

of *constants*, contrary to the nonterminal symbols which are variables. This set is denoted by V_N. The sets V_T and V_N must satisfy

$$V_T \cap V_N = \varnothing \,, \, V_T \cup V_N = V \qquad (7.2.11)$$

3. A set of *production rules*, often called *productions* or *rewriting rules*. This set is denoted by P and coupled with V_T, provides the *structure* of the given grammar.

4. A *starting symbol* (*root*) denoted by S, where $S \in V_N$.

The following example taken from the natural language English, will help to clarify the roles of the four entities of a grammar in generating an outcome, i.e. a *legitimate sentence*.

■ **Example 7.2.6** Consider the simple sentence "the baby walks." A tree structure given in Fig. 7.2.1 describes the generation of this sentence. All the symbols in Fig. 7.2.1 are included of course in the given alphabet.

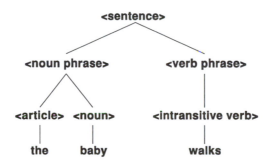

■ **Figure 7.2.1** A tree structure for generating "the baby walks." Specifically we have

$$' \text{the}' \,, \, ' \text{baby}' \,, \, ' \text{walks}' \, \in V_T$$

while

$$< \text{sentence} >, \quad < \text{noun phrase} >, \quad < \text{verb phrase} > \quad \in V_N$$

$$< \text{article} >, \quad < \text{noun} >, \quad < \text{intransitive verb} > \quad \in V_N$$

The specific production rules which are used in this example are

    I. $< \text{sentence} > \rightarrow < \text{noun phrase} > < \text{verb phrase} >$

    II. $< \text{noun phrase} > \rightarrow < \text{article} > < \text{noun} >$

    III. $< \text{verb phrase} > \rightarrow < \text{intransitive verb} >$

    IV. $< \text{article} > \rightarrow \text{the}$

    V. $< \text{noun} > \rightarrow \text{baby}$

    VI. $< \text{intransitive verb} > \rightarrow \text{walks}$

We start with a tree's root which is the abstract concept $< \text{sentence} >$. As previously requested, $< \text{sentence} >$ is an element in V_N. Next we apply production I and using substitution obtain the next level of the tree. productions II and III are applied next and provide the 3-rd level of the tree. Finally, productions IV through VI are substituted and the sentence "the baby walks" which consists only of primitives is obtained.

♠

In view of the previous example we may now furnish a general definition of a formal language.

■ **Definition 7.2.6** The *formal language* generated by a grammar $G = \{V_T, V_N, P, S\}$ is a set of strings over V, denoted by $L(G)$, which satisfy the requirements:

1. Each string is composed only of primitives.

2. Each string can be *derived* from S via substitution of productions from P.

Usually the set of productions P is restricted to include only the elements

$$A \rightarrow B \tag{7.2.12}$$

where

$$A \in (V_N \cup V_T)^+ - V_T^+ \qquad\qquad (7.2.13)$$

and

$$B \in (V_N \cup V_T)^* \qquad\qquad (7.2.14)$$

i.e. the set of productions is a set mappings $A \to B$, where A consists of at least one element of V_N i.e. at least one nonterminal and B is an arbitrary ordered arrangement of terminals and nonterminals.

It must be remembered that either side of an arbitrary production is a *sentence* in the sense of Definition 7.2.1 and that each level of a tree structure of a sentence in $L(G)$ is a *nonterminal sentence* (except for the bottom level which is the terminal sentence itself).

■ **Example 7.2.7** Consider the grammar $G = \{V_T, V_N, P, S\}$ where

$$V_T = \{a, b\}, \quad V_N = \{S\}, \quad P = \{S \to aSb, S \to ab\}$$

If the first production is applied consecutively $(n - 1)$ times we obtain

$$S \to aSb \to aaSbb \to \ldots \to a^{n-1} S b^{n-1}$$

and by substituting $S \to ab$ the final outcome is $a^n b^n$. It is easily seen that the language $L(G)$ consists only of the sentences '$a^n b^n$', $n \geq 1$

♠

A grammar can be used in one of two modes:

1. *Generative*: The grammar is applied to generate a string of primitives via productions from P. This string is a *sentence* in the language $L(G)$.

2. *Analytic*: Given a sentence in the general sense of Definition 7.2.1, and the specifications of G, check:

    I.   Is the sentence in $L(G)$, i.e. can it be generated using G?

II.   The sentence's structure if it is indeed in $L(G)$.

As previously stated (Definition 7.2.3) a language is a subset L of V^*. If only terminal symbols are considered, a general language is a subset L of V_T^*. If the number of elements in L, denoted by $|L|$ is finite, L is said to be *finite*. Clearly, many languages are infinite since V_T^* is infinite. The number of *all* languages given V_T is not even denumerable. In fact the number of all languages is (\) (i.e. the set of all languages is equivalent to the set of all real numbers). By introducing a grammar G, we select a unique formal language $L(G)$ which through the imposed set of productions P, can be used for practical applications in pattern recognition.

PROBLEMS

1. For the alphabet $V = \{0,1\}$ find all the sentences with less than four symbols.

2. For a general alphabet V, obtain necessary and sufficient conditions for two arbitrary strings s and t of lengths 3 and 2 respectively to satisfy $s \circ t = t \circ s$.

3. Let $V = \{a,b,c\}$, $L_1 = \{a,b,ab,bc\}$, $L_2 = \{a,b\}$. Find the union and intersection of the concatenations $L_1 \circ L_2$ and $L_2 \circ L_1$.

4. Consider the grammar $G = \{V_T, V_N, P, S_1\}$ where

$$V_T = \{a,b\}, \quad V_N = \{S_1, S_2\}$$

and

$$P = \{S_1 \rightarrow S_2 ab, \, S_1 \rightarrow S_2 ba, \, S_2 \rightarrow a, \, S_2 \rightarrow b\}$$

What is the formal language $L(G)$?

5. Consider the grammar $G = \{V_T, V_N, P, S\}$ where

$$V_T\{a,b,c\}\,,\quad V_N = \{S\}$$

and

$$P = \{S \to aSb^2,\ \ S \to a,\ \ S \to bc\}$$

Which of the following sentences are *legitimate*, i.e. belong to $L(G)$:

(i) $abcb^2$ (ii) a^3b^4 (iii) acb^3 (iv) cb (v) a^5b^8

7.3   GRAMMAR TYPES

Throughout this chapter the following notation will be used:

1. Nonterminals will be denoted by capital letters (possibly indexed, for example S_1).

2. Terminals will be denoted by lower-case letters (possibly indexed, for example a_1).

3. Mixed strings, i.e. strings consisting of terminals and nonterminals, will be represented by lower-case Greek letters (i.e. α, β).

A general production is given by
$$\alpha_1 \to \beta_2 \tag{7.3.1}$$

where a string α_1 is *replaced by* the string β_2. Four types of grammars are considered:

1. An *UnRestricted Grammar (UR)* has no restriction on its productions. Each production is given by Eq. (7.3.1) where $\alpha_1 \in V^+$ and $\beta_2 \in V^*$.

2. A *Context Sensitive Grammar (CS)* allows only productions (originally given by Eq. (7.3.1)) of the form

$$\alpha A_1 \beta \rightarrow \alpha \beta_2 \beta \qquad (7.3.2)$$

where

$$\alpha, \beta \in V^*, \ A_1 \in V_N, \ \beta_2 \in V^* - \varepsilon \qquad (7.3.3)$$

Any of the strings α, β may equal ε and since A_1 is a single symbol and $|\beta_2| \geq 1$, we obtain

$$|\alpha A_1 \beta| \leq |\alpha \beta_2 \beta| \qquad (7.3.4)$$

(or $|\alpha_1| \leq |\beta_2|$ in Eq. (7.3.1)). By Eq. (7.3.2) the nonterminal A_1 can be replaced by the string β_2, only when A_1 appears in the context $\alpha A_1 \beta$. This grammar is therefore context sensitive.

3. A *Context Free Grammar (CF)* has productions of the form

$$A_1 \rightarrow \beta_2 \qquad (7.3.5)$$

where $A_1 \in V_N$ and $\beta_2 \in V^* - \varepsilon$. Considering the general form of productions we get

$$1 = |\alpha_1| \leq |\beta_2| \qquad (7.3.6)$$

This grammar allows the replacement of a nonterminal A_1 independently of its context, and is therefore a context free grammar.

4. A *Finite State Grammar (FS)* has productions of the form

$$A_1 \rightarrow a \qquad (7.3.7)$$

or

$$A_1 \rightarrow aB_2 \qquad (7.3.8)$$

where $A_1, B_2 \in V_N$ and $a \in V_T$. An alternative FS grammar is obtained if Eq. (7.3.8) is replaced by

$$A_1 \rightarrow B_2 a \qquad (7.3.9)$$

However, given the productions set P, only *one* of the forms given by Eqs. (7.3.8) and (7.3.9) is allowed.

■ **Example 7.3.1**   Let $G = \{V_T, V_N, P, S\}$ where

$$V_T = \{a, b, c\}, \quad V_N = \{S, A, B\}$$

(a) An unrestricted grammar is obtained if the set of productions is for example

$$\begin{aligned}
P : S &\rightarrow abA \\
A &\rightarrow c \\
S &\rightarrow cB \\
B &\rightarrow aA \\
B &\rightarrow \varepsilon
\end{aligned}$$

(b) A context sensitive grammar is obtained if for example

$$\begin{aligned}
P : S &\rightarrow aBbc \\
S &\rightarrow ab \\
aB &\rightarrow aAc \\
Ac &\rightarrow abc \\
Bb &\rightarrow Acb
\end{aligned}$$

(c) A context free grammar is obtained from the productions set

$$\begin{aligned}
P : S &\rightarrow aAc \\
S &\rightarrow bB \\
S &\rightarrow AB \\
A &\rightarrow aB \\
A &\rightarrow c \\
B &\rightarrow b
\end{aligned}$$

(d) A finite state grammar is obtained if for example

$$P: S \rightarrow aA$$
$$S \rightarrow bB$$
$$A \rightarrow \varepsilon$$
$$A \rightarrow a$$
$$B \rightarrow b$$
$$B \rightarrow c$$

It should be noted that the production $A \rightarrow \in$ is allowed *only* in an unrestricted grammar.

Graphical Representation of an FS Grammar

The FS grammars have several properties which account for their popularity. One of the important features of these grammars, is their simple graphical representation. A graph of a finite state grammar is designed as follows:

1. The graph's nodes include all the nonterminals in V_N and an additional *terminal node* T which is not in the alphabet V.
2. Each production of the type $A_i \rightarrow aA_j$ is represented by an edge labeled a, and directed from A_i to A_j.
3. Each production of the type $A_i \rightarrow a$ is represented by an edge labeled a, and directed from A_i to T.

■ **Example 7.3.2** Consider a finite state grammar $G = \{V_T, V_N, P, S_1\}$, where

$$V_T = \{a, b, c\} , \quad V_N = \{S, A, B\}$$

and

$$P:S \rightarrow aA$$
$$S \rightarrow bB$$
$$A \rightarrow cB$$
$$B \rightarrow a$$
$$A \rightarrow c$$

The directed graph which represents this grammar is

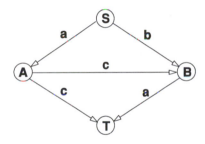

■ **Figure 7.3.1**   A graphical representation of an FS grammar

In the case of an FS grammar, the problem of *recognizing* whether an arbitrary sentence belongs to the language $L(G)$ is answered by the next result.

■ **Theorem 7.3.1**

For a given finite state grammar G, an arbitrary string $x = x_1 x_2 \ldots x_n$, $x_i \in V_T$ is in $L(G)$ if and only if there exists at least one path $(x_1, x_2, \ldots, x_n)$ from S to T.

Proof:

(a)   If $(x_1, x_2, \ldots, x_n)$ be a path from S to T, then there are $(n-1)$ productions

$$
\begin{aligned}
S &\rightarrow x_1 A_1 \\
A_1 &\rightarrow x_2 A_2 \\
&\;\;\vdots \\
A_{n-2} &\rightarrow x_{n-1} A_{n-1}
\end{aligned}
$$

and another production

$$A_{n-1} \rightarrow x_n$$

By substitution we obtain $x_1 x_2 \ldots x_n \in L(G)$.

(b) The opposite part of the theorem is left as an exercise for the reader.

□

7.4   THE SYNTACTIC PATTERN RECOGNITION PROBLEM

We may now use the concepts introduced in the previous section to establish the connection between grammars, formal languages and pattern recognition. Consider a $2-$class pattern recognition problem. Let the patterns of these classes, C_1 and C_2, be *composed* of features from a set V_T. These features are the *terminals* from Section 7.2. Thus, each pattern may be regarded as a sentence since it is composed of terminals. Let G be a grammar such that its language $L(G)$ consists only of patterns (sentences) which belong to C_1. Then, any incoming pattern can be classified in C_1 if it belongs to $L(G)$. Otherwise, it will be classified at C_2.

■ **Example 7.4.1** Consider a CF grammar $G = \{V_T, V_N, P, S\}$ where

$$V_T = \{a, b\}, \quad V_N = \{S, A\}$$

and the production set is

$$P: S \to aSb$$
$$S \to b$$

The language $L(G)$ consists of the strings $\{b; a^n b^{n+1}, n \geq 1\}$. If a $2-$class classification problem is such that C_1 includes only the patterns $\{b; a^n b^{n+1}, n \geq 1\}$ while C_2 includes only the patterns $\{a^n b^n, n \geq 1\}$, we can classify an incoming pattern x using the following rule:

$$x \in C_1 \text{ iff } x \in L(G)$$

$$(7.4.1)$$

$$x \in C_2 \text{ iff } otherwise$$

The procedure which has to answer the question whether or not a given string is *grammatically correct* is called *parsing*.

Generally we deal with m classers $\{C_i\}_{i=1}^m$ and associated languages $\{L_i\}_{i=1}^m$ formed by grammars $\{G_i\}_{i=1}^m$. An incoming pattern x is decomposed and is classified in C_i if it is a sentence in L_i. The pattern may be assigned to several classes if the languages are not disjoint but may also be rejected if does not belong to any L_i, $1 \leq i \leq n$ and represents for example 'noise'.

A most important subject regarding this process is syntactic pattern description.

7.5 SELECTING PRIMITIVES

The selection of primitives by which the patterns of interest are going to be described, depends upon the type of data and the associated application. The important requirements are that the primitives provide reasonable description of the patterns with respect to their structural relations and that they can also be easily recognized by nonsyntactic methods, since their own structural formation is not important.

■ **Example 7.5.1** Consider the problem of separating between all rectangles and all the other four sided polygons. We select the primitives

$$
\begin{array}{ll}
a: & 0^0 \text{ horizontal edge} \\
b: & 90^0 \text{ vertical edge} \\
c: & 180^0 \text{ horizontal edge} \\
d: & 270^0 \text{ vertical edge}
\end{array}
$$

and the set of all the triangles will be represented by the string *abcd*. If we want to distinguish between rectangles of different sizes we select as primitives edges a_0, b_0, c_0, d_0 of length 1 pointing at the same directions. The set of all rectangles is

$$L = \{a_0^n\, b_0^m\, c_0^n\, d_0^m \; ; \; n,m = 1,2,3,...\}$$

Constructing a Pattern Grammar

Once a set of primitives has been chosen for the pattern, we need to design a grammar whose language will describe the training patterns. As much as it would be desirable to obtain such a grammar automatically from the string of primitives which describe the patterns, it is usually the user who constructs an appropriate grammar based on personal knowledge and experience.

■ **Example 7.5.2** Consider the language

$$L = \{a^n b^n c^n \; ; \; 1 \le n \le 3\}$$

which may represent for example the set of all equilateral triangles with one horizontal side and side length 1,2,3 provided that *a,b,c* are the following primitives:

$$a: \quad 0^0 \text{ horizontal unit length}$$
$$b: \ 120^0 \text{ unit length}$$
$$c: \ 240^0 \text{ unit length}$$

This language can be obtained using the following finite state grammar $G = (V_T, V_N, P, S)$. The terminals and nonterminals are taken as

$$V_T = \{a, b, c\}$$
$$V_N = \{S, A, B, C, D, E, F, G, H, I, J, K\}$$

and the production rules (P) are set as:

$S \rightarrow aA$	$C \rightarrow bI$	$H \rightarrow bK$
$S \rightarrow aC$	$D \rightarrow bF$	$I \rightarrow c$
$A \rightarrow aB$	$F \rightarrow bJ$	$J \rightarrow cI$
$A \rightarrow aD$	$E \rightarrow bG$	$K \rightarrow cJ$
$B \rightarrow aE$	$G \rightarrow bH$	

The triangle $a^2 b^2 c^2$ for example is obtained by using the productions

$$S \rightarrow aA$$
$$A \rightarrow aD$$
$$D \rightarrow bF$$
$$F \rightarrow bJ$$
$$J \rightarrow cI$$
$$I \rightarrow c$$

♠

Finding a grammar for a language is a problem that usually does not have a unique solution. In the case of Example 7.5.2 we may use also a context free grammar $G(V_T, V_N, P, S)$ where

$$V_T = \{a, b, c\}$$
$$V_N = \{S, A, B, C, D, E, F\}$$

and

$$P = \begin{cases} S \rightarrow aAF & A \rightarrow aBF & D \rightarrow bC \\ A \rightarrow b & B \rightarrow aEF & C \rightarrow b \\ A \rightarrow aDF & E \rightarrow bD & F \rightarrow c \end{cases}$$

Clearly, this is a more attractive solution.

In the next famous example [Ledley 1965] a context free grammar describes submedian and telocentric chromosome patterns (Fig. 7.5.1).

■ **Example 7.5.3** Designing a grammar for chromosomes.

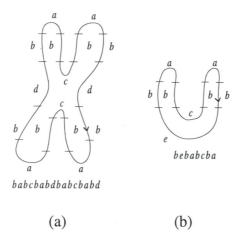

(a)   (b)

■ **Figure 7.5.1** Chromosomes: (a) submedian   (b) telocentric

The grammar has two starting symbols

$$S_1 = \langle \text{submedian chromosome} \rangle , \quad S_2 = \langle \text{telocentric chromosome} \rangle$$

and its sets of terminals and nonterminals are

$$V_T = \{ \widehat{\cap}, \; |, \; \bigcup, \; \langle, \; \smile \; \}$$
$$\phantom{V_T = \{} a \quad b \quad c \quad d \quad e$$

$$V_N = \{\langle\text{submedian chromosome}\rangle, \langle\text{telocentric chromosome}\rangle,$$
$$\langle\text{arm pair}\rangle, \langle\text{left part}\rangle, \langle\text{right part}\rangle, \langle\text{arm}\rangle, \langle\text{side}\rangle, \langle\text{bottom}\rangle\}$$

The production rules (P) are as follows:

$$\langle\text{submedian chromosome}\rangle \rightarrow \langle\text{arm pair}\rangle\langle\text{arm pair}\rangle$$
$$\langle\text{telocentric chromosome}\rangle \rightarrow \langle\text{bottom}\rangle\langle\text{arm pair}\rangle$$
$$\langle\text{arm pair}\rangle \rightarrow \langle\text{side}\rangle\langle\text{arm pair}\rangle$$
$$\langle\text{arm pair}\rangle \rightarrow \langle\text{arm pair}\rangle\langle\text{side}\rangle$$
$$\langle\text{arm pair}\rangle \rightarrow \langle\text{arm}\rangle\langle\text{right part}\rangle$$
$$\langle\text{arm pair}\rangle \rightarrow \langle\text{left part}\rangle\langle\text{arm}\rangle$$
$$\langle\text{left part}\rangle \rightarrow \langle\text{arm}\rangle c$$
$$\langle\text{right part}\rangle \rightarrow c\langle\text{arm}\rangle$$
$$\langle\text{bottom}\rangle \rightarrow b\langle\text{bottom}\rangle$$
$$\langle\text{bottom}\rangle \rightarrow \langle\text{bottom}\rangle b$$
$$\langle\text{bottom}\rangle \rightarrow e$$
$$\langle\text{side}\rangle \rightarrow b\langle\text{side}\rangle$$
$$\langle\text{side}\rangle \rightarrow \langle\text{side}\rangle b$$
$$\langle\text{side}\rangle \rightarrow b$$
$$\langle\text{side}\rangle \rightarrow d$$
$$\langle\text{arm}\rangle \rightarrow b\langle\text{arm}\rangle$$
$$\langle\text{arm}\rangle \rightarrow \langle\text{arm}\rangle b$$
$$\langle\text{arm}\rangle \rightarrow a$$

The arrows at Fig. 7.5.1 indicate the starting primitive and the direction of the chromosome's string.

PROBLEMS

1. In Example 7.5.2 obtain the triangle $a^3b^3c^3$ using the finite state grammar.

2. In Example 7.5.2 obtain the triangle $a^2b^2c^2$ using the context free grammar.

3. Obtain the submedian chromosome, using the productions set of rules in Example 7.5.3.

4. Obtain the telocentric chromosome, using the productions set of rules in Example 7.5.3.

7.6 SYNTAX ANALYSIS FOR RECOGNITION

Once a grammar is designed we want to construct a pattern recognition system that will recognize the patterns generated by the grammar. As previously stated a straightforward approach is to construct a specific grammar for each class of patterns. Let L_i, G_i, $1 \le i \le m$ be the language and grammar associated with the calsses C_i, $1 \le i \le m$ respectively. Let x be an incoming unknown pattern given as a string. The recognition problem is finding $L(G_i)$ such that

$$x \in L(G_i) \tag{7.6.1}$$

The process of determining $L(G_i)$ is *syntax analysis* or *parsing*. Apart from giving an answer to the classification problem, syntax analysis also provides the tree associated with x. The process itself can be described as follows: Given a sentence x and a grammar G construct a triangle with top vertex S and bottom side x (Fig. 7.6.1) inside which we fill the derivations tree.

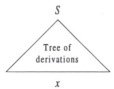

■ **Figure 7.6.1** Parsing x.

If we succeed and get x at the bottom of the tree then $x \in L(G)$. The tree can be found either by starting from the top S-'top-down' parsing or by starting from the bottom x-'bottom-up' parsing.

The parsing process can be very slow if *all* the possible trees are considered. Very seldom we are in a position where only one choice is available at every step. Usually, we have several choices and must find a way to ignore those choices that will eventually lead to nowhere.

Top Down Parsing

Consider a grammar G with

$$V_T = \{a,b,c,d,e\} \ , \ V_N = \{S, A, B\}$$

and productions

$$
\begin{aligned}
S &\rightarrow A & B &\rightarrow a \\
S &\rightarrow AdS & B &\rightarrow b \\
A &\rightarrow BeA & B &\rightarrow c \\
A &\rightarrow B
\end{aligned}
$$

and let $x = adbec$ a given sentence. To parse x top-down, we start from S and choose (the only correct choice as can be easily deduced) the production $S \rightarrow AdS$.   At the next tree level we must choose $A \rightarrow B$ and $S \rightarrow A$ otherwise we end with sentences which are not x. The next step must be $B \rightarrow a$ and $A \rightarrow BeA$.   This follows from $B \rightarrow b$ and $A \rightarrow B$. The final step is $B \rightarrow C$. The different steps of the parsing are shown in Fig. 7.6.2.

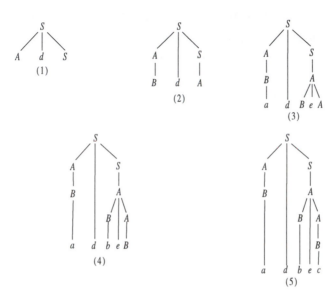

■ **Figure 7.6.2**   Top-down parsing.

There are several tests that can be helpful in avoiding wrong choices while performing the parsing. One test is the following: a nonterminal will create a terminal sequence with at least one terminal in it. Thus, if the number of the symbols still left to be analyzed is greater than the number of terminals left in the sentence, this parsing is incorrect.

Another useful test is the following: Let a denote the current leftmost symbol of the parsed sentence x which needs to be obtained and let A be the current leftmost nonterminal. If A is to be replaced by one of its productions, we need to select only those productions which start with a. To implement this test we must construct a binary matrix which for each nonterminal A determines all the terminals and nonterminals $\{\alpha\}$, such that a production $A \rightarrow \alpha \dots$ exists.

■ **Example 7.6.1**   Let $G = \{V_T, V_N, P, S\}$ where $V_T = \{a,b,c\}$, $V_N = \{S, A\}$ and

$$P = \begin{cases} S \to Ac & A \to Ab \\ S \to a & A \to c \end{cases}$$

The matrix associated with the previously mentioned test is

	S	A	a	b	c
S	0	1	1	0	0
A	0	1	0	0	1

Bottom-Up Parsing

Consider the example previously analyzed for the top-down parsing. The following procedure outlines the basics of bottom-up parsing. At each step we denote by s' the final set of end nodes of the tree. A subset of s' which is a set of leaves (end nodes) of a subtree of the current derivation tree is called a *phrase*. The leftmost phrase is called the *handle* of s'. From Fig. 7.6.2 (5) we obtain the sentence *adbec* with phrases *a,b,c, bec, adbec*. The handle here is *a*. The bottom-up parsing process starts with the final sentence s_0 and repeats the following steps:

1. Find the handle of s_i.
2. Delete the handle, subject to the productions set and obtain s_{i+1}.

In the case given by Fig. 7.6.2 we obtain

$$\begin{aligned}
s_0 &= adbec & s_5 &= AdBeA \\
s_1 &= Bdbec & s_6 &= AdA \\
s_2 &= Adbec & s_7 &= AdS \\
s_3 &= AdBec & s_8 &= S \\
s_4 &= AdBeB &
\end{aligned}$$

In bottom-up left-to-right parsing, there can be at each step many strings that can be replaced by nonterminals, thus forcing us to try many possibilities. Some grammars called *LR(k)* [Knuth 1965] grammars enable the parsing process to be deterministic, provided that it is always possible to look k symbols beyond the current one.

PROBLEMS

1. Use top-down parsing to determine whether the string $a^2b^2c^2$ belongs to $L = \{a^n b^n c^n \; ; \; 1 \leq n \leq 3\}$ with the context free grammar of Example 7.5.2.

2. Using the grammar and language of problem 1, use bottom-up parsing for $x = a^3 b^3 c^3$ and obtain the starting symbol S.

3. Obtain the tree associated with the submedian chromosome, using the productions set of rules in Example 7.5.3.

7.7 STOCHASTIC LANGUAGES

Due to measurement noise and some ambiguity regarding the characteristics of the pattern classes, it is necessary to consider a stochastic model of grammar and stochastic languages.

■ **Definiton 7.7.1** A *stochastic grammar* is a set

$$G_s = \{V_T, V_N, P, Q, S\}$$

where V_T, V_N, P, S are defined as before and Q is a set of probabilities associated with the given productions.

■ **Example 7.7.1** Let $V_T = \{a,b\}$, $V_N = \{S\}$ and

$$(P, Q) = \begin{cases} S \xrightarrow{p} aSb \\ S \xrightarrow{1-p} ab \end{cases}$$

i.e. the first production has an associated probability p and the second $(1-p)$. By applying the first and the second productions alternatively we obtain a sentence $x = a^2 b^2$ whose probability is $p(x) = p(1-p)$. If x can be obtained in several ways, its probability is adjusted accordingly.

■ **Definition 7.7.2** A *stochastic language* $L_s(G_s)$ is a language generated by a stochastic grammar.

In order for the set Q to be consistent we must have

$$\sum_{x \in L_s} p(x) = 1 \tag{7.7.1}$$

Assume that a $x \in L_s$ is generated from S by

$$S \overset{P_1}{=\!>} \alpha_1 \overset{P_2}{=\!>} \alpha_2 \ldots \overset{P_n}{=\!>} \alpha_n = x \tag{7.7.2}$$

where $\alpha_1, \alpha_2, \ldots, \alpha_n$ are intermediate strings and α_{i+1} is obtained from α_i using a production rule P_{i+1} with an associated probability $p_i = p(P_i)$. Then, the probability to obtain x is

$$p(x) = p(P_1) p(P_2 | P_1) \cdots p(P_n | P_1, P_2, \ldots, P_{n-1}) \tag{7.7.3}$$

If always $p(P_i | P_{i_1}, P_{i_2}, \ldots, P_{i_k}) = p(P_i)$, the production P_i is called *unrestricted*. The knowledge of the production probabilities reduces the time consuming of the parsing process for stochastic languages.

For more on syntactic pattern recognition the reader is referred to the excellent book by King Sun Fu (1982).

8 NEURAL NETS AND PATTERN CLASSIFICATION

8.1 INTRODUCTION TO NEURAL NETWORKS

An *artificial neural network* is an *information-processing* system which performs similarly to biological neural networks. These networks were designed as mathematical models of human cognition or neural biology. The basis to these models are the following assumptions:

1. Information processing occurs at a large number of simple elements called *neurons*.
2. Signals are transmitted between neurons along *connection links*.
3. Each connection link is assigned a *weight* which multiplies the transmitted signal.
4. Each neuron applies an *activation function* on its net input (which is the sum of the weighted input signals) to obtain its output signal.

An arbitrary neural network is characterized by

1. The connection links between the neurons which determine the *architecture* of the network.

2. The method for determining the weights, called the *learning algorithm*.
3. The activation which is usually a nonlinear function.

The Neural Net (NN) consists of a large number of neurons, also called cells, nodes or units. Each neuron is connected to other neurons by *directed* links with their associated weights. The weights represent information related to some given problem which the neural net is expected to solve. Typical problems which may be solved by neural nets are pattern classification, storing or recalling patterns and optimal control problems. After absorbing the inputs, each neuron produces its activation as an output signal to other neurons. Each neuron sends a *single* signal to *several* neurons at the same time.

■ **Example 8.1.1** Fig. 8.1.1 illustrates a single neuron Y which receives inputs from other neurons X_1, X_2, X_3. If the weights on the connection links between X_i, $1 \le i \le 3$ and Y are w_i, $1 \le i \le 3$ respectively, the total input to Y is

$$y\_in = w_1 x_1 + w_2 x_2 + w_3 x_3 \tag{8.1.1}$$

where x_i, $1 \le i \le 3$ are the assumed activations of X_i, $1 \le i \le 3$ respectively.

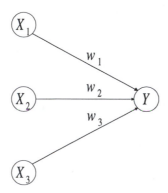

■ **Figure 8.1.1**   A simple neuron with three input connections.

The neuron Y activates its input y_in using its activation function $f(x)$ and sends a signal $y = f(y\_in)$ to the neurons Z_1 and Z_2 (Fig. 8.1.2). The signals received by Z_1 and Z_2 are yv_1 and yv_2 respectively. The neurons X_i, $1 \le i \le 3$ are the *input units*, while Z_i, $1 \le i \le 2$ are the *output units*. The intermediate neuron Y is called a *hidden unit*.

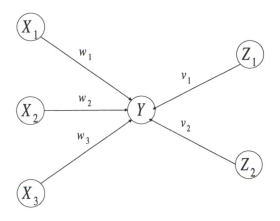

■   **Figure 8.1.2**   A simple neural network

It is usually most convenient to visualize the neurons as units arranged in layers. Within each layer, all the neurons (usually) have the same activation and the same pattern of interconnection. For example, if a neuron in layer A has a connection link to a neuron in layer B, then *each* neuron in A is connected to each neuron in B. The arrangement of the layers and the patterns of the interconnections between layers and inside a single layer is called the *architecture* (this is somewhat a broader definition than the previous one) of the net.

Single-Layer Net

A single-layer net has one layer of weights. The net consists of n input neurons X_i, $1 \le i \le n$ and m output neurons Y_j, $1 \le j \le m$. Each X_i is connected to each Y_j with an associated weight w_{ij}. Two arbitrary input neurons or output neurons are not connected. The single layer net is illustrated in Fig. 8.1.3.

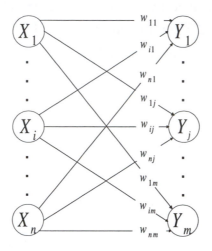

■   **Figure 8.1.3**   A general single-layer net.

A Multilayer Net

A multilayer neural net with n layers consists of one layer of input units, one layer of output units and $(n-1)$ *hidden layers*. Thus, there are $(n+1)$ layers of neurons but only n layers of weights. The first includes the weights associated with the connection links between the input layer and the first hidden layer. These weights are v_{ij} in Fig. 8.1.4 which illustrates the case $n=2$. The last layer of weights (w_{ij}) is associated with the connection links between the last hidden layer and the output layer. The remaining $(n-2)$ layers of weights are each associated with the connection links between the corresponding two consecutive hidden layers.

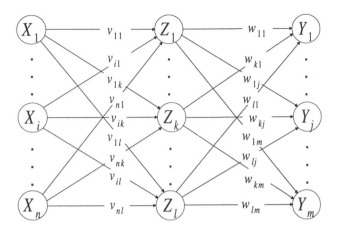

■ **Figure 8.1.4**   A two-layer neural network.

The method of *setting* the weights (*training*) is a significant feature of the neural net. In general, the appropriate process for training the neural net is strongly related to the *type* of problem that needs to be solved.

Supervised Training

In most cases we have a sequence of input vectors each associated with a corresponding target output vector. The weights are adjusted to obtain these output vectors. This process is called *supervised training* and is frequently used in pattern classification. Some of the simplest neural nets are designed so that they can be applied to perform pattern classification. Each output unit is identified with a single class. If the pattern belongs to this category the unit receives a signal of 1. Otherwise it receives −1.

Unsupervised Training

Other neural nets are designed to perform *unsupervised training*. There are no training patterns which represent typical pattern of each class. The neural net is provided a sequence of input vectors but no target output vectors are available. The net adjusts the weights so that input vectors which are 'very close' to each other will be assigned to the same output unit.

Activation Functions

The activation function is naturally application-dependent. Several types are most commonly used.

1. Identity function:

$$f(x) = x, \; all \; x \qquad\qquad (8.1.2)$$

The identity function is usually associated with input units and transfers the whole signal.

2. Binary step function:

$$f(x) = \begin{Bmatrix} 1 & , \; x \geq \theta \\ 0 & , \; x < \theta \end{Bmatrix} \qquad\qquad (8.1.3)$$

This activation function replaces the input x by a binary result. It is 1 if x exceeds or equals a given threshold θ and 0 otherwise.

3. Bipolar step function:

$$f(x) = \begin{Bmatrix} 1 & , \; x \geq \theta \\ -1 & , \; x < \theta \end{Bmatrix} \qquad\qquad (8.1.4)$$

The activation is 1 if x exceeds or equals a given threshold θ and -1 otherwise.

4. Binary sigmoid:

$$f(x) = \frac{1}{1 + \exp(-\sigma x)}, \; \sigma > 0 \qquad\qquad (8.1.5)$$

These activations (Fig. 8.1.5) are particularly useful in neural nets which are trained by *backpropogation* where the values of $f(x)$, $f'(x)$ are both evaluated for each x. Since

$$f'(x) = \frac{\sigma \exp(-\sigma x)}{[1 + \exp(-\sigma x)]^2} = \sigma\, f(x)[1 - f(x)] \qquad (8.1.6)$$

The evaluation of $f'(x)$ adds almost no cost once $f(x)$ has been calculated.

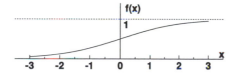

■ **Figure 8.1.5**   Binary Sigmoid, $\sigma = 1$.

5. Bipolar Sigmoid:

$$f(x) = \frac{1 - \exp(-\sigma x)}{1 + \exp(\sigma x)}$$

$$\qquad (8.1.7)$$

$$f'(x) = \frac{\sigma}{2}[1 + f(x)][1 - f(x)]$$

Net Input

Let the matrix $W = (w_{ij})$ consists of the weights associated with the connection links between the units $X_1, X_2 ..., X_n$ and the units $Y_1, Y_2 ..., Y_m$ (Fig. 8.1.3). The net input to unit Y_j is

$$y\_in_j = \mathbf{x}^T \cdot \mathbf{w}_j = \sum_{i=1}^{n} x_i w_{ij} \qquad (8.1.8)$$

where the vector $\mathbf{x} = (x_1, x_2, \ldots, x_n)^T$ consists of the outputs of $X_1, X_2, \ldots, X_n$ and $\mathbf{w}_j$ is the j-th column of W. A *bias* b_j can be included by adding the component 1 to $\mathbf{x}$ and a component b_j to $\mathbf{w}_j$. Then

$$y\_in_j = \mathbf{x}^T \cdot \mathbf{w}_j = b_j + \sum_{i=1}^{n} x_i w_{ij} \qquad (8.1.9)$$

where

$$\mathbf{x}^T = (1, x_1, x_2, \ldots, x_n)$$

$$\qquad (8.1.10)$$

$$\mathbf{w}_j^T = (b_j, w_{1j}, \ldots, w_{nj})$$

A single neuron with a bias is shown in Fig. 8.1.6.

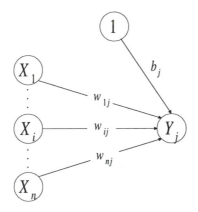

■   **Figure 8.1.6**   A neuron with a bias.

8.2   THE McCULLOCH-PITTS NEURON

The McCulloch-Pitts (MP) neuron is the earliest suggested artificial neuron which illustrates several important features common to many neural nets. It is characterized by the following rules:

Rule 1. The neurons are connected by directed weighted paths.

Rule 2. Each activation is binary, i.e. equals 1 (the neuron *fires*) or 0 (the neuron *does not fire*).

Rule 3. A connection is *excitatory* if its associated weight is positive. Otherwise it is *inhibitory*. All excitatory connections into an arbitrary neuron must have the same weights.

Rule 4. Each neuron has a fixed threshold θ such that the neuron fires if and only if its net input is greater than θ.

Rule 5. Each threshold is prefixed so that any nonzero inhibitory input will prevent the neuron from firing.

Rule 6. It takes a signal a single time step to pass a connection link.

■ **Example 8.2.1** Consider the neuron Y in Fig. 8.2.1. The connections between X_1, X_2 and Y are excitatory. By Rule 3 these connections must have the same weight (each weight is 2). Let x_i, $1 \le i \le 3$ denote the activations of X_i, $1 \le i \le 3$ respectively. Then by Rule 5, the threshold θ of Y must satisfy

$$2x_1 + 2x_2 - x_3 < \theta \qquad (8.2.1)$$

whenever $x_3 \ne 0$. Thus, Y will not fire upon receiving a negative signal from X_3. The maximum value of the left-hand side of Eq. (8.2.1) is then 3, obtained if $x_1 = 1$, $x_2 = 1$ and $x_3 = 1$. If the threshold's value is restricted to integers we must choose $\theta = 4$. If $x_3 = 0$ there is no signal from x_3 and if $x_1 = 1$ and $x_2 = 1$ the net input to Y is 4 and the neuron will fire.

The activation of Y at time t is determined by the activations of X_i, $1 \le i \le 3$ at time $t-1$ (Rule 6). This activation is always 0 except in the case $x_1 = x_2 = 1$, $x_3 = 0$.

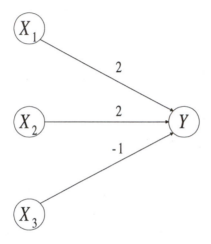

■ **Figure 8.2.1** A McCulloch-Pitts neuron.

♠

Architecture of the MP Neuron

An MP neuron is generally connected to n units via excitatory connections - each associated with a weight $w > 0$ and to m units through inhibitory connections - each associated to a negative weight $-v$ (Fig. 8.2.2).

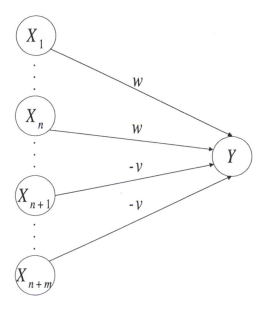

■ **Figure 8.2.2**   Architecture of the MP neuron.

The activation of Y is

$$f(y\_in) = \begin{cases} 1 & , \ y\_in \geq \theta \\ 0 & , \ y\_in < \theta \end{cases} \qquad (8.2.2)$$

where y_in is the total input to Y and θ is the threshold of the neuron. Clearly θ must be chosen so that Y will not fire even if it obtains a single negative signal, i.e. even when a single x_i, $n+1 \leq i \leq n+m$ equals 1. Therefore, θ must satisfy

$$nw - v < \theta \qquad (8.2.3)$$

If θ also satisfies

$$(k-1)w < \theta \leq kw \qquad (8.2.4)$$

Y will fire if it receives at least k excitatory inputs but no inhibitory ones.

8.3   SIMPLE APPLICATIONS OF THE MP NEURON

For simple MP neurons the values of the weights and threshold can be determined by direct analysis. The following examples present MP neurons which model single logic functions. These neurons can be later used as designing elements to obtain an arbitrary phenomenon that can be represented as a logic function.

AND

Let x_1, x_2 denote two inputs which may be 'true' (1) or 'false' (0). The 'AND' function operating on x_1 and x_2 yields the result y whose *truth table* is given in Table 8.3.1 which provides the four training (input, output) pairs. The MP neuron which models the function 'AND' is illustrated in Fig. 8.3.1.

■ **Table 8.3.1**   Truth table for 'AND'.

x_1	$x_2 \rightarrow y$	
1	1	1
1	0	0
0	1	0
0	0	0

In order to prevent Y from firing unless $x_1 = x_2 = 1$ its threshold θ must be greater than 1 and if only integer values are considered we must have $\theta = 2$.

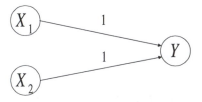

■ **Figure 8.3.1**   MP neuron for 'AND'.

OR

The truth table of 'OR' is given in Table 8.3.2.

■   **Table 8.3.2**   Truth table for 'OR'.

x_1	$x_2 \rightarrow y$	
1	1	1
1	0	1
0	1	1
0	0	0

The MP neuron which functions like 'OR' is illustrated in Fig. 8.3.2. The threshold of Y is obviously $\theta = 1$.

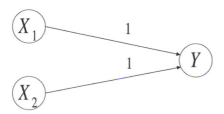

■   **Figure 8.3.2**   MP neuron for 'OR'.

AND NOT

The truth table of 'AND NOT' i.e. $[x_1 \text{ AND}(\text{NOT } x_2)]$ is given in Table 8.3.3.

■   **Table 8.3.3**   Truth table for 'AND NOT'.

x_1	$x_2 \rightarrow y$	
1	1	0
1	0	1
0	1	0
0	0	0

The MP neuron which functions like 'AND NOT' must have one inhibitory connection so that if $x_1 = x_2 = 1$, Y will not fire! Such a neuron is shown in Fig. 8.3.3. Its threshold is $\theta = 1$. The weights and the threshold are not determined uniquely. For example let w, $-v$ be the weights along (X_1, Y) and (X_2, Y) respectively and let θ denote an appropriate threshold of Y. Then, the four requirements of Table 8.3.3 yield:

$$
\begin{aligned}
w - v &< \theta \\
w &\geq \theta \\
-v &< \theta \\
0 &< \theta
\end{aligned}
\tag{8.3.1}
$$

respectively. For the particular choice $v = 1$ we obtain

$$w - 1 < \theta \leq w$$

$$0 < \theta \tag{8.3.2}$$

and if only integer values are considered we have

$$0 < \theta = w \tag{8.3.3}$$

The choice $w = \theta = 1$ is given in Fig. 8.3.3.

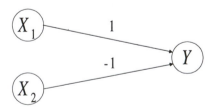

■ **Figure 8.3.3**   MP neuron for 'AND NOT'.

PROBLEMS

1. Obtain an MP neural net for 'XOR' using the relation

$$x_1 \text{ XOR } x_2 \equiv \left[x_1 \text{ AND (NOT) } x_2\right] \text{OR} \left[x_2 \text{ AND (NOT } x_1)\right] \quad (8.3.4)$$

2. If a cold stimulus is applied to a person's skin for a *very short* time, the person will perceive heat. If the stimulus, however, lasts for a longer period of time, the person perceives cold. By using discrete time steps, a simple McCulloch-Pitts neural net which models this phenomenon can be designed. We first assume that if the cold stimulus is applied for one time step, heat is perceived and if it is applied for two time steps cold is perceived.

    We now assign two neurons X_1 and X_2 to receive heat and cold signals respectively. If x_1 and x_2 are the activations of X_1 and X_2 respectively, then

    $$(x_1, x_2) = (1,0) \text{ if heat is applied}$$

    $$(x_1, x_2) = (0,1) \text{ if cold is applied}$$

    The input $(x_1, x_2) = (0,0)$ is also possible. It occurs if a cold stimulus is applied for one time step and then removed.

    Let Y_1 and Y_2 with activations y_1 and y_2 respectively denote neurons which are perceptors for heat and cold respectively. Construct a neural net which will provide *only* the first perception of either heat or cold. Design first 'cold is perceived' followed by 'heat is perceived'.

    The final net should consist of the following features:

    (a) A hot stimulus at time $(t-1)$ is detected as *perception of heat* at time t.

(b) Two consecutive cold stimulus at times $(t-2)$ and $(t-1)$ are detected as *perception of cold* at time t .

(c) A cold stimulus at time $(t-3)$ which is removed (i.e. $x_1(t-2) = x_2(t-2) = 0$) at time $(t-2)$ cause the net to detect *perception of heat* at time t .

8.4 ELEMENTARY NEURAL NETS FOR PATTERN CLASSIFICATION

An important application of neural nets is solving pattern classification problems. We will discuss several approaches, most of which assume a simple single-layer neural net.   However, real-world problems often request the use of multilayer nets.

We open this section by introducing simple neural nets which are capable of performing pattern classification problems.

Preliminaries; A Simple Model

The basic architecture of a single-layer neural net which performs classification, is different from the McCulloch-Pitts architecture.   It produces the net shown in Fig. 8.4.1.   This neural network classifies arbitrary vectors $x = (x_1, x_2, \ldots, x_n)^T$ in R^n and assumes membership in a *single* class. The net is composed of n input neurons X_i, $1 \le i \le n$ (one input unit for each component of x and a single output neuron Y). In addition there is a 'bias' unit denoted by B which adds a bias b to the net input of Y.   Let $x_i, 1 \le i \le n$ denote the activations of X_i, $1 \le i \le n$ respectively. Then, the total net input into Y is

$$net = b + \sum_{i=1}^{n} w_i x_i$$

$$\text{(8.4.1)}$$

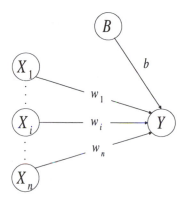

- **Figure 8.4.1**   A general single-layer neural net for pattern classification.

Consider a bipolar activation function to Y, i.e.

$$f(net) = \{ \begin{matrix} 1 \\ -1 \end{matrix} \quad \begin{matrix} , net \geq 0 \\ , net < 0 \end{matrix} \tag{8.4.2}$$

If Y's activation is 1, the output unit fires and the pattern x belongs to class C. If the activation is -1, Y does not fire and x does not belong to C. Thus

$$b + \sum_{i=1}^{n} w_i x_i \geq 0 \Rightarrow x \in C$$

$$\tag{8.4.3}$$

$$b + \sum_{i=1}^{n} w_i x_i < 0 \Rightarrow x \notin C$$

By introducing bias to the model illustrated in Fig. 8.4.1 we eliminate the necessity of assigning a threshold θ to Y. Instead we adjust the bias b and a threshold θ is equivalent to a bias $(b-\theta)$ and a vanishing threshold.

- **Example 8.4.1**   In the case $n=2$ we classify an incoming pattern $x = (x_1, x_2)^T$ in C if and only if the pattern is on the positive side of the straight line

$$b + w_1 x_1 + w_2 x_2 = 0 \tag{8.4.4}$$

which separates between C and the rest of the universe.

♠

If two classes C_1, C_2 exist such that for every incoming pattern

$$b + \sum_{i=1}^{n} w_i x_i \geq 0 \Rightarrow x \in C_1$$

$$\text{(8.4.5)}$$

$$b + \sum_{i=1}^{n} w_i x_i < 0 \Rightarrow x \in C_2$$

then the neural net of Fig. (8.4.1) models and solves a two-class classification problem. The straight line given by Eq. (8.4.4) or in general, the hyperplane

$$b + \sum_{i=1}^{n} w_i x_i = 0 \qquad \text{(8.4.6)}$$

is the familiar decision boundary which separates between two decision regions. The response of Y is +1 if x is in the *positive decision region* and −1 if x is in the negative decision region. Thus, to each x we assign a sign (+) or (−) according to the decision region in which x is a member.

■ **Example 8.4.2** The OR logic function is modeled by two input units X_1, X_2 and a single output unit T (target) with activations x_1, x_2, t respectively. If bipolar activation is applied we obtain the following table which consists of four training patterns and four required responses of the output neuron T:

■ **Table 8.4.1**   Truth table of OR using bipolar activation.

x_1	$x_2 \rightarrow$	t
1	1	1
1	−1	1
−1	1	1
−1	−1	−1

The requirements of Table 8.4.1 are illustrated in Fig. 8.4.2.

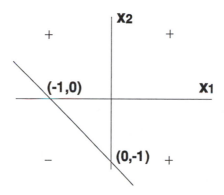

■ **Figure 8.4.2** The logic function OR.

Each of the training patterns is marked by its target value. There are infinite number of possible separation lines. One of them, for example, is $1 + x_1 + x_2 = 0$ i.e. $w_1 = w_2 = 1$ and $b = 1$. We cannot choose $w_1 = w_2 = 1$ and $b = -1$ since $(1,1)$ for example must be on the positive side of the separation line.

A more mathematical approach for obtaining a separation line is to observe the net which models OR with its free parameters w_1, w_2, b (Fig. 8.4.3).

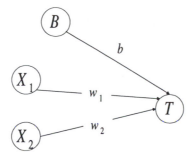

■ **Figure 8.4.3** The neural net of OR.

By substituting the four training patterns and the desired responses we get

$$
\begin{array}{ll}
(1,1) : b+w_1+w_2 \geq 0 \\
(1,-1) : b+w_1-w_2 \geq 0 \\
(-1,1) : b-w_1+w_2 \geq 0 \\
(-1,-1) : b-w_1-w_2 < 0
\end{array}
\qquad (8.4.7)
$$

The system of inequalities given by Eq. (8.4.7) has an infinite number of solutions. One of them is $w_1=w_2=b=1$ which satisfies the four inequalities. On the other hand there is no solution for which w_1 and w_2 have different signs. Indeed, if $w_1=k^2>0$ and $w_2=-l^2<0$ the third inequality of Eq. (8.4.7) implies $b \geq k^2+l^2$ which contradicts the fourth one which yields $b<k^2-l^2$. If $w_1=-k^2<0$ and $w_2=l^2>0$ the second inequality implies $b \geq k^2+l^2$ which contradicts the fourth inequality by which $b<l^2-k^2$.

♠

So far we emphasized the possibility of using single-layer neural nets to solve pattern classification problems, and presented a simple neural net which models such problems. The next step is to provide learning rules for this net. This topic will be discussed in the remainder of this chapter.

PROBLEMS

1. Obtain a truth table of XOR using bipolar activations, and show that it does not provide a linearly separable classification problem.

2. Prove algebraically that a single-layer neural net which models XOR does not exist.

8.5   HEBB NET

A simple learning rule for a neural net is Hebb rule which can be formulated as follows.

Hebb learning rule

If two interconnected neurons fire at the same time, the weight associated with their connection link should be increased.

A stronger form of learning is obtained if the weight is increased also in the case when both neurons do not fire at the same time. We thus get

The extended Hebb rule

If two interconnected neurons fire or do not fire at the same time, the weight associated with their connection link is increased.

A single-layer which is trained using the extended Hebb rule is called a *Hebb net*. If we apply bipolar activations, a possible formulation to the extended Hebb rule for a Hebb net is

$$w_i(new) = w_i(old) + x_i y \tag{8.5.1}$$

where x_i is the activation of an input unit X_i, $y-$ the activation of an output unit Y and w_i is the weight associated with the connection link between X_i and Y. In order to include bias we add the connection link between Y and an input unit B with constant activation 1, which is associated with the weight b.

The right-hand side of Eq. (8.5.1) implies that should X_i (or B) and Y fire and not fire alternately, the associated weight must be *decreased*.

The simplest form of using Hebb learning rule is to pass once through the training set and adjust the weights accordingly.

■ **Example 8.5.1** To obtain a separation line for the logic function AND one should find w_1, w_2 and b such that the truth table (Table 8.5.1).

■ **Table 8.5.1**   Truth table for AND using bipolar activations.

$$
\begin{array}{ccc}
x_1 & x_2 \to t \\
1 & 1 & 1 \\
1 & -1 & 0 \\
-1 & 1 & 0 \\
-1 & -1 & 0 \\
\end{array}
$$

will be obtained by a neural net.   Consider the initial values $w_1 = w_2 = b = 0$ and denote

$$\Delta w_i = w_i(new) - w_i(old) = x_i t, \ 1 \le i \le 2$$

$$ (8.5.2) $$

$$\Delta b = b(new) - b(old) = t$$

The four 'extended patterns', namely

$$
\begin{aligned}
x_1 &= (1,1,1) \\
x_2 &= (1,-1,1) \\
x_3 &= (-1,1,1) \\
x_4 &= (-1,-1,1)
\end{aligned}
$$

enter the neural net and w_i, $1 \le i \le 2$ and b are adjusted using Eq. (8.5.2). The process is described in Table 8.5.2.

■ **Table 8.5.2**   Hebb rule applied to AND, using bipolar activations.

Input			Target	Weight Changes			Weights		
x_1	x_2	1	t	Δw_1	Δw_2	Δb	w_1	w_2	b
1	1	1	1	1	1	1	1	1	1
1	-1	1	-1	-1	1	-1	0	2	0
-1	1	1	-1	1	-1	-1	1	1	-1
-1	-1	1	-1	1	1	-1	2	2	-2

The final separation line is $2x_1 + 2x_2 - 2 = 0$ (Fig. 8.5.1). The decision boundaries suggested by the system at the interim stages are illustrated in Figs. (8.5.2) through (8.5.4). In this case the fourth training pattern is not needed and the decision boundary after the first three training patterns is already final.

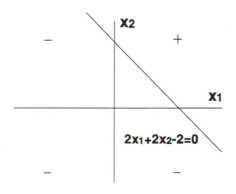

■ **Figure 8.5.1** Getting a separation line for AND.

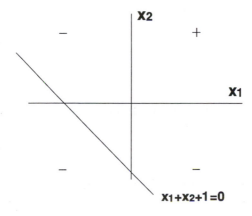

■ **Figure 8.5.2** Decision boundary after first training pattern.

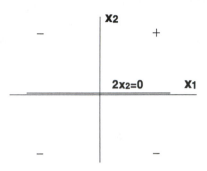

■ **Figure 8.5.3**   Decision boundary after second training pattern.

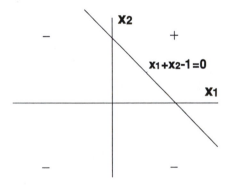

■ **Figure 8.5.4**   Decision boundary after third training pattern.

♠

The Hebb learning rule is limited and does not always provide a linear separator even if there is one. In the next example, the use of binary activations prevents the neural net from learning some of the patterns.

■ **Example 8.5.2** Consider a neural net which is assembled to model AND, using binary activations. The associated truth table is given in Table 8.3.1 and by applying Hebb rule and the initial conditions $w_1 = w_2 = b = 0$ we obtain

■ **Table 8.5.2**   Hebb rule applied unsuccessfully to AND using binary activations.

Input			Target	Weight Changes			Weights		
x_1	x_2	1	t	Δw_1	Δw_2	Δb	w_1	w_2	b
1	1	1	1	1	1	1	1	1	1
1	0	1	0	0	0	0	1	1	1
0	1	1	0	0	0	0	1	1	1
0	0	1	0	0	0	0	1	1	1

Clearly, if the target t is 0, no learning occurs.

♠

In the next example the Hebb net is applied to classify letters - represented by pixel matrices.

■ **Example 8.5.3** Consider a pattern classification problem where each pattern is either the letter 'M' or the letter 'L' represented by 5x5 pixel matrices (Fig. 8.5.5).

```
X   ·   ·   ·   X        X   ·   ·   ·   ·

X   X   ·   X   X        X   ·   ·   ·   ·

X   ·   X   ·   X        X   ·   ·   ·   ·

X   ·   ·   ·   X        X   ·   ·   ·   ·

X   ·   ·   ·   X        X   X   X   X   X
      Pattern 'M'              Pattern 'L'
```

■ **Figure 8.5.5**   Representation of 'M' and 'L' by pixels.

An arbitrary pattern is represented by a 25-component vector. The pixels 'x' and '.' are represented by the values 1 and −1 respectively and each vector is obtained by concatenating the rows of the corresponding pixel matrix starting at the top. The Hebb net consists of 25 input units and an output unit. There is no need to include here a bias unit.

The patterns 'M' and 'L' are therefore

$$\text{'M'} = (1-1-1-11,11-111,1-11-11,1-1-1-11,1-1-1-11)^T$$
$$\text{'L'} = (1\ -1\ -1\ -1\ -1,1\ -1\ -1\ -1\ -1,\ 1\ -1\ -1\ -1\ -1,\ 1\ -1\ -1\ -1\ -1,\ 11111)^T$$

and the desired outputs are 1 for 'M' and −1 for 'L'. If we start with $w_i = 0, 1 \leq i \leq 25$ and feed the system with the pattern 'M' and $t = 1$, we obtain that the weight change vector $\Delta w_1 = (\Delta w_{11}, \Delta w_{12}, \ldots, \Delta w_{1n})$ equals to 'M'. As we start with homogeneous initial conditions, the new weight vector is also 'M'. Since $t = -1$ (no response) for the training pattern 'L', the second weight change vector is '−L' and the final weight vector is

$$W_f = \text{'M'} - \text{'L'} = (0\,0\,0\,0\,2, 0\,2\,0\,2\,2, 0\,0\,2\,0\,2, 0\,0\,0\,0\,2, 0 - 2 - 2 - 2\,0)^T$$

The net input into the output unit when 'M' is fed into the system is $W_f^T \text{'M'} = 20 > 0$ and the response is 1. If 'L' enters the system, the net input is $W_f^T \text{'L'} = -20 < 0$ and the response is −1 as desired. If an incoming pattern, given as a 25-component vector, includes noise or some wrong measurements it may still be classified as 'M' or 'L' provided that the noise and the errors in measurements are significantly small. For example, the pattern in Fig. 8.5.6 is similar to 'M'. Its representation as a 25-component vector is

```
X   ·   ·   ·   ·

X   X   ·   X   X

·   ·   X   ·   X

X   ·   ·   ·   X

X   ·   ·   ·   X
```

■ **Figure 8.5.6**   A pattern which resembles M.

$$\text{`M'} = (1 \ -1 \ -1 \ -1 \ -1, 11 \ -111, \ -1 \ -11 \ -11, 1 \ -1 \ -1 \ -11, 1 \ -1 \ -1 \ -11)^T$$

and W_f^T 'M'$=16$, i.e. the pattern definitely produces a positive response and therefore classified in the M-class.

♠

We now return and discuss the limitations of the Hebb net.   In Example 8.5.2, using the Hebb rule with binary activations, prevented the *learning* of three out of four training patterns.   Consequently, the Hebb neural net could not provide a linear separator for the AND logic function, although such a separator exists (Example 8.5.1).   However, even if the Hebb net learns all the patterns and even if a linear separator exists, there is no guarantee that the final weights will indeed provide an appropriate separator.

PROBLEMS

1. Consider 3-D four bipolar training patterns and outputs given by

Input			Target
x_1	x_2	x_3	t
-1	-1	1	1
1	-1	-1	-1
1	-1	1	-1
-1	1	1	-1

Assume vanishing initial conditions $w_1 = w_2 = w_3 = b = 0$.

(a) Show that the final set of weights using the Hebb net provides the decision boundary $-2x_1 - 2 = 0$.

(b) Does this plane correctly classify all the patterns?

(c) Does a linear separator exist for this problem?

2. Repeat Example 8.5.3 for the letters 'D' and 'O'.

3. Explain the difference between the performance of the Hebb nets for Example 8.5.3 and problem 2.

8.6   THE PERCEPTRON

The limitations of the Hebb rule are not shared by another learning procedure which was also implemented in the earliest neural nets - the perceptron. Furthermore, sufficient conditions for the convergence of its iterative process exist.

The basic perceptron consists of three layers of neurons: a layer of *sensory units* S_i, $1 \leq i \leq m$; a layer of *associative units* X_i, $1 \leq i \leq n$ and a layer of *response units* Y_j, $1 \leq j \leq k$. The case of a single response unit is illustrated in Fig. 8.6.1.   Each of the associative units is randomly connected to the sensory units with connection links over which the weights are prefixed.   The sensory units transfer the stimuli from the measurement devices to the associative units and since no learning occurs at this stage, we may observe the associative units as input units and just consider the second and third layers (Fig. 8.6.2). We also assume a bias associative unit B. The activations x_i, $1 \leq i \leq n$ of the associative units are binary or bipolar, while that of Y is $1, 0$ or -1. The net input of the response unit Y is

$$y\_in = \sum_{i=1}^{n} w_i x_i + b \qquad (8.6.1)$$

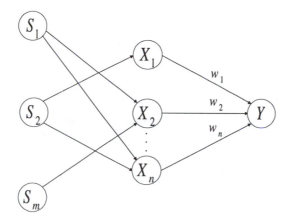

■ **Figure 8.6.1**   A perceptron model.

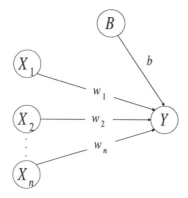

■ **Figure 8.6.2**   Associative and response units.

and its activation is defined by

$$f(y\_in) = \begin{cases} 1 & , & y\_in > \theta \\ 0 & , & -\theta \le y\_in \le \theta \\ -1 & , & y\_in < -\theta \end{cases} \qquad (8.6.2)$$

Thus, the perceptron's output is 1 if the response unit's activation exceeds a given threshold θ. If the net input falls within a band of width θ around zero, the activation is set to zero. Otherwise it equals -1. The *target* is always $+1$ or -1. If it is 1, an error occurs whenever $f(y\_in)$ is either -1 or 0 and the weights associated with the connection links between the associative units and the response unit, will be adjusted by the perceptron learning rule.

The purpose of introducing the threshold θ is to be able to decisively distinguish between a positive and a negative response. This threshold determines a *neutral zone* between the two choices, and cannot be included in the bias b. Indeed, a positive response occurs if

$$\sum_{i=1}^{n} w_i x_i + b - \theta > 0 \qquad\qquad (8.6.3)$$

while a negative one yields

$$\sum_{i=1}^{n} w_i x_i + b + \theta < 0 \qquad\qquad (8.6.4)$$

Clearly, we cannot replace b and θ by a single parameter $(b-\theta)$ in Eq. (8.6.3) since in Eq. (8.6.4) that single parameter should be $b+\theta \neq b-\theta$.

For each pattern we calculate the response unit's activation $f(y\_in)$. If it is not equal to the target t the weights are adjusted by

$$w_i(new) = w_i(old) + \alpha t x_i \qquad\qquad (8.6.5)$$

where α is a correction coefficient between 0 and 1 which can be observed as the *learning rate* of the perceptor. If, however, $f(y\_in) = t$ the weights are unchanged and the next pattern is tested. Each *iteration* consists of a complete sweep over the set of training patterns. The process stops if throughout an iteration no adjusting of w_i, $1 \leq i \leq n$ occurs, i.e. if all the training patterns provide the desired targets.

The complete perceptron algorithm is given next.

Algorithm 8.6.1.

(An algorithm for a basic perceptron: PERC)

Input: $m-$ the number of training patterns.
$n-$ the number of associative units.
$\theta-$ the perceptron threshold.
$\alpha-$ the perceptron learning rate.

$\{x_{ij}\}_{j=1}^{n}-$ The activations of the i - th pattern, $1\le i\le m$.

$t_i, 1\le i\le m-$ The correct targets of the training patterns.

$w_{j0}, 1\le j\le n-$ The initial weights.

b_0 – The initial bias.

Output: $w_j, 1\le j\le n-$ the final weights.

$b-$ the final bias.

Step 1.   Set $it=0$ and $w_{j0}^{*}=w_{j0}, 1\le j\le n, b_0^{*}=b_0$

Step 2.   Set $ichange=0$ and for $1\le i\le m$ do Steps 3-5.

Step 3.   Calculate

$$y\_in=\sum_{j=1}^{n}w_{j0}x_{ij}+b_0$$

Step 4.   Set

$$y=\begin{cases} 1 & , & y\_in>\theta \\ 0 & , & -\theta\le y\_in\le\theta \\ -1 & , & y\_in<-\theta \end{cases}$$

Step 5.   Updating the weights and bias:

If $y \neq t_i$ set

$$ichange = 1$$
$$w_j = w_{j0} + \alpha \, t_i x_{ij}, 1 \leq j \leq n$$
$$b = b_0 + \alpha \, t$$

and then $w_{j0} \leftarrow w_j, 1 \leq j \leq n$ and $b_0 \leftarrow b$.

Otherwise continue.

Step 6.   If $w_j = w_{j0}^*$, $1 \leq j \leq n$; $b = b_0^*$ and $ichange = 0$, output 'learning is successfully completed', it (no. of iterations) and stop. Otherwise, if $w_j = w_{j0}^*$, $1 \leq j \leq n$; $b = b_0^*$ and $ichange = 1$, output 'learning cannot be completed for all training patterns' and stop; otherwise set $it \leftarrow it + 1$; b_0^*, $b_0 \leftarrow b$; w_{j0}^*, $w_{j0} \leftarrow w_j$, $1 \leq j \leq n$ and go to Step 2.

A subroutine PERC which incorporates Algorithm 8.6.1 is given in the appendix.

■ **Example 8.6.1**   Consider the logic function OR where the input is binary and the targets are bipolar, i.e.

x_1	$x_2 \rightarrow t$	
1	1	1
1	0	1
0	1	1
0	0	-1

Choose $\theta = 0.3$, $\alpha = 1$ and $w_{10} = w_{20} = b_0 = 0$. The first iteration provides Table 8.6.1 which has a 'Net' column for y_in and an 'Output' column for $f(y\_in)$.

■ **Table 8.6.1**   The first perceptron iteration for OR.

Input			Net	Output	Target	Weight Changes			Weights		
x_1	x_2	1				Δw_1	Δw_2	Δb	w_1	w_2	b
1	1	1	0	0	1	1	1	1	1	1	1
1	0	1	2	1	1	0	0	0	1	1	1
0	1	1	2	1	1	0	0	0	1	1	1
0	0	1	1	1	−1	0	0	−1	1	1	0

At the end of this iteration or cycle we get the weights $w_1 = w_2 = 1$ and the bias $b = 0$ which yield a temporary *decision band* between the straight lines $x_1 + x_2 - 0.3 = 0$ and $x_1 + x_2 + 0.3 = 0$ (Fig. 8.6.3). In order for the decision band to provide correct results for all of the training patterns, the patterns with positive targets must fall on the positive side of the band, i.e. must satisfy $x_1 + x_2 - 0.3 > 0$, while the patterns with negative targets should fall on the negative side, i.e. satisfy $x_1 + x_2 + 0.3 < 0$.   The threshold is therefore a parameter which indicates the *desired extent* of the decision band as a *separating zone* between the two classes of patterns. In this example the training input pattern (0,0) falls within the decision band and the process is not terminated.   This can be also concluded by comparing the initial and final weights and bias:

$$(w_1, w_2, b) = (1,1,0) \neq (0,0,0) = (w_{10}^*, w_{20}^*, b_0^*)$$

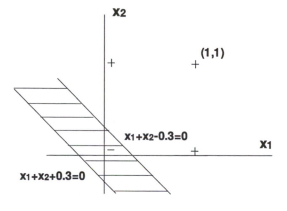

■ **Figure 8.6.3**   Decision boundary after first cycle.

The results of the next cycles are given below.

Cycle 2:

x_1	x_2	1	Net	Output	Target	Δw_1	Δw_2	Δb	w_1	w_2	b
1	1	1	2	1	1	0	0	0	1	1	0
1	0	1	2	1	1	0	0	0	1	1	0
0	1	1	2	1	1	0	0	0	1	1	0
0	0	1	0	0	-1	0	0	-1	1	1	-1

Cycle 3:

x_1	x_2	1	Net	Output	Target	Δw_1	Δw_2	Δb	w_1	w_2	b
1	1	1	1	1	1	0	0	0	1	1	-1
1	0	1	0	0	1	1	0	1	2	1	0
0	1	1	1	1	1	0	0	0	2	1	0
0	0	1	0	0	-1	0	0	-1	2	1	-1

Cycle 4:

x_1	x_2	1	Net	Output	Target	Δw_1	Δw_2	Δb	w_1	w_2	b
1	1	1	2	1	1	0	0	0	2	1	-1
1	0	1	1	1	1	0	0	0	2	1	-1
0	1	1	0	0	1	0	1	1	2	2	0
0	0	1	0	0	-1	0	0	-1	2	2	-1

Cycle 5:

x_1	x_2	1	Net	Output	Target	Δw_1	Δw_2	Δb	w_1	w_2	b
1	1	1	3	1	1	0	0	0	2	2	-1
1	0	1	1	1	1	0	0	0	2	2	-1
0	1	1	1	1	1	0	0	0	2	2	-1
0	0	1	-1	-1	-1	0	0	0	2	2	-1

Since all the training patterns produce outputs which are identical to their corresponding targets the process ends successfully after five cycles. The final weights are $w_1 = w_2 = 2$ and the final bias is $b = -1$.   The training patterns and the final separation band are illustrated in Fig. 8.6.4.

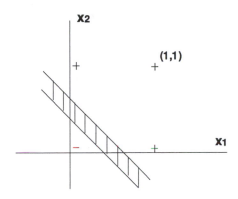

■   **Figure 8.6.4**   A final separation band for OR.

We will next prove a convergence theorem for the perceptron learning rule.

Consider a set X of input training vectors x_i, $1 \leq i \leq m$ with associated target values t_i, $1 \leq i \leq m$ respectively, such that t_i is either 1 or -1, and with an activation function $y = f(y\_in)$ such that

$$y = \begin{cases} 1 & , & y\_in > 0 \\ 0 & , & -\theta \leq y\_in \leq \theta \\ -1 & , & y\_in < -\theta \end{cases}$$

Let the new weights be updated (if $y \neq t$) by

$$w(new) = w(old) + \alpha t x$$

If $y = t$ the weights remain the same.

■ **Theorem 8.6.1**

If a vector $w*$ for which

$$f(x_i^T \cdot w*) = t_i \quad , \quad 1 \leq i \leq m \tag{8.6.6}$$

exists, the perceptron learning rule will converge to a weight vector $w**$ which satisfies

$$f(x_i^T \cdot w**) = t_i \quad , \quad 1 \leq i \leq m \tag{8.6.7}$$

in a finite number of iterations.

The finite weight vector which provides correct responds, is generally not unique.

Proof.

Define

$$T^+ = \{x_i \mid t_i = 1\} \quad , \quad T^- = \{x_i \mid t_i = -1\} \tag{8.6.8}$$

For the sake of simplicity we assume $\alpha = 1$, $\theta = 0$. Consequently, the existence of $w*$ guarantees $(\theta = 0)$

$$x^T \cdot w* > 0 \quad , \quad x \in T^+$$

$$\tag{8.6.9}$$

$$x^T \cdot w* < 0 \quad , \quad x \in T^-$$

Let $T = T^+ \cup (-T^-)$. Then

$$x^T \cdot w* > 0 \quad , \quad x \in T \tag{8.6.10}$$

If an arbitrary response is incorrect (i.e., ≤ 0) for the current weight vector w, the updating is performed $(\alpha = 1)$ by

$$w(new) = w(old) + x \qquad (8.6.11)$$

where x is the training vector which provided the incorrect response.

Let w_0 denote an initial weight vector and denote by y_0 the first training vector with an incorrect response, i.e., it is the first x_i, $1 \le i \le m$ for which $y_0^T \cdot w_0 \le 0$ (if y_0 does not exist the process terminates and $w^{**} = w_0$). To update w_0 we define

$$w_1 = w_0 + y_0$$

and take y_1 as the first training vector which satisfies $y_1^T \cdot w_1 \le 0$. If y_1 does not exist the process terminates and $w^{**} = w_1$. To update w_1 we choose

$$w_2 = w_1 + y_1 = w_0 + y_0 + y_1$$

At every step of the process we have

$$w_k = w_0 + \sum_{i=0}^{k-1} y_i \qquad (8.6.12)$$

and we will show that k cannot increase indefinitely. Let

$$a = \min_{1 \le i \le m} [x_i^T \cdot w^*] \qquad (8.6.13)$$

Clearly $a > 0$ and consequently by Eq. (8.6.12)

$$w_k^T \cdot w^* = w_0^T \cdot w^* + \sum_{i=0}^{k-1} y_i^T \cdot w^* \ge w_0^T \cdot w^* + ka \qquad (8.6.14)$$

If $w_0^T \cdot w^* + ka$ is always negative, k is bounded and the process for obtaining w^{**} is finite. Assume k in contrast to be such that

$w_0^T \cdot w * + ka$ is already positive. By combining Eq. (8.6.14) and the Cauchy-Schartz inequality we get

$$(w_0^T \cdot w * + ka)^2 \le (w_k^T \cdot w*)^2 \le \|w_k\|^2 \|w *\|^2$$

which leads to

$$\|w_k\|^2 \ge \frac{(w_0^T \cdot w * + ka)^2}{\|w *\|^2} \tag{8.6.15}$$

i.e., $\|w_k\|^2 \ge Ak^2$ for some $A > 0$. However, for arbitrary k

$$w_k = w_{k-1} + y_{k-1} \quad , \quad y_{k-1}^T \cdot w_{k-1} \le 0$$

and therefore,

$$\|w_k\|^2 = \|w_{k-1} + y_{k-1}\|^2 \le \|w_{k-1}\|^2 + \|y_{k-1}\|^2$$

This implies

$$\|w_j\|^2 \le \|w_{j-1}\|^2 + \|y_{j-1}\|^2 \quad , \qquad 1 \le j \le k \tag{8.6.16}$$

and we finally obtain

$$\|w_k\|^2 \le \|w_0\|^2 + kb \tag{8.6.17}$$

where

$$b = \max \|x_i\|^2 \quad , \quad 1 \le i \le m \tag{8.6.18}$$

Obviously, Eqs. (8.6.15) and (8.6.17) lead to contradiction if k increases indefinitely. They also provide an upper bound for k given by

$$\frac{(w_0^T \cdot w* + ka)^2}{\|w*\|^2} \le \|w_0\|^2 + kb \tag{8.6.19}$$

If we assume (without a real loss of generality) $w_0 = 0$ we get

$$k \le \frac{b\|w*\|^2}{a^2} \tag{8.6.20}$$

which concludes the proof.   □

Clearly, the bound of Eq. (8.6.20) is not exactly practical since $w*$ (and therefore, a) is unknown. If $\alpha \ne 1$ we obtain a similar proof and for $w_0 = 0$, Eq. (8.6.20) still holds. The validity of the proof for $\theta > 0$ is also straightforward. The restriction that the number of training vectors m is finite can be lifted if $0 < p \le \|x\| \le q < \infty$ for all $x \in X$. If X includes training vectors whose norms are very large or very small, the perceptron learning rule may require an extensive number of iterations to converge.

The perceptron learning rule performs better than the Hebb rule as can be seen from the next example.

■   **Example 8.6.2** Consider the 3-D four training patterns and targets given by

x_1	x_2	x_3	t
−1	−1	1	1
1	−1	−1	−1
1	−1	1	−1
−1	1	1	−1

Here the Hebb rule, starting with $w_i = 0$, $1 \le i \le 3$; $b = 0$, yields the final weights $w_1 = -2$, $w_1 = w_3 = 0$, $b = -2$ which do not provide an appropriate linear separator. If $x^T \cdot w \ge 0$ is considered a positive target and $x^T \cdot w < 0-$ a negative one, the first three patterns are properly classified but not the fourth.

   If we treat the same problem using the perceptron learning rule with $\theta = 0.3$, $\alpha = 1$ we obtain after two iterations $w_1 = w_2 = -2$, $w_3 = 0$, $b = -2$.

♠

PROBLEMS

1. Use the perceptron learning rule for the AND operator, using bipolar patterns and targets, homogeneous initial conditions, $\theta = 0.2$ and $\alpha = 1$.

2. Use the 3-D patterns and targets given by

x_1	x_2	x_3	t
2	0	0	1
2	2	0	1
1	1	1	1
2	0	2	-1
0	0	2	-1

   to train a neural net using the perceptron rule. Assume $\theta = 0.1$ and $\alpha = 0.5$.

8.7   ADALINE

   The ADALINE (ADAptive Linear NEuron) usually uses bipolar activations and targets. It is a single neuron which receives its input from several input units including one (a bias unit) which provides a constant signal 1. The ADALINE's architecture is shown in Fig. 8.7.1.

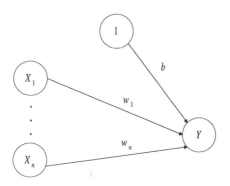

■ **Figure 8.7.1** The architecture of a single ADALINE

If several ADALINEs receive their inputs from the same units, they may create a single-layer net. However, if the outputs of several ADALINEs are the inputs for others, we obtain a multilayer net–MADALINE (Many ADAptive Linear NEurons). The training of the ADALINE is done using the *delta rule* and its general design is given next.

Algorithm 8.7.1

(An algorithm for a single ADALINE: ADAL)

Input: m – the number of training patterns.

n – the number of associate units.

α – the ADALINE learning rate.

$\{x_{ij}\}_{j=1}^{n}$ – the activations of the i-th pattern,

$$1 \leq i \leq m$$

t_i, $1 \leq i \leq m$ – the correct targets of the training

patterns.

w_{j0}, $1 \leq j \leq n$ – the initial weights.

b_0 – the initial bias.

ε – a given tolerance for determining convergence.

N – maximum number of iterations allowed.

Output: w_j, $1 \le j \le n$ – the final weights.

              b – the final bias.

              it – number of iterations.

Step 1.   Set $it = 0$, $w^*_{j0} = w_{j0}$, $1 \le j \le n$; $b^*_0 = b_0$.

Step 2.   For $i = 1, ..., m$ do Steps 3-4.

Step 3.   Compute the net input to the output unit:

$$y\_in = b^*_0 + \sum_{j=1}^{n} w^*_{j0} x_{ij}$$

Step 4.   Update the weights and bias using the *delta rule*:

$$w_j = w^*_{j0} + \alpha(t_i - y\_in)x_{ij}, \quad 1 \le j \le n$$

$$b = b^*_0 + \alpha(t_i - y\_in)$$

and set $w^*_{j0} \leftarrow w_j$, $1 \le j \le n$; $b^*_0 \leftarrow b$

Step 5.   Calculate E: the maximum weight (or bias) change in Steps 2-4; $it = it + 1$

Step 6.   If $E < \varepsilon$ output $\{w_j\}_{j=1}^{n}$, b, it and stop; otherwise if $it = N$ output 'maximum number of iterations exceeded' and stop; otherwise go to Step 2.

If the targets are bipolar we apply in Step 3 an activation function which receives y_in and provides a step function:

$$f(y\_in) = \begin{cases} 1, & y\_in \ge 0 \\ -1, & y\_in < 0 \end{cases}$$

which replaces y_in in Step 4.

The delta rule applied in Algorithm 8.7.1 is a consequence of trying to reduce the squared error of an arbitrary training pattern. This error is $E = (t - y\_in)^2$ where t is the desired output. To minimize it we apply the method of steepest descent, i.e. following the opposite direction of the error's gradient. The error is obviously a function of the current weights w_j, $1 \leq j \leq n$ and the bias b, and since we have

$$\frac{\partial E}{\partial w_j} = -2(t - y\_in)x_j \qquad (8.7.1)$$

we obtain

$$w_j(new) = w_j(old) + \alpha(t - y\_in)x_j \qquad (8.7.2)$$

where α is some prefixed learning rate.

■ **Example 8.7.1**   Consider the OR function using bipolar patterns and targets:

x_1	x_2	t
1	1	1
1	-1	1
-1	1	1
-1	-1	-1

The total squared error for given weights and bias w_1, w_2, b is

$$E = (w_1 + w_2 + b - 1)^2 + (w_1 - w_2 + b - 1)^2$$

$$+ (-w_1 + w_2 + b - 1)^2 + (-w_1 - w_2 + b + 1)^2$$

and its minimum is attained by choosing $w_1 = w_2 = b = 0.5$ i.e., the linear separator is $0.5x_1 + 0.5x_2 + 0.5 = 0$

8.8   BACKPROPAGATION NEURAL NET AND ITS APPLICATIONS

The limitations of single-layer neural networks inspired the interest in multilayer neural networks and the discovery of a general method for training such networks — the *backpropagation* method. It consists of applying the steepest descent method to minimize the error produced by the neural net's output.

The architecture of a multilayer neural network with a single hidden layer is illustrated in Fig. 8.8.1. It has input units $\{X_i\}_{i=1}^{n}$ (and a bias); hidden units $\{Z_j\}_{j=1}^{l}$ (and a bias); output units $\{Y_k\}_{k=1}^{m}$. The weights associated with the connections between the input and the hidden units are v_{ij}; $0 \leq i \leq n$, $1 \leq j \leq l$ and those between the hidden and the output units are w_{jk}; $0 \leq j \leq l$, $1 \leq k \leq m$.

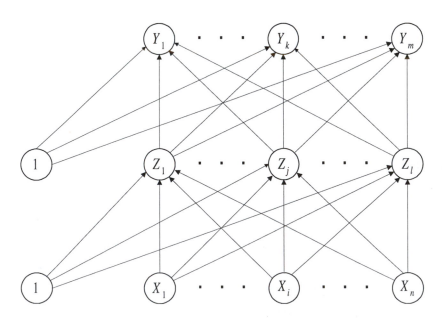

▪ **Figure 8.8.1**   A multilayer neural net with a single hidden layer.

Backpropagation Method

The training of a network using backpropagation consists of three stages: (a) feedforward the input training pattern throughout the neural network; (b) backpropagation analysis of the error; (c) updating the weights. Without loss of generality, we will consider and discuss the single hidden layer case of Fig. 8.8.1.

The feedforward is performed as follows: each input unit receives a signal and transfers it via its connections and weights to all the hidden units. Each Z_j computes its activation and transfers its own signal to all the output units. Finally, each Y_k computes its activation y_k. The set $\{y_k\}_{k=1}^m$ is the network response (or output) of the given input.

The backpropagation analysis of the error is the training stage. Each y_k is compared with its associated target value. This provides the error for that pattern with the unit Y_k. Next, a quantity of δ_k which divides this error back to the units of the previous layer, is computed. In the case of Fig. 8.8.1, these are the hidden units. After obtaining $\{\delta_k\}_{k=1}^m$ we compute similar quantities $\{\delta_j'\}_{j=1}^l$ which are associated with $\{Z_j\}_{j=1}^l$.

Once determined, the numbers $\{\delta_k\}_{k=1}^m$, $\{\delta_j'\}_{j=1}^l$ are used to adjust all the weights simultaneously. The weight w_{jk} (from Z_j to Y_k) is adjusted using δ_k and the activation z_j while v_{ij} (from X_i to Z_j) is adjusted by δ_j' and the activation x_i .

The backpropagation procedure is performed on all the training patterns and if the maximum weight adjustment is less than a given tolerance, the process is completed. The standard training algorithm for the backpropagation neural network with a single hidden layer is given next.

Algorithm 8.8.1 (Training by backpropagation).

Input: A set of M training patterns $x^{(p)} = (x_1^{(p)}, \ldots, x_n^{(p)})^T$, $1 \le p \le M$ with   targets $t^{(p)} = (t_1^{(p)}, \ldots, t_m^{(p)})^T$, $1 \le p \le M$; initial   weights $v_{ij}^{(0)}; 0 \le i \le n, \ 1 \le j \le l$ and

$w_{jk}^{(0)}$, $0 \le j \le l$, $1 \le k \le m$; a tolerance $\varepsilon > 0$; a maximum allowed number of iterations N and a learning rate α.

Output: Final weights for the neural network - v_{ij} and w_{jk} .

Step 1. Set $v_{ij} = v_{ij}^{(0)}$; $0 \le i \le n$, $1 \le j \le l$ and $w_{jk} = w_{jk}^{(0)}$; $0 \le j \le l$, $1 \le k \le m$. Set $it = 0$ (current number of iterations).

Step 2. For $1 \le p \le M$ do Steps 3-4 (feedforward) and Steps 5-7 (backpropagation of the error).

Step 3. For each hidden unit Z_j, $1 \le j \le l$ calculate the total weighted input from input layer:

$$z\_in_j^{(p)} = v_{0j} + \sum_{i=1}^{n} v_{ij} x_i^{(p)}, \ 1 \le j \le l$$

and use the activation function $f(x)$, to get the output signals obtained from the hidden units:

$$z_j^{(p)} = f\ (z\_in_j^{(p)}), \ 1 \le j \le l$$

Step 4. For each output unit Y_k, $1 \le k \le m$ calculate the total weighted input from the hidden layer:

$$y\_in_k^{(p)} = w_{0k} + \sum_{j=1}^{l} w_{jk} z_j^{(p)}, \ 1 \le k \le m$$

and use the activation function $f\ (x)$, to get the output signals

$$y_k^{(p)} = f(y\_in_k^{(p)}), \ 1 \le k \le m$$

Step 5. Calculate the error terms (steepest descent method).

$$\delta_k^{(p)} = (t_k^{(p)} - y_k^{(p)}) f'(y\_in_k), \quad 1 \leq k \leq m$$

the weight correction terms

$$\Delta w_{jk} = \alpha \delta_k^{(p)} z_j ; \quad 1 \leq j \leq l, \ 1 \leq k \leq m$$

and the bias correction terms

$$\Delta w_{0k} = \alpha \delta_k^{(p)} , \quad 1 \leq k \leq m$$

Step 6. For each hidden unit sum its *delta inputs* from the output layer:

$$\delta\_in_j = \sum_{k=1}^{m} \delta_k^{(p)} w_{jk} , \quad 1 \leq j \leq l$$

and its backward error term

$$\delta_j'^{(p)} = \delta\_in_j \ f'(z\_in_j) , \quad 1 \leq j \leq l$$

Then, obtain the weight correction terms

$$\Delta v_{ij} = \alpha \delta_j'^{(p)} x_i ; \quad 1 \leq i \leq n, \ 1 \leq j \leq l$$

and the bias correction term

$$\Delta v_{0j} = \alpha \delta_j'^{(p)} , \quad 1 \leq j \leq l$$

Step 7. Update the weights of the neural net:

$$v_{ij} \leftarrow v_{ij} + \Delta v_{ij} ; \quad 0 \leq i \leq n, \ 1 \leq j \leq l$$

$$w_{jk} \leftarrow w_{jk} + \Delta w_{jk} ; \quad 0 \leq j \leq l, \ 1 \leq k \leq m$$

Step 8. Set $it \leftarrow it + 1$ and

$$e = \sum_{p=1}^{M} \sum_{k=1}^{m} (t_k^{(p)} - y_k^{(p)})^2$$

If $it \leq N$ and $e > \varepsilon$ go to Step 2; otherwise, if $it \leq N$ and $e < \varepsilon$, output v_{ij}, w_{jk}, it and stop; else if $it > N$ output 'no convergence' and stop.

For most problems, using a single hidden layer is sufficient. Sometimes, however, a problem is better treated by using two or more hidden layers. The associated algorithms are basically similar to algorithm 8.8.1.

Mathematical Background

The backpropagation procedure is based on a popular minimization process—the steepest descent method. The learning rules of algorithm 8.8.1 are obtained as follows. For arbitrary input pattern $x = (x_1, \ldots, x_n)^T$ and target $t = (t_1, \ldots, t_m)^T$, the error to be minimized is (the factor ½ is chosen for convenience)

$$E = \frac{1}{2} \sum_{k=1}^{m} (t_k - y_k)^2 \qquad (8.8.1)$$

where

$$y_k = f(y\_in_k) \qquad (8.8.2)$$

and

$$y\_in_k = w_{0k} + \sum_{j=1}^{l} w_{jk} z_j \qquad (8.8.3)$$

Let I, J, K denote fixed values in the sets $\{0, 1, \ldots, n\}, \{0, 1, \ldots, l\}, \{1, 2, \ldots, m\}$ respectively. To apply the steepest descent method we obtain the derivatives

$$\frac{\partial E}{\partial w_{JK}} = -\left(t_K - y_K\right)\frac{\partial y_K}{\partial w_{JK}} = -\left(t_K - y_K\right)f'\left(y\_in_K\right)\frac{\partial\left(y\_in_K\right)}{\partial w_{JK}}$$

$$= -\left(t_K - y_K\right)f'\left(y\_in_K\right)z_J = -\delta_K z_J \tag{8.8.4}$$

and

$$\frac{\partial E}{\partial v_{IJ}} = -\sum_{k=1}^{m}\left(t_k - y_k\right)\frac{\partial y_k}{\partial v_{IJ}} = -\sum_{k=1}^{m}\left(t_k - y_k\right)f'\left(y\_in_k\right)\frac{\partial\left(y\_in_k\right)}{\partial v_{IJ}}$$

$$= -\sum_{k=1}^{m}\delta_k\frac{\partial\left(y\_in_k\right)}{\partial v_{IJ}} = -\sum_{k=1}^{m}\delta_k w_{Jk}\frac{\partial z_J}{\partial v_{IJ}}$$

$$= -\sum_{k=1}^{m}\delta_k w_{JK}f'\left(z\_in_J\right)x_I = -\delta\_in_J f'\left(z\_in_J\right)x_I$$

$$= -\delta_J' x_I \tag{8.8.5}$$

and update the weights using the correction terms

$$\Delta w_{jk} = -\alpha\frac{\partial E}{\partial w_{jk}} \; ; \;\; 0 \le j \le l, \; 1 \le k \le m$$

$$\tag{8.8.6}$$

$$\Delta v_{ij} = -\alpha\frac{\partial E}{\partial v_{ij}} \; ; \;\; 0 \le i \le n, \; 1 \le j \le l$$

where α is some prefixed learning rate.

Activation Function

Due to its role in the design of a neural network the activation function $f(x)$ is expected to be monotonic nondecreasing and to belong to $C^1(-\infty, \infty)$. Usually, it is also expected to *saturate*, i.e.

$$\lim_{x \to \infty} f(x) = A < \infty$$

(8.8.7)

$$\lim_{x \to -\infty} f(x) = B > -\infty$$

Finally, from computational point of view, it is desirable to apply an activation such that $f(x)$ and $f'(x)$ are easily computed. Typical activation functions are the previously defined binary and the bipolar sigmoid functions and $\tanh(x)$.

Initialization

Choosing appropriate initial values for the various weights may determine the speed of the learning process and whether we reach a global or local minimum of the error (a typical problem when applying the steepest descent method). Since updating the weights involve values of activations and their derivatives, it is preferable that these values should not vanish. Consequently it is usually advisable to choose initial weights which are not too large. For example, one could choose the initial weights randomly within the range $(-0.5, 0.5)$.

A modification to this trivial choice is the Nguyen-Widrow initialization. The initial weights and biases from the hidden layer to the output layer are chosen randomly, say between -0.5 to 0.5. As to the initial weights over the connections between the input and the hidden layers, they are determined using the following procedure. Define a scale factor

$$\beta = 0.7 \sqrt[n]{l} \qquad\qquad (8.8.8)$$

where n and l are the numbers of the units at the input and hidden layers respectively. We first choose v_{ij} randomly between -0.5 and 0.5 and denote them by $v_{ij}^{(0)}$. Let $v_j^{(0)}$ denote the vector of the weights from the input units to the hidden unit Z_j, i.e. $v_j^{(0)} = (v_{1j}^{(0)}, \ldots, v_{nj}^{(0)})^{\mathrm{T}}$. We now update $v_{ij}^{(0)}$ and use

$$v_{ij}^{(1)} = \frac{\beta v_{ij}^{(0)}}{\left\| v_{j}^{(0)} \right\|} \; ; \;\; 1 \leq i \leq n, \;\; 1 \leq j \leq l$$

as the final initial weights between X_i and Z_j. The initial biases v_{0j} are taken randomly between $-\beta$ and β.

The Nguyen-Widrow initialization procedure is based on the activation function $\tanh(x)$ but is also effective for the similarly behaving bipolar sigmoid function.

■ **Example 8.8.1** Consider a neural network with two input units, three hidden units and a single output unit, i.e. $n = 2$, $l = 3$ and $m = 1$. This network is supposed to operate as the 'XOR' function. Four training patterns which are 2-D vectors ($n = 2$) are the inputs. The outputs are four scalars ($m = 1$). If a binary representation is considered, the patterns are $(1, 1)^T$, $(1, 0)^T$, $(0, 1)^T$, $(0, 0)^T$, with targets 0, 1, 1, 0 respectively and the activation function is the binary sigmoid. For a bipolar representation the input patterns are $(1, 1)^T$, $(1, -1)^T$, $(-1, 1)^T$, $(-1, -1)^T$ with targets -1, 1, 1, -1 respectively and the activation function is the bipolar sigmoid.

The initial weights chosen randomly between -0.5 and 0.5 are:

$$
\begin{aligned}
v_{01} &= 0.396, & v_{02} &= -0.030, & v_{03} &= -0.401 \\
v_{11} &= -0.066, & v_{12} &= -0.046, & v_{13} &= 0.414 \\
v_{21} &= -0.017, & v_{22} &= 0.220, & v_{23} &= 0.231
\end{aligned}
$$

and

$$w_{01} = 0.118, \;\; w_{11} = -0.173, \;\; w_{21} = 0.204, \;\; w_{31} = -0.271$$

The training of the network continues until the total squared error is sufficiently small, i.e.

$$\sum_{p=1}^{M} \sum_{k=1}^{m} \left(y_k^{(p)} - t_k^{(p)} \right)^2 < \varepsilon$$

For a tolerance $\varepsilon = 0.05$ and learning rate $\alpha = 0.1$ we obtain the following results:

(a) Binary representation: 15342 iterations are needed for convergence and the final outputs are:

$$y_1^{(1)} = 0.112, \quad y_1^{(2)} = 0.870, \quad y_1^{(3)} = 0.899, \quad y_1^{(4)} = 0.102$$

(b) Bipolar representation: 823 iterations are needed for convergence and the final outputs are:

$$y_1^{(1)} = -0.883, \quad y_1^{(2)} = 0.910, \quad y_1^{(3)} = 0.895, \quad y_1^{(4)} = -0.869$$

♠

The next example demonstrates some advantage of using the Nguyen-Widrow initialization process.

▪ **Example 8.8.2** Consider the previous example with $\varepsilon = 0.01$ and $\alpha = 0.15$. Applying standard (ST) and Nguyen-Widrow (NW) initializations provide the following results.

(a) Binary representation:

Type of Initialization	No. of iterations
ST	12971
NW	6883

(b) Bipolar representation:

Type of Initialization	No. of iterations
ST	1534
NW	1246

♠

For fixed initial values of the weights and a given tolerance $\varepsilon > 0$, the speed by which the backpropagation network trains itself, depends on the learning-rate α.

In the next example we obtain the number of iterations needed for convergence, $I(\alpha)$, for the 'XOR' function. The weights are chosen randomly.

- **Example 8.8.3** Consider Example 8.8.1 $(\varepsilon = 0.05)$.   Fig. 8.8.2 illustrates the speed of convergence as a function of α in the case of bipolar representation.

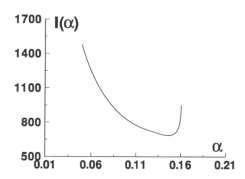

- **Figure 8.8.2** $I(\alpha)$ for the 'XOR' function-bipolar representation.

A reasonable choice for 'optimal' α is between 0.1 and 0.15.

Updating Weights Using Momentum

In order to speed up the convergence of a backpropagation network, it is sometimes recommended to derive the weights at step $(t+1)$, using not only the weights at step t but also those at step $(t-1)$. The updating is performed by

$$\Delta v_{ij}\left(t+1\right)=\alpha\delta_j x_i + \mu\,\Delta\,v_{ij}\left(t\right)$$

$$\Delta\,w_{jk}\left(t+1\right)=\alpha\delta_k z_j + \mu\Delta w_{jk}\left(t\right)$$

(8.8.9)

where

$$\Delta\,v_{ij}\left(t\right)=v_{ij}\left(t\right)-v_{ij}\left(t-1\right)$$

$$\Delta\,w_{jk}\left(t\right)=w_{jk}\left(t\right)-w_{jk}\left(t-1\right)$$

(8.8.10)

and μ , the *momentum* coefficient is between 0 and 1.

This modified updating may allow reasonably large weights adjustments and reduces the likelihood to obtain a local minimum rather than a global one while training the network.

Batch Updating

Sometimes it is more efficient to accumulate the weight adjustments for several patterns and then perform a single adjustment using the average of the various correction terms.   A possible disadvantage is that this procedure may have a smoothing effect on the correction terms and consequently may lead to a local minimum.

Updating the Learning Rate

In many applications each weight may have its own learning rate. Moreover, if the weight change is in the same direction for several steps, its associated learning rate should be increased. On the other hand, if the weight change sign alternates, the associated learning rate should be decreased.

■ **Example 8.8.4** Consider Example 8.8.1 with bipolar representation. Let $\varepsilon = 0.01$ and $\alpha = 0.1$. The standard implementation of Algorithm 8.8.1 converges after 2081 iterations. By using the momentum procedure with $\mu = 1$ the number of iterations is reduced to 30.

♠

PROBLEMS

1. Consider the XOR function with bipolar training patterns and targets and a backpropagation network with two input units, four hidden units and a single output unit. For tolerance $\varepsilon = 0.01$ and random initial weights between –0.5 and 0.5, find the number of iterations needed for convergence for a learning rate (a) 0.05 (b) 0.10 (c) 0.15 (d) 0.50. Use the same initial weights for all the cases.

2. Repeat and solve problem 1 in the case of binary representation.

3. (a) Repeat and solve problem 1 in the case of five hidden units.

   (b) Repeat part (a) using the Nguyen-Widrow modification.

4. Repeat and solve problem 1, using the momentum procedure with $\mu = 0.2, 0.4, 0.6, 0.8$.

5. (a) Repeat and solve problem 1, using the nonsaturating activation function

$$f(x) = \begin{cases} \ln(1+x), & x > 0 \\ -\ln(1-x), & x < 0 \end{cases}$$

   (b) Repeat part (a) using the momentum procedure with $\mu = 0.2, 0.4, 0.6, 0.8$.

6. Consider the following set of 6 input patterns

$$x^{(1)} = (1, 2, -1, 3, 5, 4, 0)^T$$
$$x^{(2)} = (2, 0, 6, 0, 1, 2, 3)^T$$
$$x^{(3)} = (5, 2, 1, 0, 3, 3, 7)^T$$
$$x^{(4)} = (0, 0, 0, 1, 0, 1, 2)^T$$
$$x^{(5)} = (1, 2, 3, 4, 5, 6, 1)^T$$
$$x^{(6)} = (-1, -2, 3, 1, 0, 5, 2)^T$$

with associated targets

$$t^{(1)} = (1, 1, 1)^T \ , \ t^{(2)} = (-1, 1, 1)^T \ , \ t^{(3)} = (1, -1, -1)^T$$
$$t^{(4)} = (-1, -1, -1)^T \ , \ t^{(5)} = (-1, 1, -1)^T \ , \ t^{(6)} = (-1, -1, 1)^T$$

Train the system using 7 input units, 3 output units and 3, 6, 9 hidden units, given a tolerance $\varepsilon = 0.01$, a learning rate $\alpha = 0.1$ and a momentum parameter $\mu = 0.5$.   The initial weights are chosen randomly between –0.5 and 0.5.

APPENDIX

```
      subroutine mcmp(y,n,m,np,npm,x,sumax,jmax,k)
ccccccccccccccccccccccccccccccccccccccccccccccccccccccccccccccc
c
c      This subroutine is a minimum-distance classifier.
c
c      INPUT:
c
c      n - dimension of the given patterns.
c
c      m - number of classes.
c
c      npm - maximum number of sample patterns in a class.
c
c      np - a m - dimensional vector. np(i) is the number of
c           patterns in class i.
c
c      y - the given patterns.  y(i,j,k) is the k-th component
c           of the j-th pattern in the i-th class.
c
c      x - an incoming n - dimensional pattern.
c
c      OUTPUT:
c
c      k - the number of class at which x is classified.
c
c      jmax - an m - dimensional vector. jmax(i) is the number of
c             the closest pattern in class i to the pattern x.
c
c      sumax - an m - dimensional vector. sumax(i) is
c
c                     max[x(T)*y-0.5*y(T)*y]
c
c             where T stands for 'transpose' and y is arbitrary
c             pattern in class i.
c
ccccccccccccccccccccccccccccccccccccccccccccccccccccccccccccccc
      dimension y(m,npm,n),np(m),jmax(m),sumax(m),x(n)
      do i=1,m
      sum0=-1.e10
ccccccccccccccccccccccccccccccccccccccccccccccccccccccccccccccc
c
c      It is assumed that no 'sum' is less than -1.e10.
c
ccccccccccccccccccccccccccccccccccccccccccccccccccccccccccccccc
```

```
j0=0
do j=1,np(i)
sum=0.
do k=1,n
sum=sum+x(k)*y(i,j,k)-.5*y(i,j,k)*y(i,j,k)
enddo
if (sum.gt.sum0) then
j0=j
sum0=sum
endif
enddo
jmax(i)=j0
sumax(i)=sum0
enddo
k=1
sum=sumax(1)
do i=2,m
if (sumax(i).gt.sum) then
sum=sumax(i)
k=i
endif
enddo
return
end
```

```
      subroutine mdnn(y,n,m,np,nc,iout,ic,x,k,l)
ccccccccccccccccccccccccccccccccccccccccccccccccccccccccccccccccc
c
c      This subroutine is a minimum-distance nearest - neighbor
c      classifier.
c
c      INPUT:
c
c      n - dimension of the given patterns.
c
c      m - number of classes.
c
c      np - number of given preclassified patterns.
c
c      k - the order of the classifier.
c
c      y - the given patterns.  y(i,j) is the j-th component
c          of the i-th pattern.
c
c      nc - an np - dimensional vector. nc(i) is the class number
c           the i-th pattern.
c
c      x - an incoming n - dimensional pattern.
c
c      ic - an m - dimensional vector with components all 0's.
c
c      iout - an np - dimensional vector with components all 1's.
c
c      OUTPUT:
c
c      l - the number of class at which x is classified.
c
c      ic - an m - dimensional vector. ic(i) is the number of the
c           nearest neighbors (among k) in class i.
c
c      iout - an np - dimensional vector. iout(i) is 0 if the i-th
c             pattern is one of the nearest neighbors. Otherwise
c             iout(i)=1.
c
ccccccccccccccccccccccccccccccccccccccccccccccccccccccccccccccccc
      dimension y(np,n),nc(np),x(n),ic(m),iout(np)
      sum0=1.e10
ccccccccccccccccccccccccccccccccccccccccccccccccccccccccccccccccc
c
c      It is assumed that no 'sum' is greater than 1.e10.
c
ccccccccccccccccccccccccccccccccccccccccccccccccccccccccccccccccc
      j0=0
      do i=1,np
      sum=0
```

```
      do j=1,n
      sum=sum+(y(i,j)-x(j))**2
      enddo
      if (sum.lt.sum0) then
      j0=i
      sum0=sum
      endif
      enddo
      if (k.eq.1) then
      l=nc(j0)
      return
      endif
      iout(j0)=0
      ic(nc(j0))=1
      do i0=1,k-1
      sum0=1.e10
      j0=0
      do i=1,np
      if (iout(i).eq.1) then
      sum=0
      do j=1,n
      sum=sum+(y(i,j)-x(j))**2
      enddo
      if (sum.lt.sum0) then
      j0=i
      sum0=sum
      endif
      endif
      enddo
      iout(j0)=0
      ic(nc(j0))=ic(nc(j0))+1
      enddo
      l=0
      do i=1,m
      if (ic(i).gt.l) then
      l=ic(i)
      endif
      enddo
      return
      end
```

```
      subroutine mmd(x,y,mc,lc,iout,n,m,t,k)
ccccccccccccccccccccccccccccccccccccccccccccccccccccccccccccccc
c
c     This subroutine is a max-min distance clustering procedure.
c
c     INPUT:
c
c     n - dimension of the given patterns.
c
c     m - number of patterns.
c
c     x - the given patterns.  x(i,j) is the j-th component
c         of the i-th pattern.
c
c     t - a threshold value which determines whether a new cluster
c         should be created. The smaller t is the more clusters
c         are likely to be created.
c
c     iout - an m - dimensional vector with components all 1's.
c
c     OUTPUT:
c
c     k - the number of cluster centers found. It is at least 2.
c
c     y - the k cluster centers. y(i,j) is the j-th component of
c         the i-th cluster.
c
c     mc - a k - dimensional vector. mc(i) is the number of
c          patterns in the i-th cluster.
c     lc - a matrix  (m x m). lc(i,j) is the original pattern
c          number of the i-th element in class j.
c
c     iout - an m - dimensional vector. iout(i) is 0 for all i.
c
ccccccccccccccccccccccccccccccccccccccccccccccccccccccccccccccc
      dimension x(m,n),y(m,n),mc(m),lc(m,m),iout(m)
      do i=1,n
      y(1,i)=x(1,i)
      enddo
      lc(1,1)=1
      sum0=0
      j0=0
      do i=2,m
      sum=dist(x,y,m,n,i,1)
      if (sum.gt.sum0) then
      sum0=sum
      j0=i
      endif
      enddo
      iout(1)=0
```

```
       iout(j0)=0
       do i=1,n
       y(2,i)=x(j0,i)
       enddo
       k=2
       lc(1,2)=j0
       sum=dist(y,y,m,n,1,2)
       a=sqrt(sum)
   20  sum0=0
       j0=0
       i0=0
       do j=1,m
       if (iout(j).eq.1) then
       sum00=1.e10
ccccccccccccccccccccccccccccccccccccccccccccccccccccccccccccccccc
c
c      It is assumed that no 'sum' is greater than 1.e10.
c
ccccccccccccccccccccccccccccccccccccccccccccccccccccccccccccccccc
       i00=0
       do i=1,k
       sum=dist(x,y,m,n,j,i)
       if (sum.lt.sum00) then
       sum00=sum
       i00=i
       endif
       enddo
       if (sum00.gt.sum0) then
       sum0=sum00
       j0=j
       i0=i00
       endif
       endif
       enddo
       if (sqrt(sum0).lt.(t*a)) go to 10
       k=k+1
       do i=1,n
       y(k,i)=x(j0,i)
       enddo
       lc(1,k)=j0
       iout(j0)=0
       a0=0
       do i=1,k-1
       do j=i+1,k
       sum=dist(y,y,m,n,i,j)
       a0=a0+sqrt(sum)
       enddo
       enddo
       a=(2.*a0)/(k*(k-1))
       go to 20
```

```
10      do i=1,k
        mc(i)=1
        enddo
        do i=1,m
        if (iout(i).eq.1) then
        sum0=1.e10
ccccccccccccccccccccccccccccccccccccccccccccccccccccccccccccccccc
c
c       It is assumed that no 'sum' is greater than 1.e10.
c
ccccccccccccccccccccccccccccccccccccccccccccccccccccccccccccccccc
        j0=0
        do j=1,k
        sum=dist(x,y,m,n,i,j)
        if (sum.lt.sum0) then
        sum0=sum
        j0=j
        endif
        enddo
        mc(j0)=mc(j0)+1
        lc(mc(j0),j0)=i
        endif
        enddo
        do j=1,k
        do l=1,n
        sum=0
        do i=1,mc(j)
        sum=sum+x(lc(i,j),l)
        enddo
        y(j,l)=sum/mc(j)
        enddo
        enddo
        return
        end
        function dist(x,y,m,n,i,j)
ccccccccccccccccccccccccccccccccccccccccccccccccccccccccccccccccc
c
c       This function calculates the squared distance between two
c       n - dimensional vectors x(i) and y(j)
c
ccccccccccccccccccccccccccccccccccccccccccccccccccccccccccccccccc
        dimension x(m,n),y(m,n)
        dist=0
        do k=1,n
        dist=dist+(x(i,k)-y(j,k))**2
        enddo
        return
        end
```

```
      subroutine cmi(x,y,yn,mc,lc,m,n,c,it0,it)
ccccccccccccccccccccccccccccccccccccccccccccccccccccccccccccccc
c
c      Assuming c cluster centers around which the given samples
c      cluster this subroutine calculates these centers
c      iteratively, minimizing at each iteration a set of
c      performance indices. Once the centers are modified, the
c      patterns are reclassified using min - distance principle.
c
c      The procedure terminates only when the cluster centers do
c      not change.
c
c      INPUT:
c
c      n - dimension of the given patterns.
c
c      m - number of patterns.
c
c      c - the number of clusters
c
c      x - the given patterns.  x(i,j) is the j-th component
c          of the i-th pattern.
c
c      it0 - maximum number of iterations allowed.
c
c      OUTPUT:
c
c      y - the final c cluster centers. y(i,j) is the j-th
c          component of the i-th cluster.
c
c      mc - a k - dimensional vector. mc(i) is the number of
c           patterns in the i-th cluster.
c
c      lc - a matrix  (m x c). lc(i,j) is the original pattern
c           number of the i-th element in class j.
c
c      it - the number of iterations needed for convergence. If
c           the procedure does not converge, it=it0 and the cluster
c           centers are those calculated at the last iteration.
c
ccccccccccccccccccccccccccccccccccccccccccccccccccccccccccccccc
      integer c
      dimension x(m,n),y(c,n),yn(c,n),mc(c),lc(m,c)
      it=0
      do i=1,c
      do j=1,n
      y(i,j)=x(i,j)
      enddo
      enddo
10    do i=1,c
```

```
          mc(i)=0
          enddo
          do i=1,m
          sum0=1.e10
          j0=0
          do j=1,c
          sum=dist(x,y,m,n,c,i,j)
          if (sum.lt.sum0) then
          sum0=sum
          j0=j
          endif
          enddo
          mc(j0)=mc(j0)+1
          lc(mc(j0),j0)=i
          enddo
          do i=1,c
          do l=1,n
          yn(i,l)=0
          do j=1,mc(i)
          yn(i,l)=yn(i,l)+x(lc(j,i),l)
          enddo
          yn(i,l)=yn(i,l)/mc(i)
          enddo
          enddo
          it=it+1
          sum=0
          do i=1,c
          sum=sum+dist1(y,yn,n,c,i)
          enddo
          if (sum.lt.1.e-6) then
          return
          endif
          if (it.eq.it0) go to 20
          do i=1,c
          do j=1,n
          y(i,j)=yn(i,j)
          enddo
          enddo
          go to 10
   20     write (*,*) 'too many iterations'
          return
          end
          function dist(x,y,m,n,c,i,j)
ccccccccccccccccccccccccccccccccccccccccccccccccccccccccccccccccc
c
c         This function calculates the squared distance between the
c         i-th pattern and the j-th cluster center.
c
ccccccccccccccccccccccccccccccccccccccccccccccccccccccccccccccccc
          integer c
```

```
      dimension x(m,n),y(c,n)
      dist=0
      do k=1,n
      dist=dist+(x(i,k)-y(j,k))**2
      enddo
      return
      end
      function dist1(y,yn,n,c,i)
ccccccccccccccccccccccccccccccccccccccccccccccccccccccccccccccc
c
c     This function calculates the squared distance between the
c     new and the old i-th cluster centers.
c
ccccccccccccccccccccccccccccccccccccccccccccccccccccccccccccccc
      integer c
      dimension y(c,n),yn(c,n)
      dist1=0
      do k=1,n
      dist1=dist1+(y(i,k)-yn(i,k))**2
      enddo
      return
      end
```

```
      subroutine fcmi(x,y,ch,yn,m,n,c,d,be,it0,it,eps)
cccccccccccccccccccccccccccccccccccccccccccccccccccccccccccccccc
c
c     The fuzzy c-Means algorithm
c
c     Assuming c cluster centers around which the given samples
c     cluster this subroutine performs fuzzy clustering around
c     these centers iteratively, minimizing at each iteration a
c     set of performance indices. Once the centers are modified,
c     the patterns are reclassified using min - distance
c     principle, i.e. the patterns grades of membership are
c     adjusted.
c
c     The procedure terminates only when the change in the
c     cluster centers do is less than a given tolerance.
c
c     INPUT:
c
c     n - dimension of the given patterns.
c
c     m - number of patterns.
c
c     c - the number of clusters
c
c     x - the given patterns.  x(i,j) is the j-th component
c         of the i-th pattern.
c
c     y - the initial cluster centers.
c
c     it0 - maximum number of iterations allowed.
c
c     eps - a given tolerance
c
c     OUTPUT:
c
c     yn - the final c cluster centers. y(i,j) is the j-th
c         component of the i-th cluster.
c
c     ch - the final grades of membership. ch(i,j) is the
c         grade of membership of the j-th pattern at the
c         i-th class.
c
c     it - the number of iterations needed for convegence. If
c         the procedure does not converge, it=it0 and the cluster
c         centers are those calculated at the last iteration.
c
cccccccccccccccccccccccccccccccccccccccccccccccccccccccccccccccc
      integer c
      dimension x(m,n),y(c,n),yn(c,n),ch(c,m),d(c,m)
      be1=2./(be-1.)
```

```
         it=0
  10     continue
         do i=1,c
         do j=1,m
         d(i,j)=sqrt(dist(x,y,m,n,c,i,j))
         enddo
         enddo
         do j=1,m
         do i=1,c
         ch(i,j)=0.
         do l=1,c
         if (abs(d(l,j)).lt.1.e-6) go to 20
         ch(i,j)=ch(i,j)+(d(i,j)/d(l,j))**be1
         enddo
         ch(i,j)=1./ch(i,j)
         enddo
         go to 30
  20     continue
         do k=1,c
         ch(k,j)=0
         enddo
         ch(l,j)=1
  30     continue
         enddo
         do i=1,c
         do l=1,n
         yn(i,l)=0
         temp=0
         do j=1,m
         yn(i,l)=yn(i,l)+ch(i,j)*x(j,l)
         temp=temp+ch(i,j)
         enddo
         yn(i,l)=yn(i,l)/temp
         enddo
         enddo
         it=it+1
         sum=0
         do i=1,c
         sum=sum+dist1(y,yn,n,c,i)
         enddo
         if (sqrt(sum).lt.eps) then
         return
         endif
         if (it.eq.it0) go to 40
         do i=1,c
         do j=1,n
         y(i,j)=yn(i,j)
         enddo
         enddo
         go to 10
```

```
 40     write (*,*) 'too many iterations'
        return
        end
        function dist(x,y,m,n,c,i,j)
ccccccccccccccccccccccccccccccccccccccccccccccccccccccccccccccc
c
c       This function calculates the squared distance between the
c       i-th pattern and the j-th cluster center.
c
ccccccccccccccccccccccccccccccccccccccccccccccccccccccccccccccc
        integer c
        dimension x(m,n),y(c,n)
        dist=0
        do k=1,n
        dist=dist+(x(j,k)-y(i,k))**2
        enddo
        return
        end
        function dist1(y,yn,n,c,i)
ccccccccccccccccccccccccccccccccccccccccccccccccccccccccccccccc
c
c       This function calculates the squared distance between the
c       new and the old i-th cluster centers.
c
ccccccccccccccccccccccccccccccccccccccccccccccccccccccccccccccc
        integer c
        dimension y(c,n),yn(c,n)
        dist1=0
        do k=1,n
        dist1=dist1+(y(i,k)-yn(i,k))**2
        enddo
        return
        end
```

```
      subroutine perc(x,t,w0,w,ws,m,n,b0,b,tr,al,iter,it,eps)
cccccccccccccccccccccccccccccccccccccccccccccccccccccccccccc
c
c     This subroutine incorporates the principle of the
c     principle of the perceptron.
c
c     INPUT
c
c     m - number of training patterns.
c
c     n - number of associative units.
c
c     tr - the perceptron threshold.
c
c     al - the learning rate.
c
c     x - activations ; x(i,j) - j-th activation of i-th pattern.
c
c     t - correct targets ; t(i) - target of i-th pattern.
c
c     w0 - initial weights ; w0(j) - weight of j-th unit.
c
c     b0 - initial bias.
c
c     iter - maximum allowed number of iterations.
c
c     eps - a given tolerance.
c
c
c     OUTPUT
c
c     w - final weights ; w(j) - final weight of j-th unit.
c
c     b - final bias.
c
c     it - number of iterations needed.
c
cccccccccccccccccccccccccccccccccccccccccccccccccccccccccccc
      dimension x(m,n),w0(n),w(n),t(m),ws(n)
      it=0
      bs=b0
      do j=1,n
      ws(j)=w0(j)
      enddo
  20  ich=0
      do i=1,m
      yin=b0
      do j=1,n
      yin=yin+w0(j)*x(i,j)
      enddo
```

```
       if (yin.gt.tr) then
       y=1
       elseif (yin.lt.(-tr)) then
       y=-1
       else
       y=0
       endif
       if (abs(y-t(i)).gt.1.e-6) then
       ich=1
       b=b0+al*t(i)
       do j=1,n
       w(j)=w0(j)+al*t(i)*x(i,j)
       enddo
       b0=b
       do j=1,n
       w0(j)=w(j)
       enddo
       endif
       enddo
       err=(b-bs)**2
       do j=1,n
       err=err+(w(j)-ws(j))**2
       enddo
       if (err.lt.eps.and.ich.eq.0) then
       write (*,*) 'learning completed',it
       go to 10
       elseif (err.lt.eps.and.ich.eq.1) then
       write (*,*) 'learning cannot be completed'
       go to 10
       endif
       it=it+1
       b0=b
       bs=b
       do j=1,n
       w0(j)=w(j)
       ws(j)=w(j)
       enddo
       if (it.ge.iter) then
       write (*,*) 'too many iterations'
       go to 10
       else
       go to 20
       endif
10     continue
       return
       end
```

Index